Writing Cures

The helping professions are increasingly harnessing the arts and humanities to broaden clinical understandings of the human condition. Yet writing is not widely recognised in counselling and therapy circles. *Writing Cures* demonstrates the power of expressive and reflective writing in the context of therapy, whether online or text-based, enabling the practitioner to undertake healing writing methods with clients.

Covering a range of contexts such as workplace and student counselling and therapy in medical settings, *Writing Cures* draws together a comprehensive view of cross-disciplinary research and practitioner reports. An impressive list of contributors cover subjects including:

- Ethical and practical dimensions of online writing.
- Writing by patients and therapists in cognitive and analytic therapy.
- Writing for professional development and reflective practice.

Illustrated throughout by examples from clinical experience *Writing Cures* will be of benefit to all counsellors, psychotherapists and clinical psychologists who want to use writing confidently with their clients.

Gillie Bolton, senior research fellow in medicine and the arts at King's College London, has written two books concerning therapeutic writing and reflective practice writing and is creative writing editor for three medical journals.

Stephanie Howlett is an analytical psychotherapist with a particular interest in the link between the mind and the body, and is currently working at the Royal Hallamshire Hospital in Sheffield.

Colin Lago was formerly Director of the Counselling Service at the University of Sheffield and now works as an independent practitioner.

Jeannie K. Wright, senior lecturer in counselling and psychotherapy at Derby University, has written down what she couldn't say for as long as she can remember.

Writing Cures

An introductory handbook of writing in counselling and psychotherapy

Edited by
Gillie Bolton, Stephanie Howlett,
Colin Lago and Jeannie K. Wright

LONDON AND NEW YORK

First published 2004
by Routledge
27 Church Road, Hove, East Sussex BN3 2FA

Simultaneously published in the USA and Canada
by Routledge
270 Madison Avenue, New York NY 10016

Reprinted 2006 and 2008

Routledge is an imprint of the Taylor & Francis Group, an Informa business

Typeset in Times New Roman by
Keystroke, Jacaranda Lodge, Wolverhampton
Printed and bound in Great Britain by
MPG Books Ltd, Bodmin, Cornwall
Paperback cover design by
Anú Design

This publication has been produced with paper manufactured to strict environmental standards and with pulp derived from sustainable forests.

British Library Cataloguing in Publication Data
A catalogue record for this book is available from the British Library

Library of Congress Cataloging in Publication Data
Writing cures : an introductory handbook of writing in counselling and psychotherapy / Gillie Bolton ... [et al.].
p. cm.
Includes bibliographical references and index.
ISBN 1–58391–911–2 (hbk. : alk. paper) – ISBN 1–58391–912–0 (pbk. : alk. paper)
1. Creative writing–Therapeutic use. 2. Psychotherapy.
3. Counseling. I. Bolton, Gillie.

RC489.C75W75 2004
616.89'165–dc22 2003019619

ISBN 13: 978–1–58391–911–8 (hbk)
ISBN 13: 978–1–58391–912–5 (pbk)

Contents

PART 2
Writing in therapy 57

PART 3
Writing online 131

Notes on contributors

Heather Allan is a counsellor and psychotherapist with a private practice in North London and a tutor for the Centre for Medical Humanities, University College London. She has a special interest in the psychology of medicine, therapeutic relationships and issues around birth and death, and is a founder member of Sheilia Kitzinger's Birth Crisis Network. She has facilitated workshops for both health care providers and patients, using creative arts as therapeutic tools in areas such as PTSD in childbirth, cancer and genetic disorders. She has a PhD in English literature from UCL.

Kate Anthony, MSc, runs www.OnlineCounsellors.co.uk which provides online and offline consultancy services and training for practitioners using the internet. She conducts ongoing research programmes about online therapy supervision, and is the author of one of the very few published empirical studies to be conducted into the use of email and internet relay chat in therapy. She was a main author of the BACP online counselling and psychotherapy guidelines and is a regular contributor to journals, international conferences, media programmes and articles. She is also a psychotherapist with the Oxleas Health Trust in south-east London.

Gillie Bolton. Therapeutic writing found me when I was in my thirties; it saved my sanity (what there is of it), so I thought it might do the same for other people. Since then I have devoted my working life to it – for patients and clients and for medical, healthcare, therapeutic and other caring practitioners. With the latter we call it 'reflective practice writing for professional development'. I've written two books, am creative writing editor for three medical journals, have written a heap of papers of various sorts – all about the same thing – and I'm senior research fellow in medicine and the arts at King's College London. I've also written poetry about angels among other things; and I'm council member to the Association of Medical Humanities. I owe the rest of my sanity, which wasn't saved by writing, to my two wise and funny children, and their dad.

Jaquie Daniels is Senior Lecturer in Education and Counselling at Sheffield Hallam University. She teaches on the Diploma in Counselling and the

Postgraduate Certificate in Counselling Supervision and is Course Leader for the BA Education and Training. She is also an independent therapist and counselling supervisor. She has a particular interest in personal development work and the teaching of study skills. Recent publications include *Developing Student Support Groups: A Practical Guide for Tutors* (1999) with R. Bingham and 'Whispers in the corridor and kangaroo courts: the supervisory role in mistakes and complaints' in *Taking Supervision Forward*, edited by B. Lawton and C. Feltham (2000).

Helen Drucquer. I have been involved with the therapy world for nearly three decades and for over two of them in general practice. I love the complexity and enormous variety of the work. It's also a joy working with a multitude of different professionals and students. I also have a private practice. My training as a Jungian analyst is drawing to a close – a long and worthwhile journey. Is this where the real learning begins? Apart from my cat, family and garden, a highlight of my life is the reflective writing group where I am beginning at last to let the words go free on the page. *Vive* the second half of life!

Colin Feltham, PhD, FBACP, FRSA is Reader in Counselling at Sheffield Hallam University, where he teaches on all counselling courses. He has been co-editor of the *British Journal of Guidance and Counselling* and has 17 books published, most recently *What's the Good of Counselling and Psychotherapy?: The Benefits Explained* (Sage, 2002).

Dr Stephen Goss is the Research Development Manager with the BACP and Hon. Research Fellow with the University of Strathclyde. He is a qualified counsellor and supervisor. His interests include innovative methods of service delivery in therapy as well as in research and evaluation methodologies, pluralist philosophies of science and maintenance of high practice standards. He was the lead author and editor of the recent BACP online counselling and psychotherapy guidelines. He has produced numerous research reports, journal articles and other works including the edited text *Evidence Based Counselling and Psychotherapy* with Nancy Rowland (Routledge 2000).

Lin Griffiths has a Relate certificate in Couple and Marital Therapy and a masters degree in Counselling and Psychotherapy from Sheffield Hallam University. She has been a practising counsellor for 15 years and currently has a private counselling practice from which she provides couple counselling and supervision. Lin also works for Relate as a member of their counsellor training and development team. She used her experience of working online both synchronously and asynchronously with clients as the basis for her thesis on 'Communicating therapeutically via the internet'. She lives in north Lincolnshire and is married with two children and two grandchildren.

Lisa Heller is a nurse with many years' experience of working with and for people with dementia. In her current post she works with staff groups to develop person-centred care for people with dementia receiving care in hospitals, day centres and residential homes. She is passionately committed to the improvement of care and to the development and support of staff caring for this client group.

John Hilsdon is a lecturer at the University of Plymouth where he coordinates the Learning Skills Service and is a member of the Educational Development team. He is also a counsellor at Derriford Hospital working with patients, families and supporters of those affected by cancer. John has particular interests in language and learning, and in the uses of writing for both personal and professional development. He is involved with a number of writing projects concerning these themes.

Stephanie Howlett is a psychoanalytically trained psychotherapist working at the University of Sheffield Counselling Service and in the Department of Neurology at the Royal Hallamshire Hospital in Sheffield. She has a special interest in the link between emotional functioning and physical symptoms, and has worked extensively as a psychotherapist with people with a wide range of bodily symptoms, using writing as an integral part of this work.

Celia Hunt is Senior Lecturer in Continuing Education at the University of Sussex Centre for Continuing Education, where she directs the MA in Creative Writing and Personal Development. She has a research interest in the developmental and therapeutic role of creative writing. She is the author of *Therapeutic Dimensions of Autobiography in Creative Writing* (2000) and editor (with Fiona Sampson) of *The Self on the Page: Theory and Practice of Creative Writing in Personal Development* (1998). She is currently working on a further book with Fiona Sampson under the title *Creative Writing and the Writer*.

Colin Lago is Director of the Counselling Service at the University of Sheffield. Trained initially as an engineer, Colin went on to become a full-time youth worker in London and then a teacher in Jamaica. He is an accredited counsellor and Fellow of BACP, and a registered practitioner with UKRC. Deeply committed to transcultural concerns he has had articles, videos and books published including *Race, Culture and Counselling* (with Joyce Thompson), *The Management of Counselling & Psychotherapy Agencies* (with Duncan Kitchin), *On Listening and Learning: Student Counselling in Further and Higher Education* (with Geraldine Shipton), *Experiences in Relatedness: Group Work and the Person Centred Approach* (co-edited with Mhairi Macmillan) and *Anti-Dicriminatory Counselling in Practice* (with Barbara Smith). A further co-edited book is in press, entitled *Carl Rogers Counsels a Black Client: Race and Culture in Person-Centered Counselling* (with Roy Moodley and Anissa Talahite). For leisure, Colin is a keen (but not very good!) fell runner, an enthusiastic (but incompetent) dancer and a lover of mountains, films and books. He is married with two grown up 'youngsters'.

Robert Langdon has been a volunteer with the Samaritans since 1977. His many responsibilities within the organisation have included being Branch Director for the South Devon branch, South-West Regional Representative and National Vice-Chairman. He is now overseeing the development of the organisation's email service, and is trying to ensure that there are sufficient branches and volunteers involved to respond to the 64,000 messages currently received every year. In his professional life he is a part-time mathematics teacher in a comprehensive school.

John Latham was formerly Professor of Physics at Manchester University and is now a freelance, part-time research scientist, specialising in lightning, clouds and climate. He is also a writer, with five collections of poetry published, and a first-prize winner in more than 20 national poetry competitions. Several of his plays have been broadcast on BBC radio, and many of his short stories have been broadcast or anthologised. He is creative writing tutor to the Arvon Foundation and Taliesin Trust.

Geoff Lowe is a health psychologist and honorary senior fellow in the Department of Clinical Psychology at the University of Hull. His research interests include the health-related benefits of writing along with areas such as alcohol and drug use, and psycho-neuro-immunology. He also tutors creative writing courses and workshops. His poems and short stories have appeared in a variety of publications and for many years he was founder-editor of the *Psychopoetica* poetry magazine.

Anthony Ryle qualified in medicine in 1949. He was co-founder of the Caversham Centre Group practice in Kentish Town, London, from 1952 to 1964, where he carried out a study of psychological adjustment in parents and their children. From 1964 to 1982 he was at Sussex University as Director of the University Health Service and subsequently as a Senior Research Fellow, carrying out research into the process and outcome of psychotherapy and beginning to develop what became cognitive analytic therapy (CAT). From 1982 to his retirement from the NHS he was Consultant Psychotherapist at St Thomas' Hospital, London, and since that time has been a part-time consultant and research fellow attached to Guy's Hospital, London, continuing to be involved in CAT teaching and research. He has written or co-authored and edited eight books and numerous papers.

Dr Jane Speedy is Director of the Centre for Narratives and Transformative Learning, Graduate School of Education, University of Bristol. She is a practising narrative therapist and an established academic researcher and writer with a particular interest in the transferability of ideas and practices between the therapeutic and research domains. She coordinates and teaches on master's programmes in narrative therapy and a doctoral programme in narrative and life story research at the University of Bristol. She has published and broadcast extensively in the fields of narrative therapy, writing practices in research and therapy, auto-ethnography and narrative research. She is currently engaged in research into the place of auto-ethnographic writings within counselling and therapy research. She lives in Bristol with her partner and their daughter.

Derek Steinberg teaches in the UK and internationally on treating psychiatric disorders of adolescence, staff training and team development, and on the relationship between mental and physical health and the arts, particularly the literary and visual arts. He has published seven books, including *Models for Mental Disorder* (Wiley 1998, with Peter Tyrer) and *Letters from the Clinic* (Routledge 2000). He is a member of Bethlem Royal Hospital Arts and History Collections Trust.

Kate Thompson is a counsellor in the NHS and in private practice, working with clients and providing counselling supervision. She gained a BA in English literature from Cambridge University and an MA in counselling and psychotherapy from UEL. Her thesis was on the use of metaphor by clients in counselling. Journal therapy and the use of writing in therapy and personal development synthesise her two particular interests. She uses writing extensively with clients and for herself. She also serves on the committee of Lapidus, the organisation for literary arts in personal development. She lives in north-east London but does her best thinking when fell-walking in Yorkshire or Colorado.

Claire Williamson worked in addiction recovery for three years. She has an MA in literary studies and a Certificate in Counselling. Claire is primarily a writer of poems, short stories and young-adult fiction, but has an ongoing interest in the therapeutic quality of writing. Claire also works with many community groups including adults with learning difficulties, prisoners, schoolchildren and youth groups.

Jeannie K. Wright is Senior Lecturer in Counselling and Psychotherapy at Derby University where she also practices in the Unit for Psychotherapeutic Practice and Research. She has worked in counselling and psychotherapy, mostly in educational settings in the UK and internationally, most recently at the University of the South Pacific in Fiji. Most of her published writing has been for academic journals, with occasional forays into fiction and poetry. She currently lives with her two teenage children in Nottingham.

Foreword: PS, make it two

Ian McMillan

Years ago, I was walking up the street to school with one of my kids when we found a note that the milkman had chucked away. This was in the days when milkmen left more, much more, than milk. It said 'One loaf. PS, make it two'. I took it along to show my co-tutor at the basic education class I was running. His eyes lit up. 'I've seen that kind of thing before. They've written that because they can't spell loaves but they want to order some more bread,' he said. 'They've written it to make them feel good.' That was a revelatory moment for me: writing can make you feel better, can make you feel more like the person you want to be.

Over the last 20-odd years I've worked as a writer in all kinds of settings with all kinds of people: schoolchildren, adults with mental health problems, kids who've been excluded from school, old people in a circle in a home, railway workers, police officers, football fans and prostitutes. The prostitutes all wanted to write and make art about their lives. At the start of our first session we sat on chairs and settees in a dingy upstairs room in Doncaster. There was a silence, as they say in novels. Somebody coughed. A young woman fingered the fresh tattoo on her arm. I tried to break the ice. 'I'm scared stiff!' I said. Maybe it was the wrong thing to say in such a setting, but it made them laugh. I said, 'Tell me what you've been up to lately,' and one of the women said, 'If somebody drags me in the pub today, I'll shoot myself.' We all laughed some more, and we were away. The women wrote poems and little stories about their lives and their hopes and their fears and about the way the moon looked after them and about the warning notes about bad punters they scribbled on the wall near where they all worked. 'If someone drags me/in the pub today/ I'll shoot myself' stayed as it was, a little haiku on its own in the middle of the page of the book we made.

Enjoy this book and use it to enable writing to happen, to create journals and letters and messages and poems and stories and jokes where there were none before. Write creative notes to the milkman. Let's make the milkman smile. One story, please. PS, make it two.

Acknowledgements

Writing Cures is a result of situational, vocational, personal and temporal synchronicities. All four of us editors were colleagues at the University of Sheffield when we started, three as counsellors in the University Counselling Service and one as Research Fellow in Medical Humanities. Jeannie and Colin had been involved in developing an online counselling service. Steph had used writing as part of evaluating a counselling research project with great success and appreciation from clients. Gillie, the researcher, was actively engaged on a daily basis, sharing the values of writing with medical students, practitioners and patients.

The book began to germinate after 'Writing for You, Writing for Me', the landmark conference in May 2001 organised by Colin, Jeannie and Steph at Sheffield University Counselling Service; Gillie gave the keynote talk. Our first acknowledgement, then, is to the synchronistic forces that have brought this project into being.

We are most grateful to all our chapter writers who not only have managed to keep within the editing deadlines but more importantly have produced wonderfully insightful chapters; to Wanda Palfreyman and Kerry Mellors for their support; and to Joanne Forshaw for her thoughtfulness and patience.

Colin's personal acknowledgements must firstly go to my family who are very tolerant of dad 'disappearing to the other room to write again'. One further specific and completely idiosyncratic acknowledgement I would like to make is to the teacher who got me to write an essay rather than 'do lines' once, when I had contravened some rule or other at school. The essay turned out to be somewhat longer than anything I had hitherto produced and showed me the creative potential of writing!

Thanks from Steph go first and foremost to Lindiwe and Daniel, for putting up with a mother who has been tired, distracted and absent-minded at times. I am grateful for the help and support of Julia Ginn and many other people in the Samaritans. Finally, my thanks to all the clients over the years who have shared their writing with me.

Thank you from Jeannie to all those people who talked to me about their writing and came to counselling willing to share it. Katie and Liam – sorry about being so absorbed in this book and burning so many dinners. Thank you to you and Jimmy too, and especially to mum.

Gillie would like to thank all the wonderful patients and practitioners who have inspired me in this work over many years, and my co-authors: John Latham, Helen Drucquer and Heather Allan. I particularly thank Kate Billingham, Matt Black, Alison Combes, Kath Hibberd, Rosie Field, Amanda Howe, Brian Hurwitz, Marilyn Lidster, Nigel Mathers, Richard Meakin, Bill Noble and especially Stephen Rowland.

Introduction: writing cures

Gillie Bolton

Writing is our cultural medium, particularly since the rise of the use of computers and virtuality, and the mushrooming of printed texts – books, journals, newspapers, magazines, signage, clothing. Writing is everywhere in the western world. Thinking onto the page is part of life. Therefore it would seem odd if writing were not an essential element of a therapist's, counsellor's or clinical psychologist's relationship with a client or patient. When Freud developed 'the talking cure', writing was something which special people did at special times. Some 150 years later things have changed.

Yet things have not changed fundamentally: writing has been known to be psychologically beneficial since Apollo was the god of both poetry and healing. The ancient Egyptians, one of the first peoples to write, knew that writing had tremendous power: they thought a god could be contacted directly through the written word, that a person could be damned forever, or their memory erased through writing or deletion of writing.

Writing is different from talking; it has a power all of its own, as *Writing Cures* amply demonstrates. It can allow an exploration of cognitive, emotional and spiritual areas otherwise not accessible, and an expression of elements otherwise inexpressible. The very act of creativity – of making something on the page which wasn't there before – tends to increase self-confidence, feelings of self-worth and motivation for life.

Writing can also be an unparalleled form of communication – with the self in the first instance, and later with another such as the therapist. A therapeutic session is brief; paper and pencil can always be there – in the middle of the night, for hour after hour if necessary. This can engender greater independence and self-reliance. Clients do not always need to be listened to by another; they can – to an extent – listen to themselves and work on their own understandings on their own. Writing can also (if not cathartically destroyed) create a record potentially invaluable to both client and therapist, together or separately. Writing also enables online communication, which can be a means of bringing client and therapist together when otherwise this might not be possible for geographical or personal reasons.

Writing Cures is a charting and demonstration of the theoretical underpinnings, the ways in which writing is already being used in therapy, and an indication of some of the many further avenues which can fruitfully be followed in this area. A case for writing as therapy does not need to be made; it should be as natural an element of therapy as smiling. But just as talking and listening need careful handling and training, so also the use of writing needs to be weighed, considered and used judiciously. This book will support such care, ensuring that the power of the processes and products of writing can be harnessed most effectively, beneficially and safely.

Writing Cures is a stating of the position, the theoretical background and the current situation, rather than a how-to handbook. Yet it is packed with practical experiences, drawn from knowledgeable and skilled practice. The reader can confidently follow these examples, developing and extending their own practice, as well as clearly grasping the theoretical position.

Arts therapies, such as art, music and drama have been effectively utilised for many years. Why is there no writing therapy? It might be because words are our everyday human communicating tool – no special skills or equipment are required, and so no specialism needed. Every therapist, counsellor, clinical psychologist or art therapist can include writing in their work in a fairly straightforward manner.

Process and product: writing and art

Writing Cures is about writing. The writing used in therapy is not necessarily an art form. It is probably more helpful to both therapist and client if it is seen as a very particular form of communication (with the self, as well as with others), and a way of developing thinking and awareness of experience, rather than an *art*. The very mention of *poetry* for example can be offputting to clients: 'Oh no, duck, I couldn't write a *poem*!' Yet this person might respond very effectively to the notion of writing a list, or a letter, or even a few diary entries. It is a continuum, of course: the shopping list at one end and the finished publishable poem at the other. When people find they've written some poetry, or another written art form, however, they often benefit from increased self-confidence and natural pride.

The focus of therapeutic writing is upon the *processes* of writing rather than the *products*. A focus upon the products of writing will prevent clients from finding and making use of the particular power of writing. To be therapeutic, the initial stages of writing need to be encouraged to be personal, private, free from criticism, free from the constraints of grammar, syntax and form, free from any notion of audience other than the writer and possibly the therapist or another reader. Writing as an art form necessitates an awareness of all these at some stage. Therapeutic writing need never respond to the needs of these forces.

Writing is introduced to many patients or clients by writers in residence in the community, hospitals, hospices, prisons, GP health centres and so on. These people are writers (poets, playwrights, novelists) working for a short time with patients to offer them the healing and inspirational benefit of their particular kind of art. They, along with painters, musicians and sculptors working in similar ways, are arts for health practitioners – artists who share the practice of their art with patients – they are *not* therapists. Many artists deplore the notion and practice of arts therapy, maintaining that art is art, a pure form and should not be used for a function. Art therapists, on the other hand, have sometimes felt that artists should not dabble with patients as they have no knowledge of therapy. *Writing Cures* does not address the use of writers in residence, nor does it address the use of the reading of literature for therapeutic benefit. Reading poetry, literature or plays – the *products* of writing – can be a very therapeutic activity, and useful to clients and patients; but this book is about the *process* of writing.

Writing to help the practitioner as well as the client

The client is not the only lucky one to benefit from writing. Practitioners can very fruitfully use much the same writing processes to enable them to reflect effectively upon their practice for professional development. Such writings can be an invaluable basis for supervision.

Writing reflectively, reflexively or therapeutically can also be used naturally within training. Trainees can use it both as a training therapy and to support their developing professionalism. A better and clearer understanding of writing can support the writing of more lucid and helpful letters by the therapist: referral letters, letters to clients and letters to make a closure to a course of therapy.

As well as covering all the above areas, this book also explores and examines theoretical issues in a lively debate. It looks at research into the therapeutic benefits of writing and offers an informative, in-depth, review of current literature. Words are themselves symbols and images: there is power and magic in their use, particularly in the written form. An understanding of and interest in this foundation can enhance therapists' skill and knowledge.

Text-based counselling using email is a recent and booming development, and is discussed in detail. Ethical issues, codes of practice and strategies for dealing with the potential pitfalls of text-based work (such as the lack of physical communication) are all discussed informatively and engagingly.

Within the more traditional therapies there are those in which writing is an essential and habitual element (such as cognitive analytic therapy: CAT). *Writing Cures* enters into these, as well as the potential for dynamic development of forms of therapy in which writing can be used to extend and enhance the therapeutic contact, for example by writing a journal or unsent letters.

Writing Cures is an adventure into as yet largely uncharted waters. Yet developments in the field are taking place daily. We hope and trust that you, our reader, will take heart, knowledge and confidence from these pages and dive into the invigorating waters of therapeutic writing with us.

Part I

Theory and research

Chapter 1

The passion of science, the precision of poetry:[1] therapeutic writing – a review of the literature

Jeannie K. Wright

Introduction

What is it about writing that 'strengthens' the writer and how far has research been able to answer some of the questions associated with how 'writing therapy' works? Recently, large-scale studies have tended to emerge from a cognitive behavioural perspective (Lepore and Smyth 2002), but this is not the only orientation to investigate therapeutic writing in individual counselling, psychotherapy and group work. It could be argued that 'writing therapy' has also been restimulated by the development of narrative approaches (White and Epston 1990; McLeod 1997; Pennebaker and Seagal 1999) and computer-mediated methods where keyboard and cyberspace have replaced pen and paper. This review aims to map major, cross-disciplinary developments in the therapeutic use of writing in the English language over the last 30 years. The use of writing in cognitive analytic therapy and in journal writing will be addressed in later chapters and is not the focus here.

A continuum exists in the growing body of literature on therapeutic writing between the polarities of a 'scientific' and a 'humanities' approach, or between 'mastery and mystery' (Bakan 1969 quoted in McLeod 1994). On an international basis, those practitioners and researchers who come primarily from a literary arts or creative writing background tend to describe the 'soothing and healing power of poetry' (Bolton 1999b) for example. Drawing on their experience of clinical practice (Fuchel 1985; Gilbert 1995; Moskowitz 1998) or of facilitating creative writing groups (Bolton 1995, 1999b, 2000; Hunt and Sampson 1998; Hunt 2000) the therapeutic benefits of writing are explored with an enthusiasm verging on the evangelical: 'Creativity is not a tool. It is a mystery that you enter: an unfolding: an opening process' (Rogers 1993:105).

Those who follow a more scientific paradigm, from disciplines including immunology, health and social psychology seek to 'master' the phenomenon by measuring, explaining, predicting and analysing the results of randomised, controlled trials. The Pennebaker paradigm (Pennebaker and Beall 1986) has been

[1] I am indebted to the poet Diana Syder for this part of the title which is, she says, from V. Nabokov. Unfortunately neither of us has been able to trace a reference.

critiqued, replicated and extended in North America, Europe and many other parts of the world (Pennebaker 1990; 1995; 2002). These experiments clearly demonstrate the benefits of 'writing therapy' in reducing inhibition and in improving both physical and mental health (eg. Francis and Pennebaker 1992). I would like to stress that I am not seeking to oversimplify the body of literature on writing therapy by structuring the review around the scientific/humanities continuum. If anything, I would agree with Mazza (1999) that both approaches are needed in order to develop the research base and professional practice of writing therapy.

Central to potential users' concerns and to those of counselling and psychotherapy practitioners, especially those working within the pressures of a brief/time-limited model, is the question: how can client writing enhance the psychotherapeutic process? Like other expressive therapies, it increases the client's control of and active engagement in the process: 'Perhaps there is no other system of psychotherapy in which the client has so much control over the rate, depth and intensity of his or her personal therapeutic work' (Rasmussen and Tomm 1992: 3).

It also allows the client to choose how to assimilate what emerges from the learning, in their own time, which can be less pressured than in 'talking therapies' (Lange 1994).

Comparisons between vocal and written expressions of feeling about traumatic events have been analysed (Murray and Segal 1994) and would suggest that there is similar emotional processing by vocal and written expressions of feeling. The need for caution once fleeting spoken thoughts and feelings are made more permanent and open to scrutiny in writing is an important limitation of writing therapy and will be examined in later chapters.

Definitions of 'writing therapy'

Defining 'writing therapy' is difficult: it is 'a useful but vague and poorly defined technique' in Riordan's (1996: 263) summary. Neither is there one neat theoretical model or set of empirical findings to guide the use of therapeutic writing. References to parallels with other expressive and creative therapies, art, movement, drama and music, for example, are clear but there is little systematic explanation as to why writing therapy has not developed to the same extent. For the purposes of this review, I will define writing therapy as 'client expressive and reflective writing, whether self-generated or suggested by a therapist/researcher'. Therefore, the use of writing by the therapist about the client, such as in case notes or in farewell letters, is not included.

The 'humanities' paradigm

The National Association for Poetry Therapy (USA) represents the most developed of the therapies, which uses creative writing (see e.g. Longo 1996). Standards and ethical guidelines are in place in the USA for certified poetry therapists and registered poetry therapists (Mazza 1993: 51). Mazza extends an earlier research agenda for poetry therapy and suggests that both quantitative and qualitative research methods are needed at this interface of the arts and psychology.

In the UK, Hunt and Sampson (1998) have edited detailed accounts of current practice in a wide range of British educational and health care settings. The section on theoretical contexts is a tentative collection of ideas, drawing on psychoanalytic theory, linguistics, symbolic interactionism and philosophy, ancient and modern. The need to synthesise and to work across disciplines in the field of writing therapy is apparent.

In her most recent book, Hunt (2000: 3) adopts a 'Horneyan literary-psychoanalytic approach' to case studies of four 'highly literate, self-reflective' women who took part in her 'Autobiography and the Imagination' creative writing course. Hunt explores the complexity of her chosen theoretical model with great tenacity, asking important questions about the tension between writing as art and writing as therapy. She points out the limitations of her approach, however, firstly in not focusing on broader cultural or sociological questions of class, gender or ethnicity. There is certainly very little sense of the political awareness of constructivist approaches to be found in some contributions to the field (e.g. Bacigalupe 1996) where questions of social justice and user preference are addressed.

Ethical boundaries are also less than clear: 'There are considerable risks associated with applying psychodynamic theory to the written and spoken words of people one is working with without the safe-guards which would normally be built into the therapeutic relationship' (Hunt 2000: 191). In autobiographical writing, which exemplifies both 'process' and 'product', who is best placed to understand the meaning of the writing? Hunt's interpretations are fraught with such risks.

Gillie Bolton also comes from a background of teaching creative writing. Describing her theoretical model as 'eclectic', the humanist tradition predominates, and specifically Rogers and Perls are cited. Bolton's work is criticised by some for implying that in self-directed therapeutic writing there are no risks. Conversely, as illustrated by the above and by self-report from a range of participants in writing groups, it is this very emphasis on the potential of therapeutic writing for self-help, prevention and self-directedness which makes it such a viable alternative to those who choose to write, whether or not they enter therapy.

In the setting of general medical practice, the question of for whom and under what circumstances writing therapy is most effective is addressed. Those patients for whom it was appropriate to suggest writing therapy (Bolton 2000) included those suffering from problematic life circumstances rather than chronic depression, for example. Those for whom it would not be useful included 'disturbed or psychotic patients' who, it was felt, needed more supervision than a general practitioner could offer. Bolton points out that 'poetry and medicine have gone hand in hand since Apollo was the god of both' (Bolton 1999a: 119).

Drawing from her extensive experience of running workshops with small groups of women (Bolton 1999b) and citing examples from modern poetry written by women, including Sylvia Plath and Anne Sexton, Bolton explores the particular persistence of the savage inner critic in women. She compares writing as therapy to other expressive therapies.

Although there are similarities between Bolton's methods and those of the Pennebaker paradigm, such as instructing the client/group in 'writing without thinking', a clear divergence emerges here. Practitioners and researchers from the cognitive behavioural/scientific end of the continuum, for whom client creativity and imagination are variables to be reduced if possible, underestimate this most important aspect of writing therapy.

Bolton is not a neutral observer. Her stance draws on a long tradition of the therapeutic use of human creativity in general and writing in particular (Abbs 1998): 'poems are a hotline to our hearts, and we forget this emotional power at our peril' (Motion 2000: 6).

The narrative approach and writing in family and systemic therapy

Family and systemic therapy has been a fruitful area for therapeutic writing, in particular using the narrative approach to encourage clients to re-author their own stories (White and Epston 1990; McLeod 1997). Etherington (2000) counsels and writes in collaboration with two brothers sexually abused by their grandfather, constructing the story of their recovery in diary form, poetry and prose. The resulting narrative examines and overturns many of the conventional power dynamics between client and counsellor and between participant and researcher.

Bacigalupe (1996), practising in an American family therapy and community mental health context, emphasises, like Bolton, the client centredness of writing *with* and *by* the client rather than writing *about* or *to* the client. The implications and relevance of client writing for working cross-culturally are also highlighted. Bacigalupe also links the participatory basis of writing therapy with the power imbalance within any helping relationship. By writing about particular problem areas, the client becomes expert on their own material thus challenging the boundaries between what White and Epston (1990) call 'expert knowledge' and 'local knowledge'. This is particularly crucial when the social status of the client is inherently subject to discrimination and oppression: 'The question of writing in therapy is also relevant to discussions about issues of social justice in therapy contexts (e.g. therapists working with minority families). Work in a community health clinic can challenge therapists with questions about gender inequalities, institutionalised racism, evolving ethnic and cultural values and classism' (Bacigalupe 1996: 362). Writing in this context is empowering and inclusive. Examples given from family therapy in Australia and the USA include instances where adolescents and children are encouraged to write about their experience of foster care, for example, and present that writing to the 'experts' on the panel of professionals who hold the power to make decisions over their lives.

L'Abate (1991, 1992), a family therapist working in the USA, has contributed significantly to the literature on the use of writing, specifically with distance and programmed writing materials which can be used preventively or in computer-assisted training. Known for his humorous suggestion that counsellors should be advised to tell their clients they must write 'unless they 1. like you a lot, 2. have plenty of money, 3. have excellent insurance, and 4. want to stay in therapy forever!' (1992: 48), L'Abate questions traditional modes of family psychotherapeutic practice and advocates new techniques, including writing, that do not rely on therapist-patient talk. Rasmussen and Tomm (1992) outline a 'long brief therapy' the core of which is 'respect for the client's self directedness' (p. 18).

Pragmatism, and not wanting to succumb to pressures to abandon his interest in psychotherapy in favour of prescribing medication, was largely Rasmussen's original motivation for using writing with non-psychotic patients. His approach to guided letter writing emerged in response to the time pressures of the Danish health care system and long train journeys incurred by his practice between urban and rural areas. Letters from patients could be read on the train! Within a time-limited model, Rasmussen encourages and supports his clients' existing resources, including their autonomy and creativity: 'In this method, clients are coached to search out and find what they need the most and will do so if the therapist doesn't interfere too much' (p. 18). Tomm has applied Rasmussen's approach in psychiatry in Canada, and outlines his clinical findings. There is no evidence of systematic evaluation.

The scientific paradigm

If science is the art of the soluble, then Pennebaker and other empiricists have failed. Four leading American researchers (Esterling *et al.* 1999: 84) admit that, 'Despite the beneficial effects of writing, it is not entirely clear why it is effective in bringing about such striking physical health and behaviour change'. The beneficial effects of written emotional expression are, however, clearly and precisely recorded and have been subjected to meta-analysis (Smyth 1998). Reviews of core research on written emotional expression and health (Pennebaker 1997; Esterling *et al.* 1999; Lepore and Smyth 2002) suggest various benefits (see Lowe, Chapter 2 for more detail). Headlines such as 'The Pen is more Powerful than the Pill' (Bower 1999) have drawn popular attention to the efficacy of writing. In spite of academic and popular exposure, however, on neither side of the Atlantic is writing 'part of the mainstream psychotherapeutic armamentarium.' (Esterling *et al.* 1999: 94).

Offering a critique of and advancing Pennebaker's early work on writing about traumatic experiences, Lange, Schoutrop and colleagues in the Amsterdam Writing Group have used both quantitative and qualitative studies to highlight effective and ineffective ways of writing about trauma (see Van Zuuren *et al.* 1999). The methods are directive and involve the therapist giving 'precise instructions' to the patient about 'subject matter, the manner of writing, frequency, the amount of time spent and location' (Lange 1996: 376.) Lange demonstrates through case studies how writing 'a powerful and "friendly" technique' (1996: 381) results in self-confrontation leading to cognitive reappraisal.

In subsequent studies (Schoutrop *et al.* 1997a, 1997b; Van Zuuren *et al.* 1999) the psychologists/researchers inspect the writing in a more open and reflective way. Rather than 'searching for a direct relation between writing therapy and an outcome measure' (Van Zuuren *et al.* 1999: 364) the group aims to study an overview of positive and negative textual features to identify elements in the writing which are indicative of effective or ineffective writing. They also exemplify a less prescriptive style: 'the finding that some participants deviated successfully from their assignment could be transformed into the instruction that deviation is permitted if the participant considers this useful. Clients might even be offered several types of instructions, in order to be able to choose which type will work best for them' (Van Zuuren *et al.* 1999: 377). A greater degree of client self-directedness is implied.

Implications for practice

The simplicity of the way in which writing therapy works, if not the precise mechanism, is expressed humbly, after a dense analysis of randomised controlled trials, as follows: 'Many people, perhaps most, are able to guide their own therapy. Writing itself is a powerful therapeutic technique' (Esterling *et al.* 1999: 94).

The implications of these findings for online therapy, where writing is the major therapeutic vehicle, are complex and will be considered in Part 3 of this book. An analysis comparing typing and writing longhand in terms of disclosure of negative emotions, for example Brewin and Lennard (1999), may seem trivial compared to the controversy surrounding the existence and viability of the therapeutic relationship online, but the implications for practice are urgently in need of more systematic application.

Similarly, Pennebaker's work and that of others (e.g. Cameron and Nicholls 1998; Esterling *et al.* 1994; Bastien and Jacobs 1974) in which students have been the participants in the majority of randomised controlled trials needs to be extended to use more pluralistic methodologies and into other disciplines in addition to psychology. The evidence that writing about a major transition, such as the experience of moving into higher education, results in health and other benefits, including improved academic performance (Pennebaker and Francis 1996) is clear, whether or not we can explain the mechanism that produces the benefit. Writing therapy is cost-effective and would provide students with a self-help vehicle, which some have clearly already discovered via the internet (see Part 3).

There are however indications, other than those already mentioned, that writing therapy is not always appropriate or beneficial. When the client's experience is preverbal, for instance, other expressive therapies would be preferred. When writing is associated with strong negative experiences, for example in English classes at school, clients are unlikely to want to try writing therapy. One such client, to whom I had suggested 'rotten fish' (Lange 1996) letter writing said,' I don't want to read or write about my experiences'. The initial negative mood and short-term psychological pain resulting from writing about traumatic events (Esterling *et al.* 1999) may be intolerable for some unsupported writers (e.g. online).

Table 1.1 outlines some of the circumstances in which writing therapy has been found to be beneficial and some examples of supporting evidence. Some of the studies cited in the table have started a line of research which requires consolidation. It has been suggested, for example, that writing may be more effective for males (Smyth 1998) who have, traditionally, been underrepresented in statistical analyses of the use of face-to-face counselling services.

Conclusions

What emerges from studying the process and outcomes of such diverse lines of enquiry as the randomised controlled trial (see e.g. Pennebaker *et al.* 1988) and the single case study (see e.g. Bolton *et al.* 2000) is the powerful sense of commonality. For some people, in some circumstances, expressive writing is beneficial, with or without the added value of a therapeutic relationship. As Bolton (1999a: 27) puts it: 'Poetry or story making is therapy for both the body and soul'. And one of the reasons writing therapy needs the 'scientific' approach is that the 'creative hunches' of advocates from the 'humanities' body of research are strengthened by corroborative evidence from the other end of the continuum: 'Thus scientific methodology is seen for what it truly is – a way of preventing me from deceiving myself in regard to my creatively informed hunches which have developed out of the relationship between me and my material' (Rogers 1955: 275).

Science, defined narrowly and exclusively, has been the dominant model in psychology and psychotherapy. On the other hand, Mair (1989: 68) makes a passionate case for the poetic and imaginative, the unpredictable and inexplicable mystery of how people are: 'A properly sensitive psychology of psychotherapy has been stunted in its tentative development by our massive emphasis on scientific method. It has, I think, been crushed by method, and an insistence on the prosaic and external'. This review has aimed to bring the 'evidence' for the benefits of writing together and, in the words of a client who allowed herself the 'indulgence' of writing, in between a full-time job, dependent children and elderly parents:

> I sat down and wrote two sides of A4 I think – more than I expected to – and I just sat and wrote and then suddenly it came to a natural end and I felt so much better, and then I was able . . . you know, at the start of the day I was feeling really depressed and that just kind of worked things through. It was very therapeutic and then I just suddenly seemed to lift in the afternoon and felt different again; I felt much more together, much more able to cope with things.

Elaine Feinstein in her poem 'Muse: for ET' suggests that writing strengthens our 'fierce and obstinate centres' (Feinstein 1993). Poetry may be as precise as science and science as passionate as poetry in working to understand the way in which writing works.

Table 1.1 Circumstances in which writing therapy is beneficial, and supporting evidence of this

Clients' circumstances	*Some supporting studies*
Time-limited, focused, brief therapy – some of the detail can be dealt with outside the therapy room, on paper and in private	• Advantages of 'economy and complexity' (e.g. Ryle 1983: 365; Rasmussen and Tomm 1992)
With people who have a self-directed tendency to write – journals, diaries, letters – and who have found the process of writing, especially autobiographical writing, cathartic and clarifying	• Examples from literature (e.g. Adams 1990, 1996; Brewer 1994; Gilbert 1995; De Salvo 1999)
With people who are or perceive themselves to be powerless	• Bacigalupe (1996); case material in Wright (2000)
With people who are not using their first language in the face-to-face therapy – they are able to use their first language or a mixture of both first and host language	• See Lago (Chapter 9); Wright 1999
With people who, for cultural or other reasons, are silenced by shame and feel unable to speak	• Bass and Davis (1988); Bolton (1999b); Etherington (2000)
With people who are in inner turmoil and need to 'unpack the mind', externalise and organise their thoughts and feelings	• L'Abate (1992); Riordan (1996)
With people who need to disclose and exorcise a particular memory of stressful or traumatic experience	• Pennebaker paradigm reviewed in Smyth (1998); Amsterdam Writing Group; Bolton (1999a, b); Lepore and Smyth (2002)
With people at particular stages of life associated with experiencing strong feelings (e.g. adolescence or for the dying and those in hospice care)	• Sosin (1983); Atlas *et al.* (1992); Longo (1996); Bolton (1998); Lepore and Smyth, (2002)

Acknowledgement

An earlier version of this chapter was published in the *British Journal of Guidance and Counselling* 29(3): 277–91, accessible at http://www.tandf.co.uk.

References

Abbs, P. (1998) The creative word and the created life: the cultural context for deep autobiography, in C. Hunt and F. Sampson (eds) *The Self on the Page: Theory and Practice of Creative Writing in Personal Development*. London: Jessica Kingsley.

Adams, K. (1990) *Journal to the Self: Twenty-Two Paths to Personal Growth*. New York: Warner Books.

Adams, K. (1996) Journal writing as a powerful adjunct to therapy, *Journal of Poetry Therapy*, 10(1): 31–7.

Atlas, J.A., Smith, P. and Sessoms, L. (1992) Art and poetry in brief therapy of hospitalized adolescents, *The Arts in Psychotherapy*, 19: 279–83.

Bacigalupe, G. (1996) Writing in therapy: a participatory approach, *Journal of Family Therapy*, 18: 361–73.

Bass, E. and Davis, L. (1988) *The Courage to Heal: a Guide for Women Survivors of Child Sexual Abuse*. New York: Harper & Row.

Bastien S. and Jacobs, A. (1974) Dear Shirley: an experimental study of the effectiveness of written communication as a form of psychotherapy, *Journal of Consulting and Clinical Psychology*, 42: 151.

Bolton, G. (1995) Taking the thinking out of it: writing, a therapeutic space, *The Journal of the British Association for Counselling*, 6(3): 15–218.

Bolton, G. (1998) Writing or pills: therapeutic writing in primary care, in C. Hunt and F. Sampson (eds) *The Self on the Page: Theory and Practice of Creative Writing in Personal Development*. London: Jessica Kingsley.

Bolton, G. (1999a) *The Therapeutic Potential of Creative Writing – Writing Myself*. London: Jessica Kingsley.

Bolton, G. (1999b) 'Every poem breaks a silence that had to be overcome': The therapeutic power of poetry writing, *Feminist Review*, 62: 118–32.

Bolton, G. (2000) *Reflective Practice: Writing and Professional Development*. London: Paul Chapman/Sage.

Bolton, G., Gelipter, D. and Nelson, P. (2000) 'Keep taking the words': therapeutic writing in general practice, *British Journal of General Practice* 50: 80–1.

Bower, H. (1999) The pen is mightier than the pill, *Guardian*, 13 April.

Brewer, W.D. (1994) Mary Shelley on the therapeutic value of language, *Papers on Language and Literature*, 30(4): 387–407.

Brewin, C.R. and Lennard, H. (1999) Effects of mode of writing on emotional narratives, *Journal of Traumatic Stress*, 12(2): 355–61.

Cameron, L.D. and Nicholls, G. (1998) Expression of stressful experiences through writing: effects of a self-regulatory manipulation for pessimists and optimists, *Health Psychology*, 17(1): 84–92.

De Salvo, L. (1999) *Writing as a Way of Healing*. London: The Women's Press.

Esterling, B.A., Antoni, M., Fletcher, M., Margulies, S. and Schneiderman, N. (1994) Emotional disclosure through writing or speaking modulates latent Epstein-Barr virus reactivation, *Journal of Consulting and Clinical Psychology*, 62: 130–40.

Esterling, B.A., L'Abate, L., Murray, E.J. and Pennebaker, J.W. (1999) Empirical foundations for writing in prevention and psychotherapy: mental and physical health outcomes, *Clinical Psychology Review*, 19(1): 79–96.

Etherington, K. (2000) *Narrative Approaches to Working with Adult Male Survivors of Child Sexual Abuse: The Client's, the Counsellor's and the Researcher's Story*. London: Jessica Kingsley.

Feinstein, E. (1993) Muse: For E.T. in *Sixty Women Poets*. Newcastle upon Tyne: Bloodaxe Books Ltd.

Francis, M.E. and Pennebaker, J.W. (1992) Putting stress into words: the impact of writing on physiological, absentee, and self-reported emotional well-being measures, *American*

Journal of Health Promotion, 6(4): 280–7.

Fuchel, J. C. (1985) Writing poetry can enhance the psychotherapeutic process: observations and examples, *The Arts in Psychotherapy*, 12: 89–93.

Gilbert, J. (1995) Clients as poets: reflections on personal writing in the process of psychological change, *Clinical Psychology Forum*, 75, 3–5.

Hunt, C. (2000) *Therapeutic Dimensions of Autobiography in Creative Writing*. London: Jessica Kingsley.

Hunt, C. and Sampson, F. (eds) (1998) *The Self on the Page: Theory and Practice of Creative Writing in Personal Development*. London: Jessica Kingsley.

L'Abate, L. (1991) The use of writing in psychotherapy, *American Journal of Psychotherapy*, 45(1): 87–98.

L'Abate, L. (1992) *Programmed Writing: A Paratherapeutic Approach for Intervention with Individuals, Couples and Families*. Pacific Grove, CA: Brooks/Cole.

Lange, A. (1994) Writing assignments in the treatment of grief and traumas from the past, in J. Zweig (ed.) *Eriksonian Approaches, the Essence of the Story*. New York: Brunner/Mazel.

Lange, A. (1996) Using writing assignments with families managing legacies of extreme traumas, *Journal of Family Therapy*, 18: 375–88.

Lepore, S.J. and Smyth, J.M. (eds) (2002) *The Writing Cure: How Expressive Writing Promotes Health and Emotional Well-Being*. Washington, DC: American Psychological Association.

Longo, P.J. (1996) If I had my life to live over – Stephanie's story: a case study in poetry therapy, *Journal of Poetry Therapy*, 10: 55–67.

McLeod, J. (1994) *Doing Counselling Research*. London: Sage.

Mcleod, J. (1997) *Narrative and Psychotherapy*. London: Sage.

Mair, M. (1989) *Between Psychology and Psychotherapy: A Poetics of Experience*. London: Routledge.

Mazza, N. (1993) Poetry therapy: toward a research agenda for the 1990s, *The Arts in Psychotherapy*, 20: 51–9.

Mazza, N. (1999) *Poetry Therapy: Interface of the Arts and Psychology*. Boca Raton: CRC Press.

Milner, M. (1971) *On Not Being Able to Paint*. London: Heinemann Educational Books.

Moskowitz, Z. C. (1998) The self as source: creative writing generated from personal reflection, in C. Hunt and F. Sampson (eds) *The Self on the Page: Theory and Practice of Creative Writing in Personal Development*. London: Jessica Kinglsey.

Motion, A. (2000) Hotlines to the nation's heart, *Guardian*, 11 March.

Murray, E.J. and Segal, D.L. (1994) Emotional processing in vocal and written expression of feelings about traumatic experiences, *Journal of Traumatic Stress*, 7(3): 391–405.

Pennebaker, J.W. (2002) Writing about emotional events: from past to future, in S.J. Lepore and J.M. Smyth (eds) *The Writing Cure: How Expressive Writing Promotes Health and Emotional Well-Being*. Washington, DC: American Psychological Association.

Pennebaker, J.W. (1990) *Opening Up: The Healing Power of Confiding in Others*. New York: Avon Books.

Pennebaker, J.W. (ed.) (1995) *Emotion, Disclosure and Health*. Washington, DC: American Psychological Association.

Pennebaker, J.W. (1997) Writing about emotional experiences as a therapeutic process, *Psychological Science*, 8(3): 162–6.

Pennebaker, J.W. and Beall, S.K. (1986) Confronting a traumatic event: toward an understanding of inhibition and disease, *Journal of Abnormal Psychology*, 93(3): 274–281.

Pennebaker, J.W. and Francis, M. (1996) Cognitive emotional and language processes in disclosure, *Cognition and Emotion*, 10: 601–26.

Pennebaker, J.W., Kiecolt-Glaser, J. and Glaser, R. (1988) Disclosure of traumas and immune function: health implications for psychotherapy, *Journal of Consulting and Clinical Psychology*, 56: 239–45.

Pennebaker, J.W. and Seagal, J.D. (1999) Forming a story: the health benefits of narrative, *Journal of Clinical Psychology*, 55(10): 1243–54.

Rasmussen, P.T. and Tomm, K. (1992) Guided letter writing: a long brief therapy method whereby clients carry out their own treatment, *Journal of Strategic and Systemic Therapie*, 7(4): 1–18.

Riordan, R.J. (1996) Scriptotherapy: therapeutic writing as a counseling adjunct. *Journal of Counseling and Development*, 74: 263–9.

Rogers, C.R. (1955) Persons or science? A philosophical question, *American Psychologist*, 10: 267–78.

Rogers, N. (1993) *The Creative Connection – Expressive Arts as Healing*. Palo Alto: Science & Behavior Books (reprinted Ross-on-Wye: PCCS Books 2000).

Ryle, A.(1983) The value of written communication in dynamic psychotherapy, *British Journal of Medical Psychology*, 56: 361–6.

Schoutrop, M.J.A., Lange, A., Hanewald, G., Duurland, C. and Bermond, B.(1997a) The effects of structured writing assignments on overcoming major stressful events: an uncontrolled study, *Clinical Psychology and Psychotherapy*, 4: 179–85.

Schoutrop, M.J.A., Lange, A., Brosschot, J.F. and Everaerd, W. (1997b) Reprocessing traumatic events in writing assignments: mechanisms, modes of processing and psychological physiological effects (abstract), *Psychosomatic Medicine*, 59: 83.

Smyth, J.M. (1998) Written emotional expression: effect size, outcome types, and moderating variables, *Journal of Consulting and Clinical Psychology*, 66(1): 174–84.

Sosin, D.A. (1983) The diary as a transitional object in female adolescent development, *Adolescent Psychiatry*, 11: 92–103.

Van Zuuren, F.J., Schoutrop, M.J.A., Lange, A., Louis, C.M. and Slegers, J.E.M. (1999) Effective and ineffective ways of writing about traumatic experiences: a qualitative study, *Psychotherapy Research*, 9(3): 363–80.

White, M. and Epston, D. (1990) *Narrative Means to Therapeutic Ends*. New York: Norton.

Wright, J.K. (1999) Uses of writing to counter the silence of oppression: counselling women at the University of the South Pacific, *Pacific Health Dialog*, 6(2): 305–10.

Wright, J.K. (2000) Using writing in counselling women at work, *Changes*, 18(4): 264–73.

Chapter 2

Cognitive psychology and the biomedical foundations of writing therapy

Geoff Lowe

Many studies have shown that people feel happier and healthier after writing about deeply traumatic memories. Actively confronting upsetting experiences – through writing or talking – reduces the negative effects of 'bottling things up', which can lead to long-term stress and disease. But what are the links between confronting traumatic events and long-term health? Teams of biomedical researchers led by American psychologist James W. Pennebaker have been finding out how 'verbally revealing it all' helps our immune systems to fight off infections.

Pennebaker's interest in the potential of writing therapy was sparked by conversations with government polygraph (or 'lie-detector') operators (Pennebaker *et al.* 1987). A criminal's heart rate and breathing are much slower immediately after a confession than before. Since then Pennebaker has been busy researching his belief that we can all feel better after confronting the past through writing.

According to Pennebaker and other researchers, the effect is not just emotional. In one of his early studies (Pennebaker *et al.* 1988) they found that college students had more active T-lymphocyte cells – an indication of immune system function – six weeks after writing about stressful events. First, the researchers asked healthy college students to write about either personally traumatic experiences or trivial topics, on four consecutive days. In the months afterwards, writers who revealed their particular thoughts and feelings visited the student health centre for illness much less often than any of the other writers.

The next stage was to investigate the physical links between confronting traumatic events and long-term health. In a follow-up study, another 50 healthy participants were questioned about their moods and physical symptoms. The researchers took blood samples from them before and after the four-day writing exercises. Some participants chose to write about highly personal and upsetting experiences (including loneliness, sexual conflicts, death and sexual abuse). Did such writings help them feel better? Not immediately – according to the subjective distress ratings. But their blood samples taken after the fourth day showed evidence of an enhanced immune response. Their lymphocytes (white cells that fight off bacteria and viruses) increased their reaction and sensitivity to 'invaders' more than did those of other participants who wrote about trivial things (such as their shoes or their plans for the day or a recent social event).

This trend continued over the following six weeks when blood samples were analysed once again. Individuals who showed the greatest improvements in health were those who wrote about topics that they had actively held back from telling others. The use of more self-reflective and causal thinking from the first to the last day of writing led to greater health improvements in terms of lower symptom reports and fewer doctor visits.

Other studies have found that people function better in day-to-day tasks, and score higher on tests of psychological well-being after such writing 'exercises' – especially if more positive aspects emerge. For instance, Cameron and Nicholls (1998) recruited students for short writing sessions over a three-week period. In addition to the control and disclosure groups, they also had a third group engage in 'self-regulatory' writing which also involved listing possible coping steps to deal with their disclosed problems. These 'self-regulatory' writers reported fewer clinic visits subsequently than controls. Among the 'disclosure only' writers, only students characterised as 'optimistic' reported fewer clinic visits. Both optimists and pessimists in the self-regulatory group reported increased psychological benefit and better mood states following the writing period.

In the late 1990s Smyth (1998) produced a timely review and synthesis of the best research (on written emotional expression) so far. Most studies involved healthy volunteers (physically and psychologically). Measures typically included: physiological (e.g. skin conductance, heart rate, blood pressure, immune indices); psychological (e.g. well-being, adjustment, mood); reported health (e.g. clinic visits, colds, symptoms); and general (e.g. grade point average (GPA), absenteeism, cognitive functioning).

All 13 primary (randomised control) studies identified in Smyth's review showed a positive influence of the emotional disclosure writing task. The average effect size was $d = 0.47$, which represents a 23 per cent improvement in the disclosure group compared with the control group. (This is roughly similar to that found with other psychological interventions, and may well be clinically relevant.) However, there was a lot of variability in effect size, ranging from 0.22 to 2.1. This suggests that confounding factors might be playing a part in some studies. Smyth found that overall effect sizes were increased in studies when the writing sessions were spaced over longer periods, and in those involving higher proportions of men. The increased effect size for male participants suggests that this type of writing may be more effective for men – possibly because they have lower pre-writing levels of emotional expression, and they may focus more on the trauma when writing.

Psychological well-being was enhanced more when student participants were involved, and in studies with instructions to write specifically about current traumas (rather than past experiences). All the review studies reported increases in short-term distress. But relatively more short-term distress did not appear to lead to greater benefit. Smyth suggests that the 'trauma-relevant fear network' must be activated for improvement to be made.

Putting traumatic memories into words can help ease turmoil and defuse the danger. According to Smyth, writing gives one a sense of control and a sense of understanding. To write about a stressful event, one has to break it down into little pieces, and suddenly it seems more manageable.

Although the writing task produces health benefits in healthy participants, there may be negative interactions with other treatments or in other non-healthy groups. For example, Gidron *et al.* (1996) carried out a study of trauma survivors with post-traumatic stress disorder (PTSD). Survivors in the disclosure group wrote about their most traumatic experiences; control survivors wrote about daily agenda without emotional content. The disclosure subjects reported higher negative feelings (they were more upset) immediately after writing, and more health care visits and avoidance symptoms at follow-up. There is a warning here that written disclosure without coping skills training should not be recommended for PTSD patients.

Nevertheless, writing may provide an alternative form of preventive therapy that could be valuable for individuals who otherwise would not enter therapy. And for some physical illnesses, it appears that doctors might be well advised to prescribe writing at the same time as writing a prescription.

The evidence comes from a notable study led by Joshua Smyth in the USA (Smyth *et al.* 1999). People with asthma and others with arthritis were asked to write about the most stressful experience in their lives for 20 minutes on three consecutive days. At the same time control groups of asthma and arthritis patients were asked simply to write about their plans for the day. All the patients carried on with their regular medications.

Four months later, the researchers found almost half those who wrote about stressful events showed clinical improvements in their symptoms, compared to less than a quarter in the control groups. In the asthmatic group, those who wrote out their innermost feelings experienced a 20 per cent improvement in their lung function, compared to no change in those who just planned their day. For the arthritis sufferers, emotional writing reduced the severity of their disease by almost a third, with again no change in the control group. They also monitored perceived stress, quality of sleep, substance use and medication use (7 days prior, during intervention and 14 days after). None of these were found to explain the main findings (Stone *et al.* 2000).

The researchers caution that writing should not replace prescribed treatment, and it is not yet known whether the impact of the writing task carries on beyond four months. Nevertheless, the observed health benefits appear to be a remarkably good return for an hour's writing.

So, what is it about an individual's writing that could be related to health outcomes? Pennebaker's teams (Pennebaker and Francis 1996, Pennebaker *et al.* 1997) have developed software that systematically evaluates written text and 'characterises' healthy writing. They have identified two traits that predict better health – more frequent use of positive emotion words (e.g. good, happy, love), and also a *moderate* number of negative emotion words (e.g. angry, hurt, ugly).

Moreover, it now seems that briefly bringing into play positive emotions at the start of our adult life could help us live longer. Danner *et al.* (2001) have found that nuns who disclose positive emotions in their autobiographical writing during their early twenties tend to survive longer in old age. Results from the Nun Study (a longitudinal study of older Catholic sisters) showed, in terms of mortality risk, a 2.5-fold difference between those with most and those with least positive emotional content in their early writings. It is likely that an optimistic explanatory style – in contrast to a pessimistic one – can lead to greater feelings of well-being and even to longer life. The 'healing' effect of positive emotions may reduce stress in the cardiovascular system even in the face of negative life events.

In Pennebaker's research, further text analyses showed that the use of more self-reflective and causal thinking from the first to the last day of writing predicts greater health improvements (lower symptom reports, fewer doctor visits). These changes may reflect more efficient cognitive processing of trauma, including more coherent construction of the emotional components of the experience.

The opposite of disclosure is suppression, and this is likely to influence the kinds of health-related effects arising from emotional writing. In one study (Petrie *et al.* 1998) medical students wrote about emotional or non-emotional topics, with or without thought suppression. Those in the suppression condition were asked to 'concentrate, for the next five minutes, on putting any thoughts about what you have been writing completely out of your mind'; those in the 'no suppression' condition to 'concentrate on what you have written'.

Lymphocyte levels were higher after 'emotional' writing (compared with 'neutral' writing); and lower with thought suppression. Other studies have noted that suppressing emotional thoughts and repression can lead to poorer health outcomes. 'Repressors' tend to have lower cell-mediated immune responses. It seems likely, then, that written emotional expression may free physiological resources previously used for inhibition/suppression.

We don't know yet exactly why writing about painful events can improve health, but the answer probably lies somewhere in the still-mysterious connections between stress and disease. Failure to confront traumatic experiences could well be a form of stress itself, and can increase the incidence of illness. Many studies have shown that prolonged emotional stress can weaken the immune system, promote heart disease and worsen the course of arthritis, asthma and many other diseases.

How could such writing disclosure interventions influence the immune system? Let us assume people cope with stressful experiences through psychological inhibition – 'bottling it up'. This inhibition takes a toll on the immune system by activating hormonal systems and/or sympathetic fibres that innervate lymphoid organs. The disclosure process is assumed to alleviate the resulting immune disregulation by forcing the individual to impose structure on the experience through words – and induces a sense of greater personal control. More positive appraisals can reduce negative emotions and facilitate greater discussion of the stressful experience – both of which should dampen hormonal and sympathetic activity and thereby restore immune regulation.

Research has shown that greater immune change after disclosure occurs in those individuals who show signs of adopting more positive appraisals. In line with this encouragement of positive aspects, one recent study explored the importance of writing about the perceived benefits of traumatic events as a factor in the 'healing process' of emotional writing (King and Miner 2000). Participants wrote about personal trauma or neutral topics; and in each group they either wrote about perceived benefits or did not. Those who wrote only about trauma or perceived benefits reported fewer clinic visits for illness during a period of five months after writing. Such results suggest that writing about perceived benefits from traumatic events ('looking on the positive side') may provide a less upsetting but effective way to benefit from writing.

These benefits from (emotional disclosure) writing have received much media attention. But we should be aware of some limiting factors. Most studies have used fairly standardised writing tasks – developed by Pennebaker *et al.* with college students and healthy volunteers. Indeed, most of the research, so far, has involved students and healthy volunteers (apart from notable exceptions such as Smyth *et al.* 1999 and Gidron *et al.* 1996). Not all studies have been randomised control trials (RCTs) – although the main ones were. RCT studies with particular groups of patients require special research designs and ethical procedures, and this is where writing therapy interventions need to be evaluated now. Even in RCT studies, control subjects may well realise that they are in the control condition, partly due to widespread media publicity about writing therapy interventions. We know very little about 'dose-response' aspects (i.e. is more writing therapy better than a little? How much is optimum?). And what kinds of writing, for how long, how frequent, which aspects, etc. produce particular outcomes?

Evaluation of the writing task as a potential intervention needs to consider several issues: whether specific types of trauma are related to outcomes; the role of writing parameters (e.g. use of insight words, positive and negative terms); the effect of writing tasks in clinical samples of both psychological (e.g. PTSD) and somatic (e.g. chronic disease) origin.

In sum, there's plenty of very interesting research in this area. Some of it has generated considerable media attention; so many more people – clients, consumers and practitioners alike – are becoming increasingly aware of these positive links between (creative) writing and health. But once we get beyond the simplified message stage, we realise that the situation is much more complex. Although the links have been well demonstrated, the precise causal mechanisms are less well understood.

Writing can represent a direct line from feeling and thinking to healing. But there are some signs that there may be problems with this approach. Until we have more high quality research which informs us about why, when, where, on whom, by whom, under what conditions, and with what possible after-effects or side-effects, then we should perhaps proceed with caution.

Bibliography

Berry, D.S. and Pennebaker, J.W. (1993) Nonverbal and verbal emotional expression and health, *Psychotherapy and Psychosomatics*, 59(1): 11–19.

Booth, R.J., Petrie, K.J. and Pennebaker, J.W. (1997) Changes in circulating lymphocyte numbers following emotional disclosure: evidence of buffering? *Stress Medicine*, 13(1): 23–9.

Cameron, L.D. and Nicholls, G. (1998) Expression of stressful experiences through writing: effects of a self-regulation manipulation for pessimists and optimists, *Health Psychology*, 17(1): 84–92.

Danner, D.D., Snowdon, D.A. and Friesen, W.V. (2001) Positive emotions in early life and longevity: findings from the Nun Study, *Personality Processes and Individual Differences*, 80(5): 804–13.

Esterling, B.A., L'Abate, L., Murray, E.J. and Pennebaker, J.W. (1999) Empirical foundations for writing in prevention and psychotherapy: mental and physical health outcomes, *Clinical Psychology Review*, 19(1): 79–96.

Francis, M.E. and Pennebaker, J.W. (1992) Putting stress into words: the impact of writing on physiological, absentee, and self-reported emotional well-being measures, *American Journal of Health Promotion*, 6: 280–7.

Gidron, Y., Peri, T., Connolly, J.F. and Shalev, A.Y. (1996) Written disclosure in post-traumatic stress disorder: is it beneficial for the patient? *Journal of Nervous and Mental Disease*, 184: 505–7.

Greenberg, M.A., Wortman, C.B. and Stone, A.A. (1996) Emotional expression and physical health: revising traumatic memories or fostering self-regulation? *Journal of Personality and Social Psychology*, 71(3): 588–602.

King, L.A. and Miner, K.N. (2000) Writing about the perceived benefits of traumatic events: implications for physical health, *Personality and Social Psychology Bulletin*, 26(2): 220–30.

Lepore, S.J. (1997) Expressive writing moderates the relation between intrusive thoughts and depressive symptoms, *Journal of Personality and Social Psychology*, 73(5): 1030–7.

Marlo, H. and Wagner, M.K. (1999) Expression of negative and positive events through writing: implications for psychotherapy and health, *Psychology and Health* 14(2): 193–215.

Njus, D.M., Nitschke, W. and Bryant, F.B. (1996) Positive affect, negative affect, and the moderating effect of writing on sIgA antibody levels, *Psychology and Health*, 12: 135–48.

Pennebaker, J.W. (1993) Putting stress into words: health, linguistic, and therapeutic implications, *Behavioral Research Therapy*, 31: 539–48.

Pennebaker, J.W. (1997a) Writing about emotional experiences as a therapeutic process, *Psychological Science*, 8(3): 162–6.

Pennebaker, J.W. (1997b) *Opening Up: The Healing Power of Expressing Emotions*. New York: Guilford Press.

Pennebaker, J.W. and Francis, M.E. (1996) Cognitive, emotional, and language processes in disclosure, *Cognition and Emotion*, 10(6): 601–26.

Pennebaker, J.W., Hughes, C.F. and O'Heeron, R.C. (1987) The psychophysiology of confession: linking inhibitory and psychosomatic processes, *Journal of Personality and Social Psychology*, 52: 781–93.

Pennebaker, J.W., Kiecolt-Glaser, J. and Glaser, R. (1988) Disclosure of traumas and immune function: health implications for psychotherapy, *Journal of Consulting and Clinical Psychology*, 56: 239–45.

Pennebaker, J.W., Mayne, T.J. and Francis, M.E. (1997) Linguistic predictors of adaptive bereavement, *Journal of Personality and Social Psychology*, 72(4): 863–71.

Petrie, K.J., Booth, R.J. and Pennebaker, J.W. (1998) The immunological effects of thought suppression, *Journal of Personality and Social Psychology*, 75(5): 1264–72.

Smyth, J.M. (1998) Written emotional expression: effect sizes, outcome types and moderating variables, *Journal of Consulting and Clinical Psychology*, 66(1): 174–84.

Smyth, J.M., Stone, A.A., Hurewitz, A. and Kaell, A. (1999) Effects of writing about stressful experiences on symptom reduction in patients with asthma or rheumatoid arthritis: a randomized trial, *Journal of the American Medical Association*, 281(14): 1304–9.

Stone, A.A., Smyth, J.M., Kaell, A. and Hurewitz, A. (2000) Structured writing about stressful events: exploring potential psychological mediators of positive health effects, *Health Psychology*, 19(6): 619–24.

Chapter 3

The contribution of narrative ideas and writing practices in therapy

Jane Speedy

> Among my people, questions are often answered with stories. The first story almost always evokes another, which summons another, until the answer to the question has become several stories long. A sequence of tales is thought to offer broader and deeper insight than a single story alone.
>
> (Pinkola Estes 1992: 1)

Introduction

There is growing interest across a range of disciplines and practices in 'narrative' and the co-construction of narratives as a useful root metaphor for understanding the ways that human beings construct, make sense of and transform their lives. The collection of ideas and practices that has become known as 'narrative therapy' might be regarded as a 'practice of writing ' in a number of ways. It is a 'storied' therapy that has strong roots within narrative, poststructuralist and literary theory and uses much of the language of these traditions. Narrative therapy presents quite a challenge to therapeutic practices that focus primarily on individual potential or 'inner state' psychology (see White 2001, for a discussion of these differences). It positions personal agency firmly within social and political discourses, and the cultural and historical traditions and 'local' stories that are available to people. In this way the construction of 'alternative' or preferred stories in therapeutic conversations, however fleeting or tentative, may be seen as something of an extraordinary achievement that warrants a written record in order to be more firmly captured and embraced.

Narrative therapy transparently and deliberately uses writing and the production of therapeutic documents and books on the part of therapists, the people that consult them and many of the 'outsider witnesses' to these therapeutic endeavours. Narrative practitioners also tend to subvert some of the taken-for-granted assumptions about the execution and ownership of note-taking and record keeping that have become part of the professional writing culture of therapy. These therapy notes, or reflections, are usually considered to have distinctly more therapeutic than professional purposes. More recently, poetic writing strategies that have emerged from the field of narrative inquiry and conversational research have also been used as transformational tools within therapeutic encounters.

In this chapter I shall introduce and explore some of these ideas and practices and, where possible, illustrate them with examples from the experiences of myself and others.

The 'interpretive turn', poststructuralism, literary theory and narrative therapy

It is not possible in such a short chapter to do more than briefly outline the range of ideas and practices that have come to be identified as the narrative therapies. These have been extensively described elsewhere, and readers who wish to engage with them further might start with any or all of Bird (2000), Epston and White (1992), Freedman and Combs (1996), Monk *et al.* (1997), Payne (2000) and White and Epston (1990).

To give a quick and incomplete overview, narrative therapists are interested in how people have come to make sense of their lives out of the materials lying around them in society and how they make and remake sense of this lived experience through the construction of narratives: that is to say, through the unfolding of sequences of events through time to form a plot.

Narrative therapists consider people to be multi-storied, invariably generating many stories at the same time. A narrative practitioner would be particularly curious about the ways in which people 'thicken' (or flesh out) and construct what become the most dominant stories in their lives. They are interested in asking 'deconstructing questions' in order to unpack what may have become problem-saturated, or unhelpful, or just habitual stories so as to open up space for 're-authoring conversations' that might generate 'preferred stories'. These are conversations that encourage the telling and retelling of stories. Curiosity is employed, often in a subjunctive tense, about the many possible versions that 'may be' or 'might be' available to people.

So far, I am placing narrative practice firmly within the arena of the talking therapies, and indeed it may well involve a lot of talking. These conversations are embedded within poststructuralist understandings about the fluidity and multiplicity of selves and identities. These 'selves' may constantly be regenerated and constituted in conversation and storytelling, just as they in turn are constitutive of the stories and identities of others (see Foucault 1984; Drewery and Winslade 1997; White 1997, 2002b; Thomas 2002 for a more extensive exposition of poststructuralist ideas and their interplay with narrative practices).

Thus the language of re-authoring or retelling dominant and preferred stories that is transparently used by narrative practitioners is of both a narrative and a literary nature. The work of literary theorists such as Derrida (1978), and their investigations into what makes a good story, also underpins narrative practices. People's lives are not texts, but narrative therapists are nonetheless heavily influenced by literary studies of what constitutes a text of aesthetic or literary merit, of stories that are evocative and that leave gaps or 'liminal' spaces for possibilities, rather than certainties, to abound and of the 'subjunctivation process of great narrative – the means whereby it creates not only a story, but also a sense of its contingent and uncertain variants' (Bruner 1986: 174).

Thus narrative therapists are constantly engaged with their clients in a process of co-researching these 'uncertain variants' or alternative versions of stories. Derrida's (1978) construct of the 'absent but implicit' stories being contained within, or contingent upon, any given narrative provides a particularly useful point of entry to alternative stories. Here's an example.

Sophie was a client who had come to consult me because '*things seemed to be getting out of hand*'. I was curious about the (absent but implicit) times and contexts when things had been *in hand*, or perhaps *more in hand*, and the (absent but implicit) times or circumstances when things might get *right out of hand* (see Derrida 1978 and White 2000 for further explorations of these ideas). Since things currently only *seemed* to be getting out of hand, I was also interested to find out the ways in which things were different from how they seemed. It transpired that Sophie was interested in this too, since things were *way out of hand* compared with how they seemed, and this had to do with, or at least coincided with, moving house.

Literary theory underpins therapy practice. Constructs such as deconstruction (unpacking meaning) or ways of working such as overtly looking for the absent but implicit or the 'open space' where other versions of a story might emerge are not merely tools or techniques. The narrative metaphor invites people into ways of working 'as if' stories will generate different positions, not only to view the world but also to perform our lives. A vital means of generating, capturing and embracing these stories is through writing.

Talking practices, writing practices and ethical document-keeping

In most psychotherapeutic traditions, note-taking and record keeping on the part of the therapist takes place when the client is absent. Although these notes are theoretically (and, under the current data protection act, legally) available to clients, in most cases written notes are considered part of 'professional' practices rather than therapeutic exchanges. They are connected with professional practices of supervision, practice management and professional accountability.

Notes in narrative therapy often tend to be taken as part of the therapeutic process, as a means of capturing client's words. These documents are often given to clients as a written record of key moments in the conversation. These notes may not be very lengthy, and certainly in my case are never very neat. They represent, I would suggest, a completely different take on ownership and ethical practices in therapeutic note-taking. White (1995) describes his ethical priorities in giving his notes to the person he is assisting in some detail. As a teacher of narrative practices, I notice that it is this collaborative, open writing of notes that seems to most frequently trouble the edges of taken-for-granted assumptions within the cultures of therapy. These assumptions are interesting in terms of therapeutic power relationships and the ownership of 'documents'. They also shed some light on an unquestioned privileging of 'talking' in most established therapeutic domains. I am usually asked if this kind of 'note-taking' detracts attention from clients. I can only reply that when I ask 'Would you mind if I write that down?' or 'Would it be a good idea to capture some of this on paper?' people are almost invariably very enthusiastic about 'capturing' key words and moments in writing and always seem pleased to have the notes.

Narrative practitioners do take their work to consultants of course, but again, this can take place within the session. In this way, the arcane mysteries of counselling supervision are made much more available to clients (see mad fax Sunday for instance, when David Epston was brought into a therapeutic conversation, via the fax machine, to offer his reflections: Lane *et al.* 1998). I have often asked people from my international online consultancy group for their reflections, questions and ideas about my work and have either emailed these on to clients or printed them out for the next session. Thus the whole process is made more of a collaborative and transparent venture and 'note-taking' becomes decentred rather than therapist-centred and a much more significant part of the available therapeutic process.

The writing practices of outsider witnesses and others 'on the team'

Narrative therapy invites people to explore their lives and identities in social and connected ways and this may include some kind of definitional ceremony involving 'outsider witnesses' to the stories being told (see White 2000, 2002a; Mann and Russell 2002 for more detailed explorations of these ceremonies which are complex and powerful processes that I do not have the time to describe here). These witnesses (who could be friends, family members or others with their own insider knowledge of similar circumstances or life events, for instance) become an audience to accounts of people's lives and offer reflections and retellings of the stories. Outsider witnesses may also write these reflections down, which they might then offer to the person at the centre of the ceremony. Sometimes these reflections are presented to clients in the moment and sometimes they are collected and presented as a book or record of the ceremony (see McMenamin 1998 and Hamilton 2001 for more on therapeutic bookmaking).

At other times where 'live' witnesses are not available, emails, faxes, and /or letters and poems from witnesses and supporters can be collected in support of a current client. Gregory, for example, is a young man who at one time was described as suicidal (although he preferred to think of himself as someone concerned about the future). During the course of our work together he generated a considerable amount of poetry. He and I both still have copies of all these poems, and I have his permission to give copies of them to other clients who are experiencing similar life events (see Speedy 2000b for more about this process).

Using therapeutic documents, letters and books

David Epston, who first developed many of these ideas, together with Michael White, suggested that the use of therapeutic documents increased the impact of 'talking therapy' fourfold (see White 1995). Many narrative therapists send documents to clients as a supplement to face-to-face sessions, reiterating and providing a permanent expression of what might have been key moments, asking supplementary questions that might be useful and, particularly with children, presenting certificates that acknowledge achievements. Such documents are usually tentative rather than prescriptive in tone:

> What stood out for me, and you may have seen things differently . . .
>
> Your words have stayed with me and perhaps . . .
>
> After our session I realised that there were a couple of other questions that I might have asked and I just wanted to capture them in case you would have found them helpful . . .

These documents capture words and stories from the more ephemeral, spoken, therapeutic conversations and put them into writing. In this way people can remind themselves about the ways in which their stories change over time and the ways in which they position themselves differently than they might have done at the beginning of therapy (Payne 2000: 127–57 explores this process extensively).

This emphasis on writing and therapeutic letter writing also extends to the people consulting therapists. Etherington (2000), for instance, encourages her clients to write the letters that they would never send, or it is too late to send and, in this way, to enter into the conversations they would have liked to have had in their lives. These letters represent powerful accounts from adults giving voice to stories that were silenced, forbidden or unimaginable in childhood. Clients may also regularly engage in letter and other writing practices in between face-to-face sessions as a reference point and a way of 'capturing' conversations. One such client observed: 'I began writing regular letters to Tim [a narrative therapist] about people and issues we were discussing, not letters to mail, but simply to hold onto and refer to' (Farmer forthcoming: 55).

In all the examples above, the therapeutic documents can be seen to consolidate and to thicken stories that are only faintly held on to. Putting these traces and glimmers and threads into writing not only seizes the fleeting moments and gives them some permanency, but, given the power differential between spoken and written language (and the higher status afforded to written text, outside of therapeutic exchanges, in modern society) it may also lend more authority to the stories being told. There has been some discussion of the impact of these writing practices on people who have not experienced an easy relationship with literacy in their lives (see Payne 2000). It would be interesting to explore this further. I can only say that in my own experience of working with young children and with people whose first language is not English, not being able to read the accounts did not detract from the immense value that some people attached to the documents they received. It would seem that, in these instances, writing has been constructed as a process that has far greater social and cultural significance than merely that of a 'means of communication'.

Contributions by people consulting therapists

Most therapy traditions have privileged the writings of professionals (and this book is, to a large extent, an example of this). Contributions from clients are rare and such writers are often considered to be very courageous in opening up such a very private and personal experience to public scrutiny. It is indeed courageous, but within narrative practice there is a much stronger emphasis on joining together with others and on witnessing and sustaining each other in written and other ways. Groups of people have produced collections of their words and reflections on each other's words, not only to sustain themselves but also to communicate to wider audiences and future clients (see Sue *et al.* 1999). Nelia Farmer (forthcoming) has recently written an account of her experiences in narrative therapy and included reflections from her therapist as well as other family members and supporters. Her purposes in writing and publishing this account are made transparent within the text: 'I did not write for catharsis, whatever that is. Rather the writings strengthened the teachings of the therapy and was, *of itself*, therapeutic' (p.11).

It would seem that narrative practices of writing (a second or third retelling of the story) and rereading (a third or fourth retelling perhaps) are not just secondary tools or techniques used in support of the talking therapies, but rather are a *transporting* therapeutic experience (see Gerrig 1993 on writing, reading and 'transportation'). That is to say, the acts of writing and reading perform the story differently and both reader and writer are taken to a different place.

Poetic transcription and 'liminal space'

One contribution to the writing of therapeutic documents has been the appearance of poetically transcribed 'talk' represented in stanza form. This has emerged from the work of linguists and narrative researchers engaged in the transcription of conversation (see Gee 1991; McLeod and Balamoutsou 1996; McLeod 2001 for detailed examples). Poetic transcription of talk stems from ideas about the proximity of poetry to speech and the ways in which the space that abounds in poetic transcription is somehow more evocative and richer in meanings. To quote *The Norton Anthology of Poetry*: 'A poem is a composition written for performance by the human voice. What your eye sees on the page is the composer's verbal score, waiting for your voice to bring it alive as you read it aloud, or hear it in your mind's ear' (Ferguson *et al.* 1996: lix).

Neither prose letters nor poetry can ever completely represent verbatim the words, nuances and meanings expressed in therapeutic conversations (and even if they could the meaning would still change in the retelling), but perhaps the meaning-rich writing traditions of poetry allow for more powerful re-presentations by therapists and those who consult them and thence also allow more open, liminal space for storying (see Broadhurst 1999 for an exposition of 'liminality' as a site for meaning-making). In my experience people invariably find poetry easier to read and more meaningful, and often surprise themselves by responding in kind.

Consider the differences between two versions of the same conversation, below. The first I might have sent as a letter and the second is part of a therapeutic document that I did send to Hyatt, a young woman with concerns about her histories and relationships with her extended family.

Prose

At first summarising the concerns:

> Your story suggested that it was the cruel inroads that 'patriarchy and other animals' (as you put it) made into your friendship, companionship and 'secret alliances' with your much-loved brothers and that that brought you vividly back in touch with that earlier time of being so lonely: lonely down to the whites of your bones.

And also touching on an account of alternative versions:

> And yet as you look at this all now, although this loneliness was seen as something troubling by others, particularly by those in 'authority' over you, it seems that for you, both then and now, being alone in your bones has been a way of keeping yourself safe and calm and in touch with your own ways.

Poetic stanzas

> The cruel inroads
> of patriarchy
>
> (and other animals)
>
> into friendships,
> companionships
> and secret alliances with much-loved brothers
>
> brought you vividly
> back in touch with *that time*
> of being so lonely
> lonely down to the whites of
> your bones

yet now it
seems those bones
those same authority-troubling bones
those 'alone bones'

were the very bones that kept you
safe and calm
and in touch with your ways

Summary

This chapter has by no means offered an exhaustive account of the narrative therapies, nor of narrative writing practices, which encompass a far wider range of written means of therapeutic sustenance than I have had time to mention here. Indeed, I have not even mentioned the production of memory boxes in HIV/aids work, nor the ways in which online opportunities for written reflections and definitional ceremonies can defy 'time' and geographical location. What I have tried to do here is portray the ways in which the narrative metaphor (and it is, I would suggest, vitally important to remember that it *is* a metaphor, not the new authoritative metanarrative!) invites storytelling, writing and the recruitment of other witnesses and supporters into people's lives. I have also tried to describe some of the ways in which my own therapeutic practice is increasingly shaped by practices of writing. This chapter has remained somewhat outside the box entitled 'writing cures' since it makes no attempt to replace one state of affairs (the problem) with another (the cure). I nevertheless hope that it has gone some way towards depicting the value of harnessing various practices of writing as a means of making some sense of 'the profusion of tangled events' (Foucault 1984) that make up our lives, in order to generate some preferred places to stand, in the moment and in this world.

References

Bird, J. (2000) *The Heart's Narrative: Therapy and Navigating Life's Contradictions*. Auckland: Edge Press.

Broadhurst, S. (1999) *Liminal Performance*. London: Cassell.

Bruner, J. (1986) *Actual Minds, Possible Worlds*. Cambridge, MA: Harvard University Press.

Derrida, J. (1978) *Writing and Difference*. Chicago: University of Chicago Press.

Drewery, W. and Winslade, J. (1997) The theoretical story of narrative, in G. Monk, J. Winslade, K. Crocket and D. Epston (eds) *Narrative Therapy in Practice: The Archaeology of Hope*. San Francisco: Jossey-Bass.

Epston, D. and White, M. (1992) Consulting your consultants: the documentation of alternative knowledges, in D. Epston and M. White *Experience and Contradiction, Narrative and Imagination: Situated Papers of David Epston and Michael White, 1989–1991*. Adelaide: Dulwich Centre Publications.

Etherington, K. (2000) *Narrative Approaches to Working With Adult Male Survivors of Child Sexual Abuse: The Client's, the Counsellor's and the Researcher's Story*. London: Jessica Kingsley.

Farmer, N. (forthcoming) *Narratives of the Healing Heart: a Therapist's Experience of Therapy*. New York: Random House.

Ferguson, M., Salter, M. and Stallworthy, J. (1996) *The Norton Anthology of Poetry*: New York, Norton.

Foucault, M. (1984) Nietzche, genealogy and history, in P. Rabinow (ed.) *The Foucault Reader*. Harmondsworth: Penguin.

Freedman, J. and Combs, G. (1996) *Narrative Therapy: The Social Construction of Preferred Realities*. New York: Norton.

Gee, J. (1991) A linguistic approach to narrative, *Journal Of Narrative and Life History*, 1: 15–39.

Gerrig, R. (1993) *Experiencing Narrative Worlds: Psychological Activities of Reading*. Boulder, CO: Westview.

Hamilton, F. (2001) Using personal books as therapeutic documents, *Gecko: A Journal of Deconstruction and Narrative Ideas in Therapeutic Practice*, 3: 26–34.

Lane, K., Epston, D. and Winter, S. (1998) Mad fax Sunday: are some virtual communities more real than virtual? *Gecko: A Journal of Deconstruction and Narrative Ideas in Therapeutic Practice*, 1: 45–61.

McLeod, J. (2001) The analysis of conversation, discourse and narrative, in: *Qualitative Research in Counselling and Psychotherapy*, pp. 90–119, London: Sage.

Mcleod, J. and Balamoutsou, S. (1996) Representing narrative process in therapy: qualitative analysis of a single case, *Counselling Psychology Quarterly*, 9: 61–76.

McMenamin, D. (1998) Documenting work in schools, *Gecko: A Journal of Deconstruction and Narrative Ideas in Therapeutic Practice*, 3: 54–61.

Mann, S. and Russell, S. (2002) Narrative ways of working with woman survivors of childhood sexual abuse, *The International Journal of Narrative Therapy and Community Work*, 3: 3–21.

Monk, G., Winslade, J., Crockett, K. and Epston, D. (eds) (1997) *Narrative Therapy In Practice: The Archaeology Of Hope*. San Francisco: Jossey-Bass.

Payne, M. (2000) *Narrative Therapy: An Introduction for Counsellors*. London: Sage.

Pinkola Estes, C. (1992) *Women Who Run With the Wolves*. London: Rider.

Speedy, J. (2000) The storied helper: an introduction to narrative ideas in counselling and psychotherapy, *The European Journal of Psychotherapy, Counselling and Health*, 3(3): 361–75.

Sue, Mem and Veronica (1999) Documents and treasures, power to our journeys, in *Narrative Therapy and Community Work: A Conference Collection*. Adelaide: Dulwich Centre Publications.

Thomas, L. (2002) Poststructuralism and therapy: what's it all about? *International Journal of Narrative Therapy and Community Work*, 2: 85–90.

White, M. (1995) Reflecting teamwork as definitional ceremony, *Re-authoring lives: Interviews and Essays*. Adelaide: Dulwich Centre Publications.

White, M. (1997) *Narratives of Therapists Lives*. Adelaide: Dulwich Centre Publications.

White, M. (2000) *Reflections on Narrative Practice: Essays and Interviews*. Adelaide: Dulwich Centre Publications.

White, M. (2001) Folk psychology and narrative practice, *Dulwich Centre Journal*, 2: 1–37.

White, M. (2002a) *Workshop Notes*. www.dulwichcentre.com.au/articles/mwworkshop notes (accessed November 2002).

White, M. (2002b) Addressing personal failure, *International Journal of Narrative Therapy and Community Work*, 3: 33–76.

White, M. and Epston, D. (1990) *Narrative Means to Therapeutic Ends*. New York: Norton.

Chapter 4

Reading ourselves: imagining the reader in the writing process

Celia Hunt

> You are always listening . . . when you write, for the voice which answers.
> (Duncker 1997: 152)

Introduction

Some years ago when I was engaged in research into the therapeutic benefits to creative writing students of writing fictional autobiography as part of a writing apprenticeship, I noticed that some of them found it difficult to use themselves as a basis for fiction because of fears of how they might be seen by others (see Hunt 2000, Chs 2, 4). This was not always a fully conscious phenomenon; indeed on closer examination it appeared that these writers were not so much anticipating the reaction of real people in the outside world as that of an imaginary reader or audience implicit in the writing process itself. Subsequently I set out to explore this phenomenon further through a writing workshop with groups of students and others. I used a guided fantasy and gathered information on the experience through questionnaires. I am grateful to those who participated in this project for permission to quote from their material in this chapter. The chapter looks at what those experiences can tell us about the effect of imagining the reader implicit in the writing process (or the 'implicit reader' for short), both on our relationship with ourselves and with ourselves as writers.

The implicit reader

When I first started thinking about the reader in the writing process I was using Wolfgang Iser's term 'implied reader' to describe it (Iser 1980). The 'implied reader' is a role that a piece of writing persuades its reader to adopt, the ideal implied reader being the reader who understands the intentions of the implied author and shares his or her facts and values (Booth 1991: 422). The writer may not be fully conscious of imbuing the writing with an implied reader, but for Iser it is an integral part of the finished text and essential for its interpretation.

I soon realised that this was not wholly satisfactory for my purposes, as the experience I was investigating was not so much a role in the text as *a sense of readership or audience in the mind of the writer when a piece of writing was in progress*. The closest I could get to what I was looking for was Peter Rabinowitz's 'authorial audience' or 'intended reader': 'the person who the author hope[s] or expect[s] [will] pick up the text', who 'may not be marked by or "present in" the text at all but may rather be silently presupposed by it' (Rabinowitz 1989: 85). The idea that the reader is 'silently presupposed' by the text is useful, but the relationship with the reader here is too pragmatic and conscious for my liking.

Ultimately I have opted for 'implicit reader', a variant of Iser's term. This retains the idea that the reader gets into the writing more by chance than by design and that therefore the writer may not be fully aware of it. But by using 'implicit' rather than 'implied', I shift its connotation from the past tense of the finished product to the continuous present of the act of writing. My term also differs from Iser's in that I am not suggesting that one particular reader inhabits all the occasions of writing (although some writers may certainly experience the same – positive or negative – sense of readership whenever they sit down to write). My thinking draws on the Bakhtinian idea that a reader or audience is always present in the utterance and contributes to its shaping. As Voloshinov says: 'the word is a two-sided act. It is determined equally by whose word it is and for whom it is meant. As word, it is precisely the product of the reciprocal relationship between speaker and listener, addresser and addressee . . . I give myself verbal shape from another's point of view' (Voloshinov 1973: 86). Thus the implicit reader may not be discernible in the text, as Rabinowitz suggests, but its presence in the writing process will affect what is written and the way writers represent themselves through their writing.

The guided fantasy

In a guided fantasy the facilitator sketches out a scenario they want participants to imagine, suggesting a number of triggers, to which they respond by writing. In my exercise participants are asked to imagine that they can go anywhere in the world on their own for a year to write. They describe the location and say why they have chosen it. On arrival they describe the room and what is outside the window; they find a place for a treasured object they have brought with them, arrange a workspace and set up their equipment. Eventually they settle down to write, free-associating from a single word that comes to mind. They are then asked to imagine that as they sit there writing, they have a sense of presence in the room, not an actual physical presence but a sense of someone there in the moment of writing. They have to identify this person, say what it feels like to have him or her in the room and what he or she wants of them in relation to the writing.

The scene now shifts forward six months. Participants are told that the writer has disappeared before the year was out, but that the room has been left intact. They are asked to bring into the room the person who the writer imagined was there when the writing was being done. They take on the role of this person – the reader – walk around the room looking at the things the writer has left behind, pick up the writing and read it. Their task now is to write from the point of view of the reader as he or she reads the writing.

Findings

Twenty-five people sent me completed questionnaires, some attaching extracts from the writing itself. Of these, 8 found the exercise very useful or very helpful, 13 found it useful or helpful, 3 found it not useful or helpful, and 1 found it positively unhelpful: an overall positive response of 84 per cent. The exercise was helpful in three main ways:

- in identifying and rehabilitating unresolved relations with family members;
- in redressing an imbalance in the relationship with a harsh inner critic;
- in clarifying writer identity.

Identifying and rehabilitating unresolved relations with family members

People are taken by surprise by what they encounter in the imagined space created by the guided fantasy. Several discover unresolved family relationships hovering just below the threshold of consciousness. Gwen's implicit reader is her brother who died as a child but who is present in the room as an adult. He is helpful and supportive and wants her to write his story. The single word that emerges for Maxine is 'family'. When she writes in the voice of the reader, it is her father who speaks, scathingly critical of her writing and her exposure of the family's secrets. She very much wants to empathise with him, to compensate 'for his lost dreams' and realises how much her family acts as a block to her writing.

Yvonne's reader is a sympathetic female, possibly her mother or sister. When she writes from the reader's point of view, though, it is 'a different side of myself' that emerges, 'slightly antagonistic, probing, challenging of me'. She struggles against a block to complete the second part of the exercise, but something highly significant emerges: 'The ending of my story revealed to me a long-forgotten, repressed, almost taboo family secret – I did not know who my maternal grandparents were. This was simply a no-go area and we managed to avoid ever asking about my mother's origins.'

Confrontation with these unresolved family relationships is disturbing but ultimately beneficial both to the writing process and to the writer's sense of self. Gwen finds her brother's presence upsetting but freeing; she learns that the lack of connection with someone so close to her but whom she never really knew bothers her. Being an only child, she tends not to refer to him as her brother when talking to people, but the exercise gives her the right to do so. Maxine abandons the novel she is struggling to write and begins another in which she is able to fictionalise successfully autobiographical material relating to her family. For

Yvonne, 'uncovering this huge repressed desire to know more about my background' is 'a great shock', and she realises how important her mother's history is for her own sense of identity. In writing up the exercise she feels that she is 'writing the missing piece, the piece of me that I never knew but could only feel the emptiness of'.

Redressing an imbalance in the relationship with a harsh inner critic

Sometimes the emergence of family members into the imagined space is not welcome. When Nora's father emerges as reader, she 'tried to get rid of him . . . but it didn't work. I felt panicky and upset. Angry that I was back in that scenario. Helpless. Not in control'. Her father is curious about her writing: 'judgemental, patronising, not understanding'. She realises 'how important [he] is as my implied reader – adored, God-like figure I want to impress and please with my masculine writing prowess, hated judge I know I can never please and whom I want to shock and confound'. The exercise makes her feel vulnerable and angry: 'I was upset to discover that even in fantasy, in a distant place, he comes into my room. He invades my consciousness, I can't get rid of him . . . Because I need him and want him.' Unexpectedly, though, the emergence of this highly negative reader provokes the emergence of a second, more supportive one, a woman this time, who respects the writer and recognises her character and writing potential. This development of a more supportive reader implies a subtle shifting of the internal balance of power, the writer's positive inner forces motivated in the struggle to write.

Other participants report the presence of more than one reader. Alice says: 'this indirect, creeping up on [my inner critic] by stealth, caught me out, broke through my defences – found me out with my two, both ineffective, critics – one too lenient, one too harsh'. Giving them the opportunity of engaging in a dialogue is, she finds, important: 'I realised how reluctant I had become to let in my [harsh sister] critic because she was very undermining', but she now understands that 'she is worth befriending and listening to without fear'. She learns that she needs to 'trust this amalgamation' of the critical and supportive readers and that this has brought 'a lot of clarity and openness – and light' to areas of her life that she had been working on.

Clarifying writer identity

Keri didn't have an immediate sense of a reader: 'In the absence of a person or presence', she says, 'the feeling was: "Only *me* that hinders, only *me* that helps"', and this led her to realise that 'my belief in myself as a writer was non-existent'. In the latter part of the exercise, however, she becomes her own reader. Entering the room her writer-self has vacated, she finds it littered with 'a hundred thousand tearings of paper, the paper itself covered in looping scrawls of brightly coloured ink'. She identifies completely with this 'fleeing phantom' who has destroyed every scrap of writing, but she is always slightly out of reach and Keri is disappointed that, yet again, she cannot grasp her. Then she realises that she *has* grasped something new: 'a deeper hurt that cannot be explained and which has no desire to be verbalised'. She gathers up the torn pieces of writing, 'afraid to disturb what I don't understand. Then I see it – a large red "I" stares accusingly up at me from the floor . . . She has been here all along waiting for me to recognise her'. She sits down at the desk and begins to write.

Becoming a reader of herself helps Keri to clarify the part of herself from which she writes, the part that is hurt and sad, that is characterised by 'the fear of not being heard, the fear of the lack of courage eating away inside'. The exercise 'helped me to tap into the place I rarely reach but is incredibly powerful when I do – the part of me that does not judge or criticise but writes freely and honestly – uncensored'. The resulting writing was 'without doubt the most valuable piece I produced all term from the aspect of personal development. Like the open window in the writer's room, it opened up a new vista for me to gaze upon . . . The important point . . . was not so much in discovering my imagined reader but in solidifying my self as a writer'.

Discussion

Creating space for the arrival of news from the self

When I devised the exercise, I didn't realise how important the creation of an ideal writing space would be; I simply wanted to provide a framework within which the appearance of a reader could be effected. With few exceptions, participants record intense excitement at the prospect of spending a year in a locale of their choice for the sole purpose of writing. There is a remarkable consonance in the locales they choose and the descriptions of their writing spaces. Most opt for remote locations – mountain slopes, tropical islands, deserts – where the natural world is abundantly present. A physical sense of space is crucial. For the most part rooms are simple and functional, but it is the way the outside and inside relate to each other that is striking: the sky and the landscape are massively visible via large windows and balconies; the clarity and quality of light is emphasised repeatedly. Loved ones are present in photos or represented by cuddly toys, but they are symbolic presences, their pictures sometimes turned away when the writing begins. Space, it seems, is a longed-for commodity, difficult to obtain in everyday life and jealously guarded when found. Yet the excitement of having it is, in most cases, matched by fear. Maxine's comment is typical: 'It felt as if a tremendous space was opening up in front of me. This was both exciting and scary. What if I couldn't negotiate that space, what if I have nothing to say?'

This reaction is not surprising. The exercise demands the 'letting go' of shared everyday reality and immersion in Winnicott's 'potential space', that transitional realm that partakes of both psychic reality and the outside world (Winnicott 1991).

Magda describes this perfectly: '[Creating a writing space] gave me a floaty panoramic sensation . . . the effort of writing seemed almost futile but necessary. I felt I could be more easily objective as well as subjective'. In this 'potential space' a greater psychic flexibility becomes possible, the opportunity to be oneself and not oneself simultaneously: 'watching oneself responding to the stimulus of an imagined scenario', as Briony puts it. But the space is not necessarily benign; once the customary sense of self is suspended, there may be a disconcerting sense of chaos. In order to hold open the space for the imagination we have to 'tolerate chaos as a temporary stage' (Milner 1971: 76), and that requires trust and a special kind of 'holding'.

The idea of a 'holding framework' is central to Winnicott's and Marion Milner's view of the necessary conditions both for creativity and for healthy self-development. In Winnicott's thinking the mother's role is to provide a safe, nurturing environment for the child not only in the early stages when the baby does not yet have a sense of itself as separate, but also during the transitional period when the child is beginning to acquire a sense of its own identity. In order to be able to make effective use of separateness, whether for creativity or self-relating, the child needs first to be able to be alone in the presence of someone, so that the space for the imagination is experienced as 'safe enough' (Winnicott 1965). In adult creativity or self-relating, according to Milner, the space for the imagination is held open by the critical faculty which, relinquishing its 'narrow focused penetrating' mode of attention and taking, as it were, an internal step back, provides a frame for a different kind of attention – the 'wide unfocused stare' of attending with the imaginative body (Milner 1952: 81). This 'framed gap' needs to be reliable enough so that, in our passive role as observers of ourselves or our creative processes, we can allow unconscious or semiconscious material to emerge freely. In the consulting room it is the therapist as the 'ideal listener' who does the 'framing' or 'holding', creating a safe imaginative space between them and the patient; in creative writing it is the page and the words that have to take on this role. In a writing group the supportive presence of other group members and the relationship of trust which the facilitator generates will also contribute to the sense of safety.

In my guided fantasy the setting up of a powerful visual scenario seems particularly to contribute to the holding framework. Participants create a room, which is not only their own special place chosen and furnished to meet their needs, but a space into which they bring a connection with significant others through a treasured object. This distant link to loved ones contributes to the safety of the potential space: they are alone but in the presence of someone dear to them. Once this space is established as safe enough (and the exercise allows a fair amount of time for this preliminary setting up), participants can more easily open themselves to the exciting but scary larger space, the less controllable realms of the unconscious represented by the chaotic natural world beyond the window. From the safe enough perspective of their holding environment, they can relinquish their usual controls and make room for what Christopher Bollas calls 'the arrival of news from the self', for things which at some level are 'known' but, until they are given the right opportunity, cannot be thought – the 'unthought known' (Bollas 1987: 236, 276).

'Cracking up' the self

The creation in the guided fantasy of a safe enough internal space involves, then, a dividing of the dominant sense of self into two, 'a generative splitting of the ego, so that [one becomes] simultaneously observer and observed' (Bollas 1987: 236). Instead of its usual role of director or driver of the self, the ego is required to relinquish its power, to retract and become part of the holding framework. In literary terms it becomes the governing consciousness or 'global author' (Palmieri 1998: 47) that oversees the scenario developing in the imaginative space but does not interfere; rather its role is to facilitate (and document) the events taking place. Indeed, once this initial splitting of the self occurs, there is a further splitting of the 'observed' into the writer-self resident in the room and the reader-self who enters after the writer-self has left. Thus participants find themselves divided up into three (or even four, in instances where there are two reader-selves) different self-entities. As some of them found, this splitting offers the possibility of seeing themselves simultaneously from a number of different angles, so that they get new and unexpected perspectives and find different aspects of themselves emerging more clearly. Thus, a debilitating inner critic becomes identifiable as a particular kind of character rather than an unconscious or semiconscious internal force against which writers have to defend themselves (with the consequent interference with, or blocks to, the writing process). Less powerful parts of the self are brought to life and given a voice. Critic and writer enter into dialogue with each other on more equal terms, so that writers have the chance of establishing themselves as negotiators rather than victims. The internal balance of power begins subtly to shift.

The objectification of self that occurs in this exercise fulfils Bakhtin's prerequisite for self-understanding, according to which: 'In order to understand it is immensely important for the person who understands to be *located outside* the object of his or her creative understanding – in time, in space, in culture' (Bakhtin 1986: 7, original emphasis). And this 'reflexive outsideness' (Palmieri 1998: 48) leads to what Bollas calls the 'cracking up' of the self (Bollas 1995), not in the negative sense of breakdown but in the more positive sense of our being shifted out of what might be a defended, single version of ourselves into a contained multiplicity. Emerging from the fantasy and back into everyday reality, participants bring with them not only increased insight into different aspects of themselves but also a new or more developed way of self-relating or 'self-sensing' (Bollas 1995: 154).

In *The Shadow of the Object*, Bollas refers to 'the self-analytic function', the adopting of a stance in relation to oneself that is as important outside as inside the therapeutic setting. What he is referring to here is a state of receptivity, 'a relaxed not vigilant state of mind' that maintains 'a receptive space for the arrival of news from within the self' and allows new internal objects to be evoked or created, objects which can then be subjected to the more rigorous process of interpretation (Bollas 1987: 239–41). This state of receptivity involves recognition of the fact that 'being and experiencing are prior to the knowing of that which is there to be understood', and that interpretation, 'the more active agent, follows being and experiencing'. Imagining the reader in the writing process seems to be a helpful device for developing the stance of which Bollas speaks. It enables us to create and maintain a safe enough space for the imagination, thus helping us to open ourselves up to the possibility of change and of 'rewriting' – both metaphorically and literally in the creative writing context – our relations with the voices that 'speak' us.

Implications for therapeutic practice

While my workshops were not carried out as a specific therapeutic intervention, they were in the main offered in an environment where the developmental or therapeutic nature of the writing exercise was explicit. As usual in my area of work, the participants were predominantly female and, not surprisingly, highly literate, and these factors would need to be taken into account in the choice of clients with whom to use this particular exercise. While some participants found the exercise disturbing, only one reported an adverse reaction: rather than helping her towards a more flexible sense of self, it made her more aware of how blocked she was, and this was upsetting. This was an occasion where I used the exercise in a non-therapeutically oriented group and where the environment wasn't wholly conducive to working through the emerging feelings. I would suggest that the exercise is most suitable for writing groups, whether therapeutically oriented or not, where the group itself can act as a support for the emergence of difficult feelings or material.

References

Bakhtin, M.M. (1986) *Speech Genres and Other Late Essays*, trans V.W. McGee. Austin, TX: University of Texas Press.

Bollas, C. (1987) *The Shadow of the Object*. London: Free Association Books.

Bollas, C. (1995) *Cracking Up*. London: Routledge.

Booth, W. (1991) *The Rhetoric of Fiction*, 2nd edn. London: Penguin.

Duncker, P. (1997) *Hallucinating Foucault*. London: Picador.

Hunt, C. (2000) *Therapeutic Dimensions of Autobiography in Creative Writing*. London: Jessica Kingsley.

Iser, W. (1980) *The Implied Reader*. London: Johns Hopkins University Press.

Milner, M. (1952) The framed gap, in *The Suppressed Madness of Sane Men*, pp. 79–82. London: Tavistock, 1987.

Milner, M. (1971) *On Not Being Able to Paint*. London: Heinemann.

Palmieri, G. (1998) 'The author' according to Bakhtin, and Bakhtin the author, in D. Shepherd (ed.) *The Contexts of Bakhtin*, pp. 45–56. Amsterdam: Harwood.

Rabinowitz, P.J. (1989) Whirl without end: audience-oriented criticism, in G.D. Atkins and L. Morrow (eds) *Contemporary Literary Theory*, pp. 81–100. London: Macmillan.

Voloshinov, V.N. (1973) *Marxism and the Philosophy of Language*, trans L. Matejka and I.R. Titunik. New York: Seminar.
Winnicott, D.W. (1965) The capacity to be alone, in *The Maturational Processes and the Facilitating Environment*, pp. 29–36. New York: International Universities Press.
Winnicott, D.W. (1991) *Playing and Reality*. London: Routledge.

Chapter 5

From archetype to impressions: the magic of words

Derek Steinberg

Introduction

Written words can raise goose pimples: they work, when even the most appropriate of physical treatments, dietary therapies and psychological approaches haven't succeeded. The vitality of words may have something to do with the nature of language and the magic of storytelling and poetry in a way that reaches well beyond psychological theories into the fundamental qualities of being human, and which may underpin or short-circuit treatments. This chapter explores what some of the roots of this vitality may be, and how they might help us understand how writing helps.

Words to letters

Our health and care industries produce a vast acreage of writing – records, minutes, reports, inquiries, correspondence and so on in an administrative papyrosphere accumulating on a grand scale – yet the writing itself is largely unthought about and untaught about. The routine letters written to and for our patients, for example, deserve more attention than they get.

I will borrow from the concept of writing and therapy as discussed in this book, propose a theoretical perspective developed from Burnshaw's (1970) account of the inherent continuity between the life sciences, psychology, mythology and the arts, and show how specifically consultative approaches to our clientele, with their quite radical implications for therapeutic work, can contribute to writing as therapy. Thoughtful and reflective letter-writing is given as an exemplar, demonstrating how we can add teaching, learning and a new dimension to therapy to administrative necessity. But first I want to consider how extraordinary words are.

Words : more than meets the I

Symbols and imagery have astonishing power, the more so because we largely take them for granted. As much as we shape them they shape *us*, and words, spoken or written, indeed any sort of notation, share this potency. Words carry more than meets the eye, or ear : they are like packets of communication, replete with multiple meanings, ambiguities and implications, and when therapist and client exchange even ordinary words, emotional resonances accompany them.

The alternative and unconscious meaning of words is of course the stuff of psychoanalysis (e.g. Freud 1901, 1922; Jung 1906, 1964), but even elaborate psychodynamic theories have their limitations; many would agree that literature and poetry soar way beyond them. *Poesis* means making: creating. We may not all be competent poets, but even without necessarily or even usually realising it we think of, select and use words which contain a poetic wealth of meaning and emotional significance. This theme is explored, magnificently I think, by Cox and Thielgaard (1987) though their discussion *is* literary and poetic, and perhaps beyond the nuts and bolts of the ordinary language of day-to-day moments in therapeutic work which I want to discuss.

Words are monumental. They contain, record and represent packets of information that commemorate the experiences and relationships, often emotionally loaded and traumatic, in which they were first forged; words contain aeons of human and perhaps pre-human experience in them and in their implications and resonances. It would be nice to think that some of this poetic energy is released, metaphorically speaking, when we use them, just as burning oil or gas warms (or burns) us with the *actual* energy of a long-past hot and sunny Jurassic day. Conceivably – I would put it no stronger – some nuances of some words could reoccur as unconscious influences when we use words in therapy, perhaps in therapy's own primitive, even primally evocative moments.

As self-conscious, imaginative, creative beings we are made of words no less than we make them. Niels Bohr, who like other pioneers of quantum physics was as familiar with the task of describing the indescribable as are we and our clients, said 'we are suspended in language' (Pais 1991). Elsewhere I have suggested that our sense of ourselves owes as much to our suspension in poetry and imagery as our material brain needs suspension in an environment of the right sort of fluid (Steinberg forthcoming). We are made of metaphors; they are part of our thinking, our expression and our sense of others and of ourselves, the myth of the supposedly hard-headed, wholly rational, no-nonsense scientist no less than that of the crazy poet. Freudian theory is constructed of metaphors and, ironically, is regularly dismissed by its detractors in metaphors (such as 'crap') – presumably unconsciously (see Tyrer and Steinberg forthcoming). In a critique of Freud, Bloom (2002) observes that much as Freud's detractors try to throw him out, they can't: 'he is now within us'.

Where do words come from? How do they get there?

To me, the magic of words, of writing and reading, is enhanced rather than diminished by regarding it as something capable of being illuminated by science.

There is of course a science and philosophy of language, communication and the study of linguistics; but biology plays a part too, and unless one's philosophy is that language was placed within us by supernatural means, its ultimate origin, and I would say aesthetics and spirituality too, must be in our genes, in that extraordinary dictionary and recipe book written in DNA from whose instructions we are made.

There is, naturally, controversy about the part genetics and evolutionary theory may play in the development of words and language (with Pinker 1994 in favour and Chomsky 1991 broadly against) but it seems to me inherently unlikely that the capacity to attend to and interpret others' utterances and symbols, and respond with our own, was not highly significant in our remote ancestors' lives, both as evolutionary necessity and pivotal phenomenon. The human race has survived not because of strong teeth and claws or high speed or flight, but by being social, cooperative animals. The human infant, born biologically premature so that the large human head can pass through the birth canal, is helpless for an extraordinarily long period by animal standards, and relies entirely on its ability to attract and sustain adult care and attention. It is reasonable to suggest that the developing individual's ability to make sense of itself and its environment (including complex and ambiguous emotional atmospheres, for example of affection or hostility), and to encapsulate such experiences in symbols, imagery and words, could have been as vital a capacity as the ability to metabolise oxygen, so much so that such capacities are now evolved into us (see e.g. Stevens 1990; Stevens and Price 1996; Steinberg forthcoming).

This notion is consistent with the wider reaches of attachment theory (see e.g. Bowlby 1969). Further, the present state of neuroscience supports the notion that internal image-making, symbol formation, memory, fantasy and language formation is integral to the nature of human self-consciousness, and has evolved 'hard-wired' into the brain (see e.g. Edelman 1987, 1994; Damasio 1999; Carter 2002). Lewis-Williams (2002) has recently proposed that arts in the wider sense have their origins in our Cro-Magnon ancestors being able, because of the nature of their brains, to make something (cave paintings) of their internal imagery. Communication between the developing human brain and developing human culture has also been described in terms of replicating units of communication which Blackmore (1999), after Dawkins (1976) calls 'memes', and memes too can evolve, underlying and indeed underwriting cultural evolution.

David Bohm, another quantum physicist and holistic philosopher, has described words and phrases as a kind of archaeology of our thought processes (1980). The direction of all this work supports the idea that words have a remarkably rich and long history, whose evolution intertwines and reciprocates with our own. All this is consistent with much new thinking in cultural psychology and social science (e.g Gray 1996; Cole 1998) and provides a basis for the idea of hierarchies of meaning and implied meaning in language (see e.g. Bandler and Grinder 1975; Grinder and Bandler 1976). It may mean that we could reconsider the rather geological, hydrodynamic model for the unconscious implied in Freud's theories (influenced, of course, by the science and technology of his time and part of the nineteenth century's story), and speculate instead whether what we call the unconscious might not be composed of layers of seething strata within our minds (itself a potent metaphor and myth, and one that causes misconceptions about illness) but in fact actually *is* an unconscious chain reaction of implied and potential meanings and imagery, set off every time by words we hear, read, write, say and think about (Tyrer and Steinberg forthcoming).

But for all this, why 'magic'? Magic is both powerful and inexplicable. Words represent a nice paradox, because (just as Winnicott says of art) they are the ingredients of an infinity of possibilities of thought, feeling and language and they generate their own conventions and rules as language develops. The range of mental life that words reflect is both 'out there' in aspects of our culture of which we may be unaware (making sense of the jargon cliché 'raising awareness') and of an equivalent inaccessibility within, hence the rationale of psychoanalysis.

The capacity for fantasy, day-dreaming, imagination and new ideas has survival value and sanity value (which are very close to each other, for the human race), and the palette of these intellectual and emotional possibilities is bequeathed to us encapsulated in words; one wonders what combination of tones initiated and spelled out such such vital qualities as, say, hope, faith, courage and altruism. If any natural phenomenon deserves the epithet magic I think it is language, particularly in the formality of the written word. It intrigues me that 'grammar' derives from *grammaire*, a book of magic spells. Glamour has the same origin. If the spell is to work, watch the spelling and the grammar, and have a dictionary at hand.

From words to writing

Small marks on paper, the 'little bugs' that baffled Tarzan in Edgar Rice Burroughs' classic story (1912), have the most extraordinary power to move us. Within a few lines of a well written piece of fiction these small black imprints on paper can lead us rapidly to imagine whole worlds, and even be concerned about imaginary characters and what might happen to them. The magic is no less in the reading than in the writing. Of course speech and sounds move us, and perhaps can be too readily manipulated by the totality of the situation and the status and manner of the speaker, using transient words and impressions as if playing an instrument. But the written word on paper has a status, autonomy and visible accessibility of its own; you can go back to it. Yet there is also something tentative and provisional about it. All this has a bearing on therapy conducted around writing rather than focused on speech.

There was a time when the spoken word (*logos*) was considered closer to the speaker's meaning and thus closer to pure thought, while writing was considered secondary, as if no more than sounds rendered into writing; but this isn't generally regarded as either an adequate explanation or even a likely story (see e.g. Harris 1986; Crystal 1987). Words, probably starting as grunts and exclamations, primitive marks, carvings and paintings, are likely to have arisen separately, albeit eventually interacting with the spoken word.

Writing, then, is different. It isn't freeze-dried speech, but something else. 'As dead as the spoken word' said John Betjeman, in 'Death in Leamington' (1932), an intriguing observation from so deceptively mischievous and deadly serious a poet. Writing is inseparable from reading, even if the only reader is the writer. As words represent the definition of experience (Bruner 1990), the act of writing demands even greater sustained attention – mindfulness – to its highly interactive cognitive and organisational components (Kellogg 1994). It involves preparation, planning, physical action and tools; Tonfoni and Richardson (1994) have likened it to pottery and Josipovici (1982) stressed its nature as a physically as well as intellectually demanding activity – it can cause *cramp*; it is conceived, reflected about, shaped, finished, used. Or left unfinished for next time, or abandoned.

Writing isn't the same as 'literature', which as Josipovici points out is abstract and idealistic. Like any creative production, it can be accompanied by particular types of anxiety and inhibition, a sense of risk and 'letting go' and powerful feelings about the outcome (Ehrenzweig 1967): about how it will *look*; and it belongs to its maker. This can be true of a therapeutic conversation, in a sense, but *only* in a sense; a conversation between two people, whether recorded or remembered or not, is different from the production of a material piece of work. Writing has authority, status, survival power and a vitality of its own, separate from the currents and undercurrents of personal reflection and interaction.

Made art also has the qualities of a transitional object (Winnicott 1965). It is not entirely imaginary, nor yet quite fixed in reality, but occupies an intermediate position and role which Winnicott identified as cultural. As with the ambiguities of words and phrases, art also is tentative and paradoxical, yet real, solid, pluripotent. In a sense, although made, it still stands for whatever its creator or observer yet cares to make of it. In therapy, art, like writing, is a useful container of whatever is to come, and in transit between one session and the next. 'In the artist of all kinds', Winnicott wrote, 'I think one can detect an inherent dilemma, which belongs to the coexistence of two trends, the urgent need to communicate and the still more urgent need not to be found. This might account for the fact that we cannot conceive of an artist's coming to the end of the task that occupies his whole nature.' (Winnicott 1965: 185). On the one hand this may seem the vaguest of task descriptions; and yet it is very close to the philosophy of science where all *facts* are necessarily provisional, leading only to more questions, more experiments and more provisional facts and working knowledge.

The story so far, then, is that in its status as something visual, material and separated from conversation, the written word has qualities that facilitate shared curiosity and joint exploration. Like science and art, writing promotes curiosity rather than reaching premature or infelicitous conclusions; the written word doesn't *guarantee* this, but it has characteristics that enable it; hence we keep minutes of meetings and make agendas. This, I think, has a direct bearing on the contribution writing makes to any non-diagnostic, non-prescriptive form of therapy; and why, it seems to me, writing, including letter writing, can have some of the qualities of the consultative style of work described below.

When I once wrote that psychotherapy was 'negotiated misunderstanding' (Steinberg 2000b) a lot of people seemed to like the description. It seems to me that in many traditional psychotherapies the therapist holds most of the best cards in this negotiation; rightly so, for some purposes of some therapies, as specialist and expert. But when the focus for therapist and client is a piece of writing, there is the possibility of a more equally shared relationship which is appropriate for the purpose in therapy: for example, to enhance the autonomy and responsibility of the client. The written piece, like a piece of art, has its own authority, and shares it with its maker. Its details are fixed, unlike conversation, its nuances less ephemeral and more open to reconsideration, review and revision. It is more of a public property. You could get a second opinion on it.

It is not only that, in contemplating a piece, art therapist and client become more equal partners; the transitional and provisional qualities of the work also prevent therapist or client jumping to conclusions. In the paradox already identified, it is a definite statement and *therefore* negotiable. Conversely there is nothing so rigid as the attitudes and feelings framed in nebulous, infinitely adaptable phrases. The 'fixity' of a piece of art or writing provides a fixed base around which discussion and development is possible. This metaphor relates to the notion in attachment theory where a safe enough base permits secure enough exploration.

The absence of a dominating or at least influential other person doesn't necessarily make things easy, however. Unlike conversation, normally with a listener, writing may generate only the possibility of there ultimately being a readership. It may be a fantasy readership, hoped for or feared. Thus Thomas Hardy described the burden for the writer who, aspiring to address a hall full of people, instead finds before him only a blank page. Or it may be a quite different sort of fantasy: that of evading the audience. This may include the therapist or the self.

Writing, narratives and real myths

An inherited capacity for internal imagery that has survival value could include not only recognition of the significance of such things as teeth, claws and certain facial expressions, but perhaps the more elaborate archetypes (wise old men and women, witches, wizards, heroes, monsters) that people our tales. Campbell (1974) described myths as public dreams, dreams as private myths, thus affirming something of the nature of both individual and communal fantasy. Jung was aware that his theory of the archetypes of the collective unconscious (1959, 1964) was widely misunderstood as the inheritance of formed images, like a witch on a broomstick, when what he meant was not the inheritance of ideas and images but the inherited *potentiality* – the neural hardware – to develop them (1959).

Our clientele and their families develop myths too, telling stories to and about themselves which may be grandiose, deprecatory, frightening and delusional. The power of the 'family script'(or myth) – all the more powerful for being unwritten, oral history – that casts one member as good or bad, well or sick, or a child as scholar, failure or family joker, is familiar to therapists as is the difficulty of turning down a typecast role to seek another, especially if it is a leading (or misleading) part. Telling new stories, and writing, as strategies for understanding and treating our clients is of course well established in therapy (see e.g. White and Epston 1990; Gersie 1991; Wallas 1991; Dwivedi and Gardner 1997; Bolton 1999; Roberts and Holmes 1999). We should also be prepared to stand back and see the therapeutic encounter itself as having mythic qualities. The personal conception of being unwell, of recognising disability or need, and the related expectation that human culture will make available some kind of shaman or healer or their prototypes are precisely the kind of myths that I would argue have evolutionary advantage within the human group and could be inherited like complex instincts. To the extent that they may influence the story and script of being a therapist and being a patient, it could be helpful if we recognise (= know again) this.

Regard for the imagination and creativity of the client does not rest on the model of an expert simply advising a listening client. As therapists, the insight and understanding that we, too, are engaged in contributing to myths and narratives about our clients should at least be as significant in our thinking as, say, the pursuit of scientific method or a treatment model. When the narrative is in writing it has a special authority, its material existence a challenge to any evasion or sophistry, however well meant.

Writing to clients

When we write a letter back to the patient or their referrer, we are writing a short story about them. It should be a fragment of biography, one for which the patient has provided authentic material, rather than fiction. Though valuing psychoanalytic theory, I am also deeply suspicious of the clever but facile 'interpretation': 'You say this, by which' (of course) 'you mean that.' But this is the therapist's poetry, not the patient's. Contributions from both are needed to make sense of pathological and therapeutic developments.

This would, one hopes, be obvious where a piece of writing is the focus of a piece of therapy. However, when we construct routine letters there is the likelihood of reverting to our professional ideologies, jargon and conceptual models. If we set out to make a letter something therapeutically helpful as well as informative, we should ensure that this too is something other than one-sided fantasy. Writing such letters as a joint therapist-patient enterprise could be an excellent idea, and no doubt someone, somewhere, is doing it. However, for the purposes of this section I want to discuss making our ordinary clinical correspondence rise beyond record-keeping and other administrative needs.

The letters I have in mind are those we write routinely to or about our patients, for example to tell a GP how things are going, to clarify the development of a session or even to discuss some practical matter like an appointment. They will be letters which we intend the patient or client to read, either by writing directly to them, with a copy to whoever else (and with permission) needs to know; or by sending patients copies of letters which are about them.

Why write?

First, why not? It seems to me that there are incontestable ethical reasons for people knowing what is being said about them, and if it is difficult to put something in writing, that gives us something important to think about. In any case, recent legislation requires people to be able to see their own notes (with some qualifications). Why not write all notes as if we would not mind, or even prefer, patients seeing what is written about them? Practising with our letters is a good way of starting.

Writing such letters can contribute to therapy and to our own wider professional skill and understanding as well. A letter for ourselves, our clientele and the referrer should be clear, positive and something from which all three can learn. We know that therapy isn't simple; it involves chaos and complexity, and one of our professional tasks is to move, with the patient, from this complexity to relative simplicity; not to fudge issues to make them *seem* simple. That has the reverse effect: the therapist may go home happy to have packaged a problem neatly and tidily, but the patient has to take home a doggy bag full of indigestible bits and pieces that don't fit the therapist's ideas. Writing however, for therapist and patient to reflect upon, comment on and modify to fit the facts, concentrates the mind and clarifies thinking. If this means we have to replace jargon with plain language, that's good. If the jargon is a genuinely new and useful technical term, that too is fine, but we have to explain it. The challenge here is that we have to know what it means.

The letter can also serve as an agreement, or at least an agenda for the next session, about what the therapist thinks and intends and what the client thinks and intends. Thus it can serve as a contract, or be the basis for one. Such a transaction can help shape the finer points of using help, but could help significantly in more acute issues – for example if someone (perhaps a third party, e.g. a child) is at risk, literally spelling out how a situation seems and what it needs.

Should there be a problem about how to say something – for example when someone is putting someone else at risk (not uncommon when working with children and families), or it is thought that one member may not persist with agreed commitments or is not telling the truth, or if the therapist isn't sure about what to do yet is being looked to for confidence and support – all the more reason to think about and work at how to put it in writing. How, for example, to be straightforward, non-euphemistic, yet neither hurtful nor libellous? Whatever such effort does for the letter, it does still more for the therapist's skills.

A letter also links one session with the next, authentically and not merely as a formality; it keeps up the therapeutic momentum and can keep a particular matter in focus. It does this while affirming the sessions and their boundaries and limits. At the same time it should complement sessions, not supplement them with extraneous comments.

The letter is also a tangible token; sent through the post it is a reminder that therapist, patient and therapy are rooted in real life. It is private, and has an intimacy of its own, yet the fact and existence of a letter is public too. A letter is a bit special; but not too special.

The letter should serve as an accurate, concise record, though not an alternative to properly kept notes, which can be a temptation and a hazard. A letter can be a handy guide to what is in the notes, and, who knows, an interest and growing skill in writing letters may even make the chore of note-making more enjoyable. Taking letters seriously develops the writer's writing skills as a bonus.

Whether one is instinctively democratic or paternalist, there is no feasible future, practically, philosophically or economically, for any therapeutic system which sets out to take all the responsibility. Perhaps the coarsest example of this is the enormous loss of health and care services' funds, time and energy into litigation or its prevention. 'Open' letters that affirm agreements and decisions made along consultative lines make an open and transparent therapist-client partnership a feasible reality.

Letter writing along the lines described here is intrinsically consultative. The consultative approach as developed by Caplan (1970) in Harvard and subsequently the Tavistock Institute in London is a strategy widely used in child and family psychiatry (see e.g. Steinberg 1989, 2000a), where the complex demands of ethical and legal matters, practicalities of management and the issues of consent are commonly both hard to resolve and imperative. Discussion, negotiation, clarity and transparency are a necessity for effective work. As originally developed, consultation was about how professional workers negotiate – for example, psychologists, teachers, social workers and careworkers. However, the joint, peer-peer exploration of what is wanted, what is needed and what is possible which forms the basis of consultation can be transferred, if we wish, to many aspects of the therapist-patient relationship too, where there are just as many ambiguities about authority, responsibility, action and consent (Steinberg 1992). Regarding the client as a peer and an expert in his or her own problems and in the possible solutions has similarities with person-centred counselling (Rogers 1951) and has been applied in creative therapies too (see e.g. Silverstone 1993).

Now a letter, something fixed, visible and in writing (and, as said, negotiable *because* it is in black and white), cannot be written usefully or with integrity unless it at least acknowledges both the therapist's and client's positions and feelings. It does not have to do so fully and in depth, but it must represent them well enough to be either acceptable as it stands or open to modification or even rethinking. Willingness and ability to write in this way depends on a relationship in which the authority, autonomy and responsibility of the client is in some sort of agreed balance with that of the therapist. This is the contribution of a consultative approach to our work, and it lends itself to reflective letter writing.

This reflection is necessarily on both sides. The transitional yet material nature of a piece of writing creates time and space for reflecting about its message on more than one occasion, or in more than one mood. In making this an explicitly shared piece of work which has a real existence outside the relationship and between the sessions, it both unites and divides, helping to establish boundaries and the means of transcending them. This is part of the magic of symbols: they touch important depths of feeling, but their form and formality keeps useful fantasy and the capacity for change afloat.

Side-effects of letters and some precautions

Anything effective in therapy has pitfalls. The existence of the letter as a visible, readable object with a life of its own requires particular vigilance about privacy and confidentiality. Patients' permissions to write about them to someone else, and letters which reflect the social and domestic context, may well contain things about people whose permission you might not have thought of asking. By the same token one should check addresses, mark letters 'Confidential' as a routine and bear in mind that as not all of our clients are fortunate enough to live in safety and privacy, there are times when a letter should be handed to the person it is for, rather than posted. Such practical things underpin trust, which underpins everything else.

Details like legibility, the quality of the paper and letter headings matter. We are back to archetypal symbols again: design can inform, amuse, reassure, encourage, deceive, put down, impress or intimidate. Details such as how to address the recipient and how to sign off, how friendly, formal or informal to be, may be as important as the attention to detail we apply in psychotherapy (examples are given in Steinberg 2000b).

The ownership of a letter is not always crystal clear. Is it yours, your organisation's or the recipient's, or is it shared? Whether you write such shared letters occasionally or as a matter of policy, all concerned have a right to know about it. I think one should check with an 'outside' colleague – for example, a GP, teacher or social worker, who might not have expected a letter received to have been copied to the patient.

Spelling it out

Words shape inchoate feelings in an astonishingly elaborate network of meaning and implied meaning; there are as many possibilities of neuronal interconnections as there are atoms in the universe, and even more potential words. We can have no idea what words may show us next, despite the fact that the whole of all that has ever been written or said, or ever will be, can be made from, say, 25 letters in a grid, 5 letters by 5 in size. This vast potential space of words and their implications is where the problems we deal with take shape, have their form and perhaps can be reshaped. In verbal psychotherapy, as in personal reflection, we necessarily grope in the dark as we try to make sense.

With the written word, the exploration and negotiation of meaning can be literally seen as it is shaped up and shared as work in progress. We can pause, reflect and consult about it. We can do this with ourselves: from mysticism to contemporary neuroscience the existential necessity for self to gaze upon self is a recurring theme.

Writing provides real, shareable, visual guidance; leverage and feedback for a difficult, abstract exercise. Therapist and client can share authority and responsibility to develop a story line, script and performance together like director and actor, or writer and editor. The psychotherapist as biographer, evolutionary archivist, literary critic, editor and agent: now *there* would be a thing.

References

Bandler, R. and Grinder, J. (1975) *The Structure of Magic: A Book about Language and Therapy*. Santa Clara, CA: Science and Behavior Books Inc.
Betjeman, J. (1932) Death in Leamington, in *Collected Poems* 4th edn. London: John Murray, 1980.
Blackmore, S. (1999) *The Meme Machine*. Oxford: Oxford University Press.
Bloom, H. (2002) *Genius*. London: Fourth Estate.
Bohm, D. (1980) *Wholeness and the Implicate Order*. London: Routledge & Kegan Paul.
Bolton, G. (1999) *The Therapeutic Potential of Creative Writing*. London: Jessica Kingsley.
Bowlby, J. (1969) *Attachment and Loss. Volume 1: Attachment*. London: Hogarth Press.
Bruner, J.S. (1990) *Acts of Meaning*. Cambridge, MA: Harvard University Press.
Burnshaw, S. (1970) *The Seamless Web*. New York: George Braziller.
Burroughs, E.R. (1912) *Tarzan of the Apes*. All Story Magazine.
Campbell, J. (1974) *The Masks of God – Volume 4: Creative Mythology*. London: Viking.
Caplan, G. (1970) *The Theory and Practice of Mental Health Consultation*. London: Tavistock.
Carter, R. (2002) *Consciousness*. London: Weidenfeld and Nicolson.
Chomsky, N. (1991) Linguistics and Cognitive Science: Problems and Mysteries, in Kasher, A. (ed.) *The Chomskyan Turn*. Cambridge, MA: Blackwell.
Cole, M. (1998) *Cultural Psychology*. London: Belknap Press.
Cox, M. and Thielgaard, A. (1987) *Mutative Metaphors in Psychotherapy*. London: Tavistock.
Crystal, D. (1987) *The Encyclopaedia of Language*. Cambridge: Cambridge University Press.
Damasio, A. (1999) *The Feeling of What Happens*. London: William Heinemann.
Dawkins, R. (1976) *The Selfish Gene*. Oxford: Oxford University Press.
Dwivedi, K. N. and Gardner, D. (1997) Theoretical perspectives and clinical approaches, in K.N. Dwivedi (ed.) *TheTherapeutic Use of Stories*. London: Routledge.
Edelman, G. (1987) *Neural Darwinism*. New York: Basic Books.
Edelman, G. (1994) *Bright Air, Brilliant Fire*. London: Penguin Books.
Ehrenzweig, A. (1967) *The Hidden Order of Art*. London: Weidenfeld & Nicolson.
Freud, S. (1901) *The Psychopathology of Everyday Life*, standard edition of the collected works, Vol. VI, ed. J. Strachey. London: Hogarth Press.
Freud, S. (1922) *Introductory Lectures on Psychoanalysis*. London: George Allen & Unwin.
Gersie, A. (1991) *Storymaking in Bereavement*. London: Jessica Kingsley.
Gray, R.M. (1996) *Archetypal Explorations*. London: Routledge.
Grinder, J. and Bandler, R. (1976) *The Structure of Magic*. Palo Alto, CA: Science and Behavior Books Inc.
Harris, R. (1986) *The Origin of Writing*. Springfield, IL: Open Court Publishing.
Josipovici, G. (1982) *Writing and the Body*. Princeton, NJ: Princeton University Press.
Jung, C.G. (1906) *Studies in Word Association*, in A. Stevens (ed.) *On Jung*. London: Penguin Books, 1990.
Jung, C.G. (1959) *The Archetypes and the Collective Unconscious*, trans R.F.C. Hall. London: Routledge & Kegan Paul.
Jung, C.G. (1964) *Man and His Symbols*. London: Aldus Books.

Kellogg, R.T. (1994) *The Psychology of Writing*. Oxford: Oxford University Press.
Lewis-Williams, D. (2002) *The Mind in the Cave*. London: Thames and Hudson.
Pais, A. (1991) Niels Bohr's times, in *Physics, Philosophy and Polity*. Oxford: Clarendon Press.
Pinker, S. (1994) *The Language Instinct*. London: Penguin Books.
Roberts, G. and Holmes, J. (eds) (1999) *Healing Stories: Narrative in Psychiatry and Psychotherapy*. Oxford: Oxford University Press.
Rogers, C.R. (1951) *Client-Centred Therapy*. Boston, MA: Houghton-Mifflin.
Silverstone, L. (1993) *Art Therapy the Person-Centred Way*. London: Autonomy Books.
Steinberg, D. (1989) *Interprofessional Consultation: Innovation and Imagination in Working Relationships*. Oxford: Blackwell Science.
Steinberg, D. (1992) Informed consent: consultation as a basis for collaboration between disciplines and between professionals and their patients, *Journal of Interprofessional Care*, 61: 43–8.
Steinberg, D. (2000a) The child psychiatrist as consultant to schools and colleges, in M. Gelder, J.J. Lopez-Ibor and N.C. Andreasen (eds) *The New Oxford Textbook of Psychiatry*, pp. 45–50. Oxford: Oxford Univerity Press.
Steinberg, D. (2000b) *Letters to the Clinic: Letter Writing in Clinical Practice for Mental Health Professionals*. London: Brunner-Routledge.
Steinberg, D. (forthcoming) *The Other Side of Organisations: Consultation and Complexity in Health Care*. Abingdon: Radcliffe Medical Press.
Stevens, A. (ed.) (1990) *On Jung*. London: Penguin Books.
Stevens, A. and Price, J. (1996) *Evolutionary Psychiatry*. London: Routledge.
Tonfoni, G. and Richardson, J. (1994) *Writing as a Visual Art*. Oxford: Intellect Books.
Tyrer, P. and Steinberg, D. (forthcoming) *Models for Mental Disorder: Conceptual Models in Psychiatry*, 4th edn. Chichester: Wiley.
Wallas, L. (1991) *Stories that Heal*. New York: W.W. Norton.
White, M. and and Epston, D. (1990) *Narrative Means to Therapeutic Ends*. New York: W.W. Norton.
Winnicott, D.W. (1965) *The Maturational Process and the Facilitating Environment*. London: Hogarth Press.

Part II

Writing in therapy

Chapter 6

Writing by patients and therapists in cognitive analytic therapy

Anthony Ryle

Introduction

In cognitive analytic therapy (CAT), change in therapy is understood to depend on the effective use of a reliable human relationship within which hope and morale can be restored (Frank 1961). These are aspects common to nearly all psychotherapies, and for many less disturbed patients nothing more specific is needed. As the extent of personality restriction and distortion increases, however, so the containment of a patient's self-destructive ways of thinking and action, their liberation from restrictive, defensive solutions and the maintenance of the working relationship of therapy become more problematic. For these patients, who form the great majority of those receiving formal psychotherapy, CAT makes considerable use of writing.

The time spent in the presence of the therapist is a small proportion of a patient's life, especially when therapy is time-limited, as is the case in CAT, where 16–24 sessions is the usual duration. The vital work of therapy must be to focus upon fundamental issues, be memorable and of high emotional impact. Recording the specific understandings arrived at by patients and therapists in writing and diagrams, and using written materials to guide reflection and exploration, are important elements of the approach. They support therapists in the provision of intense, reparative, non-collusive relationships. They represent psychological tools through which patients expand their capacity for self-reflection and control.

Background considerations

The human genotype has not changed for at least 125,000 years. Over this period, man's unique symbol-making and symbol-using capacity, manifest in artefacts and in speech, has been applied to the physical world, the social world and the process of thinking itself. The additional development, only 10,000 years ago, of external written symbols resulted in a massively accelerated rate of growth in the accumulating storehouse of knowledge. As a result new kinds of minds in new kinds of people have emerged.

In some ways the development of the individual recapitulates this evolution. The emotionally various and intense interactions between infants and their caretakers depend upon the reciprocal use of sounds, gestures, rituals, rhythms and facial expressions, some innate and some created in each caretaker-infant interaction. Through these mimetic means, communication is established long before speech emerges. Such non-verbal communication persists alongside speech, serving in particular to convey emotion.

The conversation between patients and therapists concerns facts and feelings and is always delivered expressively. Tone of voice, hesitations and repetitions may all serve to emphasise or contradict the spoken word. Because what is unspoken is likely to be felt to be unacceptable, it can be important in therapy to name and consider non-verbal communications which contradict what is said. To that extent writing can never entirely replace face-to-face meetings. But nor is it simply factual, for writing can also be expressive and is itself a part of thinking. The act of producing descriptions or explorations of experiences or beliefs can increase patients' awareness and understanding of their own feelings and processes. There are some patients for whom the distance and indirection involved in writing allows painful memories and feelings to be described in ways not possible in face-to-face meetings.

Psychoanalytic therapists have usually been wary of receiving written communications from their patients and even more reluctant to write to them. Except when justified by external factors such as illness or geographical distance (see Ryle 1983) the use of writing was conceived of as a departure from, or an evasion of, the real work of therapy, rather than as an extension of it. To find an illuminating and amusing exception to this one must turn to fiction: the book-length *The Confessions of Zeno* was elicited, in a move acknowledged as unorthodox, by his psychoanalyst Dr S. (Svevo 1958). Nowadays, however, as the present volume demonstrates, both dynamic and cognitive therapists are much more likely to invite their patients to use creative, biographical and exploratory writing and to suggest various forms of diary keeping. In CAT, writing by both therapist and patient plays an important part.

The uses of writing in CAT

Writing by therapists

Written communications from therapists to patients offer transparency and memorability and are open to discussion and correction. These advantages were recognised early in the development of CAT. Further developments were in line with Bruner's (1986) important distinction between two different, complementary ways of conveying knowledge, which he called the *narrative* and the *paradigmatic*. The narrative mode is concerned with the different ways in which experience is viewed, constructed and made sense of, while the paradigmatic mode, formally enshrined in scientific thought, aims at consistency, verifiability, abstraction and neutrality and is heavily dependent on written words and other symbols.

In CAT practice both narrative and paradigmatic modes of communication are employed, the aim being to help patients apply conscious, objective thought to the recognition, understanding and modification of the idiosyncratic meanings and dysfunctional patterns of thinking, feeling and acting which underlie their distress.

Recollection of spoken speech is limited by short-term memory capacity and is always liable to be distorted by preconceptions. These factors are particularly likely to limit a patient's capacity to recall the content of a therapy conversation which may have challenged established beliefs and assumptions about emotionally disturbing topics. Moreover, the descriptions needed to understand interactions between, and the sequences of, mental and behavioural phenomena are inevitably complex and are often beyond what can be expressed in, or retained from, speech alone. When therapists write to patients, or recapitulate in writing what has been spoken, a far higher level of shared understanding can be achieved and such writing provides a record which can be corrected, reconsulted and argued with – processes that aid accuracy and assist internalisation.

Writing by patients

Expressive and exploratory writing by patients may be offered to any therapist who is prepared to receive it and who responds with an adequately subtle attention. By externalising and giving a form to unassimilated memories and affects, writing of this sort is directly therapeutic and reading it gives the therapist a deeper level of understanding. In CAT, such writing will be accepted but is not routinely requested, although autobiographical writing, self-descriptions and other focused tasks are commonly employed.

Specific uses of writing in CAT practice

In CAT practice the early sessions culminate in the joint development of written descriptions of the recurrent dysfunctional processes determining self-management and relationships which cause or maintain the patient's distress. In the early development of CAT, three general patterns underlying the non-revision of problematic experiences and behaviours were identified as *traps*, *dilemmas* and *snags*. These were examples of what came to be called *procedures*; they are recurrent, largely self-reinforcing sequences, the descriptions of which link context, aims, cognitive, affective and behavioural features and the consequences of action. The latter include, in particular, the responses of others. Combining environmental, mental and behavioural elements in a single descriptive unit in this way is a distinguishing feature of CAT reformulation.

The procedures of concern to therapists are those involved in the patient's self-management and in their formation and maintaining of relationships with others. In enacting a role procedure the aim is to elicit the expected or desired response from the other. Such *reciprocal role procedures*, representing a revised account of object relations ideas, are the 'building blocks' of the CAT model of personality. They are formed in early, pre-verbal life and are stable, both because they are not directly available to introspection and because we are usually able to elicit (or to seem to elicit) from others the expected reciprocations. These sources of stability account for the persistence of the damaging reciprocal role procedures underlying most psychological distress; recognising, describing and avoiding collusive reinforcement of the patient's repertoire of damaging reciprocal role procedures is therefore a crucial task in therapy. A main use of writing is to record descriptions of these patterns in order to guide patients' self-observation and to support accurate understanding and non-collusion in therapists.

The Psychotherapy File

The *Psychotherapy File* was the first document developed for routine use in CAT. It was designed to introduce patients to the way of thinking on which therapy would build and to engage them in active work from the first session. The *File* has been added to and modified over the years and is a strange collage, but it is acceptable and useful to the great majority of patients. Versions will be found in Ryle (1990, 1995, 1997) and in Ryle and Kerr (2002). The *File* opens with a paragraph proposing that learning to recognise one's personal patterns is the first step in gaining control over those causing problems. It then describes self-monitoring of moods and symptoms in a way based on cognitive therapy practice. Following this, three sections describe traps, dilemmas and snags, the common patterns underlying non-revision of problem procedures. Traps are patterns whereby negative assumptions generate actions which elicit apparent confirmation of the assumptions. Dilemmas are false dichotomies whereby the options for action or roles appear to be limited to polarised opposites. Snags involve the abandonment or undoing of appropriate aims due to irrational guilt or the anticipated reactions of others. A general description of each of these patterns is given, followed by a number of examples; patients are invited to rate how far they recognise each of these as applying to them. Finally, a section labelled 'Difficult and unstable states of mind' describes experiences and behaviours typical of patients with borderline personality problems.

It should be emphasised that the *File* is not a questionnaire yielding scores; it is a structured enquiry which invites and generates self-reflection on the part of patients and discussion between patient and therapist. It is usually completed by the patient after the first session and brought to the next for discussion. In this discussion, examples of each of the features identified by the patient as applying will be discussed, a process often extending the history in important ways and demonstrating that most patients have accurately identified their patterns. This discussion of the *File* helps to define the agenda of therapy as being the recognition and control of what the patients do – in terms of behaviour, relationships and thought – to maintain their problems. It therefore plays an important role in the creation of a shared understanding of the agenda and process of therapy and in recruiting patients to active participation.

Structured explorations

Two techniques have played a part in the development of CAT and may still be of value in particular cases, namely the *personal sources questionnaire* (Ryle 1990) and *repertory grid techniques*. The former asks individuals to identify the most salient sources of their self-esteem and then to rate, against a range of descriptions, how they feel when such sources are available or achieved. It frequently reveals, usually to the patient's surprise, that some of the sources relied upon have negative effects, indicating where therapeutic work needs to be done. Repertory grid studies using patient-selected individuals or relationships as elements played a large part in the development of CAT; clinical uses are described in Ryle (1975, 1990, 1995, 1997). The use of the 'states grid' in which the elements were the partially dissociated states of a borderline patient is described in Ryle and Kerr (2002). Identifying and describing the dissociated self states in borderline patients, which this case study illustrated, is a crucial step in therapy in the CAT model (Ryle 1997) and is assisted by the use of the eight-item personality structure questionnaire (PSQ) (Pollock *et al.* 2001), high scores on which offer a reliable indication of the presence of dissociated states. The PSQ provides a basis for systematic enquiry through which the characteristics of the different states can be established.

An additional standard patient-completed procedure (the states description procedure) is currently being piloted. This provides information about the characteristics of the states, in terms of their duration and the accompanying sense of self and others, mood and symptoms, and of switches between them as regards rapidity, provocations and so on.

These various procedures all provide more detailed information than can be elicited in conversation; all point to issues which can be further explored verbally, and all involve patients in highly relevant, focused self-reflection.

Diary keeping and self-monitoring

Bearing in mind the time limit of CAT (and the Spanish proverb which suggests that keeping a diary is like blowing your nose and then looking at the handkerchief), diary keeping and self-monitoring in CAT are designed to refer to specific issues. In the early stages of therapy the focus will be on symptoms and unwanted behaviours, the monitoring of which commonly reduces the frequency of their occurrence, as well as identifying the antecedent events and accompanying thoughts and action. Diaries, biographical writing and self-monitoring contribute to the construction of written and diagrammatic descriptions of the patient's repeated dysfunctional procedures as they are evident in relationships or self-management. Once reformulation is accomplished, the focus will shift to the recognition of these procedures as they are enacted in order to create the possibility of their conscious revision.

The early sessions in CAT are devoted to the reformulation of the patient's history and current problems in written and diagrammatic form. The aim is to summarise the origins and manifestations of the individual patient's problematic procedures. These will be described:

- in a letter describing past experience, how it was dealt with and how it affects present-day life (a narrative reconstruction);
- in words and diagrams providing a model of current patterns (fulfilling a paradigmatic function).

The two forms of description, developed collaboratively with the patient, define a common agenda for therapy. Change is seen to involve the patient's use of these conceptual tools to extend the capacity for self-reflection, from which, in due course, control and replacement of harmful procedures can be developed. The same tools support the therapist in avoiding techniques or responses which might reinforce negative role procedures. Experience has shown that the development of paradigmatic tools aids rather than inhibits the exploratory aspects of therapy, unless they are used defensively by the patient or applied obsessively by the therapist. The challenge facing therapists is to find the best way to help their patients apply paradigmatic thinking to the shifting, affect-laden narratives and experiences which are mobilised by the exploratory aspects of therapy.

In clinical practice it is made clear at the first meeting that the first few (usually four) sessions of therapy are devoted to getting to know the patient and constructing the reformulation. The explicit aim is to produce a provisional written account of the patient's problems and problem procedures, summarising, but also clarifying and extending, what has been learned during the assessment interviews and making use of data from the discussion of the *Psychotherapy File*, the structured enquiries and the patient's self-monitoring and diary keeping. The therapist's first aim is to demonstrate that the patient's distress has been heard and to offer a thoughtful and empathic description of it. On this basis, non-blaming models of how problems have been caused and maintained will be suggested. These will include descriptions of the patient's destructiveness to self and others and, importantly, will anticipate how this may be manifest in the therapy relationship.

There are two parts of the reformulation. The first, in the form of a letter, offers a narrative reconstruction of the patient's life history and the second, using words and diagrams, describes the currently operating procedures through which problems remain unsolved and needs remain unmet.

Reformulation letters

These letters, written by the therapist, are presented as provisional; they will be discussed and revised if they do not make sense to the patient. They usually open with a statement of what has brought the patient to therapy. The key aspects of the life history will then be summarised, the aim being to highlight experiences likely to have played a part in the generation of current problems. The 'conclusions' (that is, the values, assumptions and procedures) drawn from early experiences are then outlined, it being proposed in most cases that they were understandable given the context, powerlessness and immaturity of the patient and hence challenging the patient's irrational guilt.

Current problem procedures are described either as continuations of the reciprocal role patterns experienced in childhood or as restrictive, symptomatic and defensive alternatives which have become self-perpetuating. If evidence of fragmentation is apparent, a preliminary description of partially dissociated reciprocal role patterns (self states) will be suggested. How these features have already been evident in, or might in the future come to influence, the relationship with the therapist is then described. The aim of therapy is identified as the recognition and control of these harmful procedures and, in the case of fragmented patients, their integration.

The following is an abbreviated example of such a letter to a 19-year-old ex-student who was referred on account of self-cutting, violence to others, alcohol abuse and depression.

> Dear Mark,
>
> Here is the letter I promised, in which I try to record what I understand about your life and present difficulties; we will discuss it and make any changes if it is incorrect or unclear.
>
> It seems you have been depressed and angry for a long time. This started in early childhood but got worse three years ago when your uncle died. He had been very important to you, offering the support which your parents, with their heavy drinking and fighting, seldom provided. You were particularly upset by his death because you felt you had not been allowed to say goodbye to him. Your relationship with him was almost the only exception to what you saw and experienced in your immediate family where you learned to assume that relationships inevitably involve patterns of conflict and abuse. Coming from this background it is not surprising that, when others reject you or ignore your needs (or when you perceive or expect them to do so), you can be overwhelmed by unmanageable sadness and rage. You seem to have developed various ways of avoiding these feelings. Sometimes being helpful to your younger brother makes you feel better and he gives you some affection back. Often, however, you just conceal your feelings and pretend to be fine. In recent years you have been using alcohol several times each week as a way of blanking off, a self-harming behaviour which led to your having to leave college. At times, however, you flip into violent rages in which you smash things, may cut yourself and sometimes attack and hurt your older brother. Deep down, you always feel threatened; perhaps that explains why you feel you have to keep a knife hidden in your room. Another problem is the snag you identified in the *Psychotherapy File*; you saw how, if things do go well, you sabotage them as if you did not deserve them. Because of this irrational guilt and because you are not able to show what you are feeling, you can never ask others for help

> or care so that your real (and normal) emotional needs are never met. In addition, your violence and drinking make many people reject you.
>
> Coming to therapy has meant acknowledging that you do have needs. Our aim over the next 20 weeks will be to help you to find better ways of getting these normal needs recognised, both by you and by others. To start with, we will need to identify the thoughts and events which either make you blank off with drink or dope or which provoke your scary switches into rage and doing harm; this will involve developing and using the diagram we began to sketch out in the last session. It will also mean monitoring and greatly reducing your drinking and other drug use. We must also be alert to what happens between us; it was difficult for you to come and while so far it feels good to be listened to, it is likely that discussing painful feelings will sometimes provoke your 'I feel fine' pretend state and that at other times disappointment with me may provoke your anger. Recognising these and dealing with them together can help you get more control over your confusing switches. Losing the support of therapy after our 24 sessions may well put you in touch with feelings similar to those experienced in relation to all your past losses and deprivations, but I believe that the work and understanding of therapy will make it possible this time to move on and find more satisfying ways of being.

Mark's sequential diagram is shown in Figure 6.1.

Sequential diagrams

Relatively simple therapies can often be conducted in relation to a small number of written problem procedures (traps, dilemmas and snags) but a fuller understanding of these may be achieved by linking them to the underlying *reciprocal role repertoire*. For example, a patient, in going through the *Psychotherapy File*, might recognise the three traps of depressed thinking, trying to please and low self-esteem, the two dilemmas of *either* trying to be perfect but feeling angry *or* not trying and feeling guilty and '*If* I must *then* I won't', and the snag of self-sabotage *as if* guilty. Descriptions of each of these, modified to reflect the patient's own language and detailed experience, are easily accessible and useful. But they show many overlaps and could all be manifestations of a single core reciprocal role procedure such as *critical rejection* (from others or self) in relation to either *guilty striving* or *passive resistance*. This formulation in terms of the core reciprocal role repertoire offers a more general understanding and also alerts the therapist to be prepared to be invited into, or be seen as playing, any one of the described roles. That is to say, it offers a guide to likely transference-countertransference interactions. The difficulty patients experience in changing can thus be understood not only in terms of their low level self-reinforcing patterns of traps, dilemmas and snags but also through the way in which their relationships and self-care are conducted and interpreted in terms of their historical role repertoire.

This higher order understanding is, of course, unfamiliar and complex. Describing the ways in which reciprocal roles are maintained involves spelling out how self and others are perceived, how relationships with others are appraised, how the way the individual acts elicits the expected reciprocation and how the responses of others are interpreted. Describing this in prose can produce complex sentences, which are hard to follow and remember, whereas sequential diagrams can offer a succinct, paradigmatic, conceptual tool summarising the key sequences.

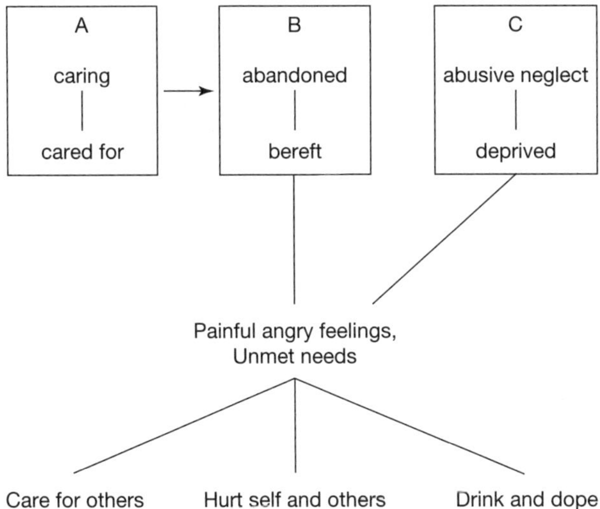

Figure 6.1 Marks provisional self-state diagram

Figure 6.1 is a provisional self-state sequential diagram for Mark, whose reformulation letter is given above. It summarises the main structure in terms of dissociated self-states. The boxes represent three partially dissociated self-states. At this stage not all the details are given, the aim being to clarify the overall pattern. In the course of the ensuing sessions details of procedural enactments of the various roles towards self and others and of the consequences evoked can be added and, as therapy continues, new procedures revising the system may be indicated. The self-state B (*abandoned* to *bereft*) was epitomised by the death of Mark's uncle but he had also experienced many other losses and was highly sensitive to any hint of being left. The self-state C was derived from the whole pattern of his childhood and A from the care he had received from his uncle and was able to offer his younger brother. It would be important to explore how far Mark might himself play the abandoning and rejecting roles towards others and to anticipate how they might lead to him leaving therapy; it was evident that he did play them towards himself. The diagram describes how, faced with actual or perceived abandonment or rejection, his sense of unmet needs generates unmanageable feelings which might be expressed in violence but which were usually replaced by pretending that all was well or were blanked off by drink. None of these procedures enabled him to fulfil his needs. The construction and use of diagrams is described in detail in Ryle and Kerr (2002).

Midway letters

Reformulation usually generates a positive, working therapy relationship, but either because early idealisation has not been adequately challenged, or because of inevitable disappointments and shortcomings leading to the emergence of established destructive procedures, it is common for the atmosphere to change around the tenth session. The hitherto cooperative patient misses a session, arrives late, becomes silent or fails to complete agreed homework tasks and the initially engaged and hopeful therapist becomes bored or frustrated. It is often helpful at such points for the therapist (with the help of supervision) to write a brief letter linking what has happened in therapy so far to the procedures identified at reformulation. It usually emerges that the therapist has been drawn into a collusive position, most commonly involving a shared avoidance of negative feelings. These *midway letters*, which may involve acknowledgement of this collusion, can make it possible for patients to express negative feelings directly in the knowledge that they are understood and will not evoke counter-hostility.

No-send letters

Reformulation usually serves to cement an early working alliance and the safety experienced as a result frequently allows patients to access more fully feelings and memories associated with past losses or past traumas. It can be helpful, in such cases, to suggest that the patient writes a letter to the person concerned, not with the intention of sending it but as a way of exploring and expressing their incompletely assimilated feelings. In the case of incomplete mourning for past losses, these letters may both express grief and acknowledge angry feelings which have stood in the way of grieving; writing them may be linked to forms of ritual, such as burying or burning the letter, which express a final acceptance of the loss. Letters to past abusers are frequently simple, direct expressions of outrage but some signal that the anger is now finished or, in a few cases, may convey forgiveness based on a fuller understanding of the abuser's own experiences.

Goodbye letters

Termination is a difficult process in all therapies. In time-limited work the aim is to give an experience which, as is true of all therapies, cannot make up for past losses but which can offer a real human engagement and new understandings and, on this basis, a manageable disappointment. The fact and meaning of the end will have been on the agenda from the beginning. For patients who are both aware and scared of their potential for unhelpful dependency, time limits offer safety, but even they will often be sad and resentful at the end.

CAT therapists write a goodbye letter to the patient, which is discussed at the last or next to last session. This should offer a sober assessment of what has and has not been achieved in terms of a greater access to memory and feeling and of recognising and revising the problem procedures identified at the time of the reformulation. The letter should acknowledge and 'permit' both the positive and the negative feelings associated with termination and should suggest what are the main issues still needing work. Brief therapy allows little time for assimilating what has been experienced and the consolidation of change depends on the patient's continuing capacity for self-reflection, often in the form of a conversation with the internalised therapist. It may be helpful to point out that breaking off or changing the terms of current relationships which have, in the past, offered unhelpful reciprocations to problematic role procedures, is likely to be painful and to take time.

These letters will usually repeat what has already been discussed but, by writing down baldly what has and has not been achieved, by naming the feelings associated with ending and by pointing to areas which need further work, they make it less likely that patients will deal with the ending by either denial or idealisation. It is helpful if patients, too, write letters at this stage as a way of consolidating their capacity for realistic self-reflection, but in some cases the emotional turmoil around termination is too great.

The following is a shortened version of a therapist's goodbye letter:

> Dear Sarah,
>
> This is the promised letter in which I will summarise how I see what your therapy has achieved. You came depressed, uncertain who you were and with difficult memories of a very unhappy childhood and of more recent hurts and disappointments with a series of boyfriends. When we started to meet you had just entered a new relationship with Pete; although this felt better than earlier ones you quickly fell into the familiar pattern whereby being close made you feel so exposed that you retreated or became angrily dismissive of him. Our relationship too provoked a similar pattern. But you persisted and, as it became clearer how this pattern was a legacy of the past, being derived from the painful neglect and unmet needs of your childhood, you began to control your reactions and to work at maintaining what was real and possible in the present. Slowly you were able to acknowledge your feelings without dismissing them as childish and to resist the old impulse to attack those from whom you needed love. Visiting your mother was an important moment; keeping your feelings under control enabled you to tell her directly how painful your childhood had been and to your surprise she was able to listen and also to support you in your plans to seek further education. Now you begin to feel you can determine your own future and have even experienced some unfamiliar moments of happiness. Ending therapy will mean facing some sadness and disappointment and maybe anger (perhaps more than you realise at this point) for there is much still to do and it was not any kind of magic cure. But I believe you will be able to hold

onto what you have learned and will continue to remember the experience and use the writing and diagrams we have made. I have enjoyed working with you and look forward to our follow-up meeting in three months' time.

Conclusion

In this chapter the advantages and limitations of writing in psychotherapy have been considered and the various uses made of writing by therapists and patients in CAT have been described and illustrated. The creation of agreed descriptions of the processes underlying patients' distresses is a particular feature of CAT and the use of writing and diagrams to describe these has been developed because it generates greater accuracy and because such conceptual tools remain available for repeated consultation.

While many psychotherapists welcome patients' exploratory writing, there is less recognition of the way in which clearly expressed accounts of the conceptual understandings achieved in the course of psychotherapy, as well as providing a new basis for self-reflection, are containing and facilitate access to memory and feeling. The various ways of exploring and describing underlying processes which have been described may sound too structured and 'cognitive' to many dynamic therapists, but in practice they contain and allow feeling, generate detailed understandings and extend patients' self-understanding. I believe they deserve wider use.

Therapists working within time limits in whatever model must aim to ensure that their interventions are accurate and focused on the patient's key issues and that their understandings become an active part of the therapeutic conversation. The uses of writing described in this chapter, many of which could be adapted to other models of therapy, can contribute to achieving this aim.

References

Bruner, J. (1986) *Actual Minds, Possible Worlds*. Cambridge, MA: Harvard University Press.

Frank, J.D. (1961) *Persuasion and Healing*. Baltimore, MD: Johns Hopkins University Press.

Pollock, P.H., Broadbent, M., Clarke, S., Dorrian, A.J. and Ryle, A. (2001) The personality structure questionnaire (PSQ): a measure of the multiple self states model of identity disturbance in cognitive analytic therapy, *Clinical Psychology and Psychotherapy*, 8: 59–72.

Ryle, A. (1975) *Frames and Cages*. London: Sussex University Press.

Ryle, A. (1983) The value of written communications in dynamic psychotherapy, *British Journal of Medical Psychology*, 56: 361–6.

Ryle, A. (1990) *Cognitive Analytic Therapy: Active Participation in Change*. Chichester: Wiley.

Ryle, A. (ed.) (1995) *Cognitive Analytic Therapy: Developments in Theory and Practice*. Chichester: Wiley.

Ryle, A. (1997) *Cognitive Analytic Therapy and Borderline Personality Disorder: The Model and the Method*. Chichester: Wiley.
Ryle, A. and Kerr, I.B. (2002) *Introducing Cognitive Analytic Therapy: Principles and Practice*. Chichester: Wiley.
Svevo, I. (1958) *The Confessions of Zeno*. New York: Random House.

Chapter 7

Journal writing as a therapeutic tool

Kate Thompson

Introduction

Journal therapy is the purposeful and intentional use of reflective or process writing to facilitate psychological, emotional or physical healing and to further therapeutic goals (Adams 1990). The development of writing therapy, though still embryonic, is growing through both the work of individuals and the expansion of organisations such as Lapidus (UK) and the National Association of Poetry Therapy (USA) and is supported by a research base (Pennebaker 1990; Bolton 1999; Lowe 2000; Wright and Chung 2001). This movement comprises a continuum of different methods and sets of techniques of which journal therapy is part. They have much in common despite avowals of difference dependent on context, background or philosophy. Burghild Nina Holzer, who changes the name of her journal writing courses depending on the context, illustrates this idea of similarity: 'in the end it didn't matter what the title was, I was always teaching the same thing. I could have called it "The expansion and integration of consciousness through writing" or I could have called it "Learning to Write in Curves"' (Holzer 1994: 3).

Journal writing can be a prelude to talking therapy; techniques can be used between therapy sessions to provide a greater continuity of the work done or within the session as a basis for the work. Talking in therapy about the process of journal writing can be more productive than reading journal extracts aloud, although clients sometimes want to read something they have written as a way of communicating difficult or painful material. Writing can express material which is previously unexpressed or access previously inaccessible material, allowing it to come to the surface. Paradoxically, a tightly structured task can circumvent the defences and allow some surprising realisations to emerge. By occupying the conscious mind with a defined task the unconscious mind can be allowed to step forward (see 'Lists of 100', p. 77). Clients bring the insights they have gained in their out-of-session journal work, often saying, 'I realise . . .', 'I learned . . .'.

The word 'journal' comes from the French *journée*: day. In the seventeenth century it meant a day's travel and the record of a day's events. Journal-*journée*-journey: the word contains both continuity and change, temporal and geographical, with direction and movement. This becomes a powerful metaphor for the relationship between person and life. A journal is a journey, a way of finding a voice.

The journal is a means of establishing relationships with the self and with others; Progoff talks about both the river and the road of individual experience (1975). The terms 'diary' (from the Latin *dies* – day, time and continuity again) and 'journal' are more or less interchangeable and used by different people to mean the same thing: *Diary of a Grief* (Woods 1998), *The New Diary* (Rainer 1978), *At a Journal Workshop* (Progoff 1975), *Journal to the Self* (Adams 1990). Conventionally perhaps, a diary is a daily record of someone's life whereas a journal may have connotations of being a more subjective record, concentrating more on the emotional and interior life.

Journal therapy developed in America. In the 1960s New York psychologist Ira Progoff began using 'psychological notebooks' with clients from which he developed the intensive journal method, published in *At a Journal Workshop* (Progoff 1975). The intensive journal uses a structured complexity of sections as a way of integrating different aspects of personal experience. Other books on the subject appeared in the 1970s (Baldwin 1977; Rainer 1978). In 1985 Kathleen Adams founded The Center for Journal Therapy in Denver, Colorado and published *Journal to the Self* in 1990. Journal writing was then adopted by education in England. Many National Vocational Qualification (NVQ) courses included a 'reflective journal module' in which students were encouraged to look at their own learning.

Journal keeping is available to everyone. Journal writing as a therapeutic tool can be introduced by therapists as part of therapy; it can also be used by clients as a self-directed method of personal development. Some clients will seem more obvious candidates for journal therapy than others. Prior experience of journal or diary keeping may be a positive indicator for the use of journal writing as a therapeutic tool in adulthood (for many people the Letts Schoolgirl or Schoolboy Diary is the first experience of regular writing about the self). Another helpful indicator is a positive relationship with writing.

> Andrea talked with great enthusiasm of writing in childhood, of writing a diary, poems and stories. We discussed journal writing and the ways in which it could be beneficial to her in her present circumstances and how she might begin again. In subsequent sessions we explored the reasons for her not writing. She began to keep a journal as our therapeutic work was ending.

Journal therapy may be particularly suitable for introverted personality types for whom the idea of talking to someone about personal or painful matter would be beyond contemplation. Confiding in a journal could be the first step in expressing such difficult material. When it is not possible for someone to speak about the content of their journal in therapy it may be useful to explore the process of writing about such things and the insights and feelings evoked.

Like introversion, a lack of support networks may be another positive indicator. When someone has no immediate intimate relationships, or circles of available acquaintance, the journal provides a place to talk, to sound out ideas, to explore feelings. It can provide an opportunity to think about and express things before talking about them; it can be a prelude to talking therapy. For people who are lonely and isolated, for example through illness or changes in their social world, or because psychologically their trust in human relationships has been damaged, the development of intimacy with the self can be a precursor to re-establishing links with other people. Thus journal therapy may make therapy of some sort accessible to a group of people otherwise excluded: 'Journal writing is an accessible trip even the most housebound can take' (Aldrich 1998: xiv).

Some second language speakers find that writing a journal in their mother tongue while undergoing therapy in their second language provides a way of making the transition between areas of experience.

> Dorita, a refugee from Kosovo, said, 'I write about what happened in my country then, so when I talk I leave it behind and think of now.' Her journal became a bridge between her past and present, the home which no longer existed and the trauma she experienced there and the country to which she was trying to find a way of belonging.

Reasons for journal therapy

There are many reasons why journal writing is useful as a therapeutic tool, either as an adjunct to therapy or as a method of self-directed therapy. A journal is an immediately accessible container available at any time, not dependent on the presence of others. It is available when no one else is, at 3 a.m., in the middle of a panic attack.

It is possible for someone to create a relationship with a journal which is *sustainable* over a period of time and is not subject to the whims of others. The ongoing and continuous relationship with a journal becomes a metaphor for the relationship with the self. It is a way of developing intimacy with the self. This is particularly useful in cases where lack of relationships in the world are part of the client's experience and contributing to distress. This can be the first step in reconnecting with other people.

A journal provides a place for *catharsis*. When intense emotion calls for immediate expression the journal is a ready container. It is a place for the expression of highly affective states, the scream on the paper, a place to vent emotion with no fear of reprisal or judgement. A journal is as tolerant of *repetition* as whoever writes in it.

Karen said, 'I wrote about what he'd done to me over and over again until I got bored with it and then I didn't need to any more.'

Part of the healing process can be the repeated telling of the story. Recounting apparently *ad infinitum* exhausts the patience of the most sympathetic of listeners but the journal receives it without demur.

Journal writing can provide people with a way of validating their own experience; a way of *capturing the reality of the moment*, the reality of the lived experience as perceived by the writer. One of my clients once told me that 'writing it down makes it real', thus giving validity to the experience.

It makes it harder to stay in patterns of denial when thoughts and feelings have been externalised in this way. In *Experience*, Martin Amis quotes his father, Kingsley: ' "In vino veritas – I don't know," Anthony Powell once said to me, "but in scribendo veritas – a certainty." ' [Martin Amis then goes on to say] 'In vino and in scribendo alike, the conscious mind steps back and the unconscious mind steps forward' (Amis 2001: 337).

A journal provides a way of *communicating with oneself*. A client once said, 'I'm getting to know myself through my journal, it's like meeting myself for the first time.' Through the journal the writer can develop intimacy with the self; the emphasis is on the encounter with the self. Speaking of the American people, Anais Nin (1976) said: 'the lack of intimacy with one's self and consequently with others is what created the loneliest and most alienated people in the world'. A journal also provides a way of communicating with others, both primary and secondary relationships, either through the actual selective sharing of written material or by recognising insights about relationships which are then integrated into the lived experience.

Scribo ergo sum. The physical act of writing, the appearance of words on the page, is an affirmation of existence. One client said in wonder, 'So I do have a voice', another said, 'I feel so empty but when I write I fill pages, so I can't be empty after all, can I?'

A consequence of cumulative writing is often the development of clarity about behaviour and feelings. Clients often say 'I realise now . . .' 'It isn't that we use writing to deny what we have experienced. Rather, we use it to shift our perspective' (deSalvo 1999: 11).

Over a period of time a *record of healing* is created, a map of the healing journey which is available for reference and consultation. *Diary of a Grief* (Woods 1998) offers a map of one person's journey through bereavement which can provide a guide for others. Woods told me that he was grateful if his book helped someone in the way that other texts had helped him.

Journal therapy techniques

Kathleen Adams (1998) developed a ladder of journal techniques, 'the developmental continuum of journal therapy'. At the bottom of the ladder are structured and boundaried techniques. These highly containing techniques are particularly suitable for the inexperienced or chaotic journal writer. They are practical and concrete. Progress up the ladder introduces more open and abstract techniques, ending with free writing, the technique with which many people and classes begin.

While there are no rules for journal writing, which is designed to liberate rather than to restrict, it is however useful to date every entry (including the year), so that reviewing previous journals provides a context for the writer's life and the material presented.

Five-minute sprint

A short burst of writing, contained by its own time limit, allows for the expression of deep emotion without loss of connection to the present. The leverage of the defined time can deepen the experience. Five-minute sprints can be on any topic and can emerge from other pieces of writing or matters arising. They can be a useful initial foray, safe in the knowledge that there is containment built in while also allowing catharsis. Clients are encouraged to keep a page of prompts for five-minute sprints for use when time permits: Who am I? Why am I here? What do I want? These questions can be used at any time, as the introduction to a longer session of writing, or to ground the self in the present. They can be interpreted on many different levels and the responses will be different each time they are addressed to reflect the writer in that moment.

Lists

Almost everybody will have made lists at some time so this has a very easy and familiar aspect. Lists are useful for prioritising and organising (to-do lists, wish lists), looking at identity (lists of roles or relationships), for positive reinforcement (list three pleasant moments/achievements/experiences each day). Ticking items off a list realises achievement and ability.

Clustering

Sometimes known as mindmapping or spidergrams, this technique commits lots of information expeditiously to paper. It is particularly useful when feeling overwhelmed and, not relying on grammar or structure, can be embraced by people with literacy needs or lacking confidence in their ability to put pen to paper. As a technique used in business it is familiar to a group of clients who might initially be sceptical of more intuitive techniques. It is useful for organising things in the midst of chaos. More extended writing can follow.

Captured moments

These are short exercises in which the writer attempts to capture the essence and the emotional experience of a memory.

Jennifer wrote a captured moment about climbing a peak in the Lake District and vividly recovered the euphoria of achievement and her glory in both the natural beauty and her physical effort. This was important for her to recall as the onset of heart disease now prevented her from repeating such experiences.

A captured moment allowed Julia to recognise the moment at which she first acknowledged that she loved women.

Lists of 100 (Adams 1990)

These are extended lists. The rules are:

- Write fast
- Repeat as much as you like
- Number the items
- Don't censor.

After reaching 100 (daunting in prospect but surprisingly manageable in practice, taking 20 to 30 minutes), items are grouped (include a 'miscellaneous' category). The taxonomy can produce surprising results.

Bernadette was vaguely dissatisfied with her life; she thought perhaps her home was making her unhappy and needed to change. She wrote 'List of 100 things I would like to change' and found that the items about her flat were all relatively trivial and manageable; the real source of her dissatisfaction was her job, appearing in 45 items. She was then able to begin to explore her options and ultimately began to retrain for a different career.

Sally was an angry woman, a lot of things irritated her and she had a lot to cope with. After writing 'List of 100 things I'm angry about' she discovered that the underlying object of her frustration was her own physical health problems and ultimately not the noisy neighbour and the uncooperative council.

Unsent letters

This is one of the most popular journal techniques. Writing letters is already a familiar activity, although for many people it is being superseded by email (Unsent emails are perhaps an unwise idea – one click and an email is sent). There is licence in the promise that the letter will never be sent. This can silence the internal censor and allow the expression of raw feeling and unprocessed thought. Unsent letters is journal writing with an external focus; the imagined reader has an identity and usually a past, present or future relationship with the writer. Letters can build on some aspect of this relationship.

Susan, a woman in her forties seen in a primary care setting for time-limited counselling, was referred with stress and anxiety manifesting in panic attacks. She revealed that her husband was in prison and refusing to communicate with her although she continued to write to him, sending him news and beseeching him to reply or send her a visiting order. She experienced feelings of sadness, hurt and bewilderment at his lack of response but there seemed to be a lot of unexpressed feeling which she could not access or acknowledge. As she was already writing him letters it was an easy progression to writing letters which would never be sent. This would allow her to express the things she needed to say to him without fear of offending him or alienating him further. She returned the following week astonished by the experience – in her unsent letters had emerged a powerful anger towards him which she had never allowed herself to acknowledge. It did not fit her image of herself; she was uncomfortable with the idea of being angry and had suppressed it. The unsent letters circumvented her defences and allowed her to begin to recognise this. The ensuing fruitful work in our counselling sessions would not have been possible without her writing.

Although the putative recipient is usually known to the writer and vice versa, this is not always the case as, most famously, when Ann Frank wrote her diary to her imagined friend Kitty. Other recipients can include deities, famous people, younger or older selves or objects. Writing unsent letters to a younger self can allow survivors of childhood sexual abuse to begin to heal the relationship with the self.

In working with issues connected to bereavement, unsent letters can provide a way of working through the grieving process, particularly after a sudden or unexpected death. In her poem 'The Hooded Hawk' Anne Michaels (2000) writes:

> Colette said, when one we love dies
> there's no reason to stop
> writing them letters

Jill Truman's book, *Letter to My Husband* (1998) is her way of working through her grief after his death.

Elaine, a woman in her forties whose sister had died the previous year from breast cancer is very involved with the care of her nephews and nieces, particularly the youngest. She began to write letters to her sister which helped her to process many of her feelings about the bereavement and her own loss and also, by telling her sister about the children, she was able to become much clearer about her own role in their lives (not usurping her sister's role as mother).

Unsent letters are also useful for resolving difficult situations. A writer can tell someone what they really think without fear of reprisal or of causing more difficulty with infelicitous expression.

Dialogue

Writing dialogues can seem a strange, counterintuitive technique to those who have never tried it before, but on further investigation few people have never had a conversation with themselves.

Steven said with wonder after early experiments with dialogues, 'It's all me, isn't it?' from which point he was able to go on to begin to develop an intimacy with himself by giving voice to his apparently inconsistent thoughts.

Dialogue techniques are a part of the repertoire of various psychotherapy orientations, for example the challenging of negative thought patterns in cognitive behavioural therapy or the 'two chairs' exercise in Gestalt therapy. Ira Progoff developed the use of dialogues to an art form; they provide the deeper work of the intensive journal (Progoff 1975). He identified six main categories of dialogue:

- Dialogue with persons
- Dialogue with events
- Dialogue with the body
- Dialogue with societies
- Dialogue with inner wisdom.

Kathleen Adams (1990) adds three more categories:

- Dialogue with emotions
- Dialogue with sub-personalities
- Dialogue with resistance/block.

I would make a distinct category of: 'dialogue with younger/older self'.

Cheryl Moskowitz (1998), a writer and psychotherapist, developed a technique which she calls 'The Self as Source' and ultimately uses dialogue to begin to integrate parts of the self.

Jenny, a teacher in her late thirties, was emerging from depression triggered by work-related stress. She had had quite a long period away from work and in one session expressed concern about her drinking. She was drinking red wine in what she was beginning to feel were excessive quantities but in therapy appeared unsure what role it was really playing in her life. She wrote a dialogue with the wine bottle which helped her to clarify her thoughts:

Jenny: Tonight you are sly, all you have to do is lie in the fridge and you and I both know you'll be opened. Tonight I'm drinking you out of habit.

Wine bottle: We're close friends. Well I'm not your friend, you make me your friend, I don't need you, I do nothing to perpetuate or develop the friendship, it is totally governed by you.

Jenny: At the moment I'm in control of you, except that I'm always in control of you, I just choose not to be in control . . . drink you and drink you and then blame you for the state I get into, torturing myself with guilt, which I've learnt to feel every day of my life, instead of rewarding myself with the pleasures of self-control.

Wine bottle: Don't talk to me, talk to yourself.

What emerged from this exercise was the realisation that she used the wine bottle to allow her to abnegate responsibility for her drinking and in turn for her life. She then had a dialogue with herself:

Why are you drinking?
  I don't know.
Why did you start drinking tonight?
  As a reward.
Why did you continue?
  Because it tasted good.
Why are you still drinking?
  I don't know.
Why are you still drinking?
  Because it's there.

The use of the dialogue tool at this point progressed our work; realisations emerged at a pace which Jenny herself was determining. From this she was able to recognise her own responsibility for her habitual drinking and to observe what was happening. Ultimately she understood the available options and the choices she was making.

> Lesley was a non-compliant diabetic who, through a series of dialogues with diabetes was able to begin to acknowledge her denial of her condition and from that, while not embracing diabetes, was at least able to begin to accept it and to learn how to manage it in a way that was less destructive.

Dialogues are also useful for anticipating and preparing for situations, and thinking about difficult or confrontational conversations.

> Simon came to a therapeutic writing group after a hard day at work. His (female) boss had been picking on him. He wrote a dialogue with her in which he was able to explain how he felt about her attitude towards him. He then stopped taking it personally and decided what he needed to say.

Perspectives

This category includes the technique of writing from the projected future. Placing a future date at the top of the page and writing for that day can help people to think about the decisions they have to make and the implications of their choices. This can help clients to set goals or courses of action for the forthcoming period or to begin to see what they really want. It can also illuminate what is being postponed or ignored.

> Alan wrote a perspectives entry for six months in the future which allowed him to realise what it would be like to be still living alone; he therefore resolved to ask his girlfriend to marry him.

Perspectives can also be a way of exploring roads not taken, past or future. Perspective entries can help the writer to identify things which may be wanting or which are present but unrecognised.

Free writing

Adams (1998: 6) says:

> When it is used purposefully and intentionally, Free Writing can be a highly effective technique that offers clarity, insight and intuitive connection. But as a default technique it can feel uncontrolled and risky, like a colt without a bridle or a free-fall with a dubious parachute. At other times it can feel like a dog leashed to a clothesline, going nowhere in tight, unsatisfying circles.

For clients with no prior experience of writing, or of therapeutic writing in particular, the exhortation to 'just write whatever comes into your head' will often produce the response 'I don't know where to begin' or stronger feelings of near panic. Other people find the liberation of free writing a way of escaping from the over-zealous internal censor, sometimes the product of early educational experiences. Julia Cameron's (1992) technique of 'morning pages' consists of writing two pages of free writing every morning.

Completing the Loop

One way of reinforcing the relationship with the self in the journal is by the use of the *feedback statement*. This reflective mechanism allows the writer to become aware of what arises during the writing.

Some experiences can be completed by the physical destruction of the written page – this is writing as artefact. This might be the case where security and privacy are concerns, or, as in the case of a client whose husband had had a series of affairs, a form of expulsion. She wrote him an unsent letter in which she expressed 20 years of pent-up anger. Catharsis was completed by the physical act of tearing the paper into shreds and flushing them down the lavatory in an act that was both symbolic and satisfying.

There are times when catharsis is not enough and a period of reflection can make the work more productive. The *feedback mechanism* can be used to deepen understanding; it is a way of completing the loop, of repossessing the self.

Reading through a journal entry is in itself a way of owning the words and the experiences contained therein. Reading aloud, hearing one's own words received by the external world, whether to oneself or to an audience, is a powerful experience. Releasing words gives them a different kind of reality; it is a way of owning, hearing and acknowledging the personal truth. The feedback statement takes this process further by requiring the writer to notice and comment upon what is being expressed:

Feedback statement

1	When I read this	I notice . . .
		I am surprised that . . .
		I realise . . .
2	As I read this	I am aware that . . .
		I feel . . .

The first group of statements asks people to reflect and comment on what they have written, to notice anything about the content or the feelings expressed in the writing. The second group asks people to reflect on their experience of reading their words, to notice what feelings are evoked as they read and their reactions. This can produce some startling insights which can be brought into therapy, illuminating connections which might otherwise not have been made.

After reflecting on an entry about her parents, Carol was able to see their relationship in a different light. Their relative strength and power within the family was different from what she had experienced when growing up.

Feedback statements can also bring people more into their living experience. A therapy session will often be concerned with feedback questions. Sometimes people are struck by the emergence in their journal of feelings previously buried or denied; their incontrovertible presence in the written words can then be worked through in therapy. Reading through a journal entry can bring understanding and insight into the content of the writing and can bring a changed perspective on past relationships.

The feedback mechanism can be used at many stages; it can be used immediately on completion of a journal entry or it can be used later, perhaps on ending one journal and before opening a new one. Some people use the last few of pages of their notebook to give themselves feedback before moving on to the next; it becomes a kind of closure and is useful for identifying recurring themes and patterns (although one client said 'I don't need to read it, I know the themes – I'm still living them' she still found herself surprised by what she read).

The process is:

WRITING → FEEDBACK → RECOGNITION → OWNING → INTEGRATING

During the writing of this chapter I used many of the techniques described as part of my own process. This helped to develop clarity about what I wanted to say as well as finding ways to say it. My journal from this period contains a number of dialogues with various partners including myself (What is it you are trying to say?), a reader, the empty page and writer's block.

References

Amis, M. (2001) *Experience*. London: Vintage.
Adams, K. (1990) *Journal to the Self*. New York: Warner Books.
Adams, K. (1994) *Mightier than the Sword*. New York: Warner Books.
Adams, K. (1998) *Clinical Journal Therapy*. Denver, CO: Center for Journal Therapy.
Aldrich, A.H. (1998) *Notes from Myself*. New York: Carroll & Graf.
Baldwin, C. (1977) *One to One*. New York: M. Evans.
Bolton, G. (1999) *Therapeutic Potential of Creative Writing*. London: Jessica Kingsley.
Cameron, J. (1992) *The Artist's Way*. Los Angeles: J.P. Tarcher.
deSalvo, L. (1999) *Writing as a Way of Healing*. London: The Women's Press.
Holzer, B.N. (1994) *A Walk Between Heaven and Earth*. New York: Bell Tower.
Lowe, G. (2000) Reading and writing: pleasure, guilt and health, *Context Magazine for Family Therapy and Systemic Practice*, 47: 2–3.
Michaels, A. (2000) *Poems*. London: Bloomsbury.

Moskowitz, C. (1998) The self as source: creative writing generated from personal reflection, in C. Hunt and F. Sampson (eds) *The Self on the Page: Theory & Practice of Creative Writing in Personal Development*. London: Jessica Kingsley.

Nin, A. (1976) *In Favor of the Sensitive Man*. New York: Harcourt.

Oliver, M. (1986) *Dreamwork*. New York: The Atlantic Monthly Press.

Pennebaker, J. (1990) *Opening Up*. New York: Guilford Press.

Progoff, I. (1975) *At a Journal Workshop*. New York: Dialogue House Library.

Rainer, T. (1978) *The New Diary*. Los Angeles: J.P. Tarcher.

Truman, J. (1998) *Letter to my Husband*. London: Hodder & Stoughton.

Woods, P. (1998) *Diary of a Grief*. York: Sessions.

Wright, J. and Chung, M.C. (2001) Mastery or mystery? Therapeutic writing: a review of the literature, *British Journal of Guidance & Counselling*, 29: 3.

Chapter 8

Writing the link between body and mind: the use of writing with clients suffering from chronic stress-related medical disorders

Stephanie Howlett

Introduction

The idea that there is a link between emotional state and physical health is not new, this view having been held, albeit by a minority of physicians, since the time of Hippocrates. However, as any GP is well aware, there are some people who are particularly prone to develop physical symptoms in response to stress or the hardships of life. These people are often frequent attenders at GP practices, the 'complex' or 'heart-sink' patients with diverse problems or long-term chronic illnesses, seeking a cure for symptoms that do not seem to respond to conventional medical interventions.

GPs, aware of the family and life circumstances of their patients, may suspect that it is these emotional difficulties that are being expressed through their symptoms. However, this is a group of patients who are notoriously difficult to work with psychologically, and who often do not respond to conventional counselling and therapeutic approaches.

In this chapter, working from a basis of psychoanalytic theory and drawing on clinical experience gained in a range of settings, I explore the diverse ways in which writing can be used to supplement therapeutic work with this client group and why they may find it particularly useful.

Psyche-soma link – a psychoanalytical perspective

This link between the mind and body has been long recognised in psychoanalytical theory. Freud never used the term 'psychosomatic', but he did believe that feelings of depression could bring about organic disease in predisposed individuals, whereas happiness could have a rejuvenating effect (Freud 1905).

Later theorists focused on the gradual development of emotions and thought processes as they start to separate out from physical sensations in the weeks and months after birth. Winnicott (1960) suggests that this begins in very early infancy, and depends on reliable and responsive physical care of the infant by the parents or carers. It is this that allows the very young baby to start to make sense of the world, of being separate from the mother and other people, gradually able to tolerate her absence, and to start to experience emotions as different from physical sensations, differentiating the psychic from the somatic.

Bick (1968, 1986) and Meltzer (1974) focused on the role played by the skin and the physical sensations conveyed through it by adequate and responsive maternal care. They saw this as having a crucial impact on an infant's ability to develop a sense of an integrated and separate self, and an internal emotional world. They felt that if things did not happen properly at this stage then the child's emotional life was likely to be characterised by 'adhesive identifications'. Such a child growing up would not have a clear sense of who they were, and would tend to get their values from other people, often by imitation. They might have a strong need for physical proximity to the people they were close to. They would not have much sense of an inner life, and might not know or be able to describe what they were feeling emotionally. They would tend to deal with emotional issues that arose in a very physical, functional way, by looking for practical solutions, through energetic sport, through talking a lot rather than thinking or feeling, or by expressing them through the body as symptoms.

This very physical, sensory way of experiencing the world is normally dominant in the first few weeks of life, and all being well gradually becomes less so as the child grows up. But in cases where healthy development is not facilitated it can continue as a predominant way of functioning into adult life. In addition, where people have had very traumatic experiences, so overwhelming that they can't be processed afterwards and need to be blocked off, they can be tipped back on a longer-term basis into a more physical way of expressing things. This can also happen with more chronic emotional issues that a person for whatever reason is unable to express or deal with in their lives.

This links with the concept of 'alexithymia' (also sometimes referred to as operatory thinking), a term coined by Nemiah and Sifneos (1970), which has been associated with psychosomatic tendencies: 'This refers to the discovery that certain people have no words to describe their emotional states, either because they are not aware of them or because they are incapable of distinguishing one emotion from another' (McDougall 1989: 24). Such people often react apparently with little emotion to major life events, which increases their vulnerability to psychosomatic symptoms.

In summary, for many people with a tendency to persistent functional or psychosomatic type illness, emotional processing is not easily available and their reactions to life's vicissitudes are expressed in a physical way. This is increasingly being borne out by research in other disciplines (see Lowe, Chapter 2).

Linking theory to therapeutic aims

If, as outlined above, the key psychological issue making people prone to unexplained physical symptoms is a difficulty with feeling and expressing painful emotions, then the main aims of therapy in working with such clients follow on logically:

1. To identify the key area where feelings can not be expressed.
2. To help the client to understand the link between the unexpressed emotions and their symptoms, in the context of their life history and current relationships.
3. To encourage the recognition and expression of the emotions in the safe space of therapy.
4. To encourage the client to communicate about their feelings within their interpersonal relationships.
5. To encourage changes in the client's life and interpersonal relationships that would reflect and take forward these changes in expressiveness, foster their sense of their own identity, and enable them to become less merged with and dependent on other people.

Using writing to further the therapeutic aims

Writing can play a key role in furthering these aims in a range of ways, limited only by the imagination of the therapist. Described below are some techniques that I have used in diverse therapeutic contexts. The examples given are fictionalised composites of typical cases.

Journal writing

This can be introduced in various ways. The client can be asked to keep a daily journal, recording both their physical symptoms and also what is happening in their lives, particularly in terms of feelings. This helps therapist and client together to identify the links between the client's symptoms and other factors in their lives. Another aim is to encourage people who often experience life very largely in terms of their physical symptoms to start to focus on, and acknowledge the existence of, an emotional dimension to their lives.

The way that people use the diaries or journals can be very revealing. It is very common in my experience for people to write a terse description of their physical symptoms and omit any reference to other aspects of their lives. This demonstrates how much the emotional dimension goes unacknowledged. These often seem to be the people who are the most difficult to work with therapeutically. It can be helpful to look with them at the omissions, and the difficulties of engaging with this aspect of the writing task. It may also be helpful to ask them to keep a journal focusing exclusively on their feelings, to encourage them to acknowledge and value their emotions and also as a means of bringing their emotional life into therapy.

Of course, non-completion of any writing assignment may also be an expression of resistance to the therapeutic task, or a manifestation of underlying transference issues, which can be worked with in the same way as lateness for sessions or other attacks on the therapeutic boundaries.

Example

One undergraduate with a chronic fear of cancer, who insisted that he had no other problems whatsoever, wrote initially in his diary exclusively about his symptoms (spots on his legs and undefined physical sensations). I persisted in asking him to write about other aspects of his life, and eventually he wrote some 'unimportant details' about friendship difficulties, which enabled us to start discussing his acute loneliness. The severity of his symptoms began to diminish from that point.

Other people would write about symptoms and what was happening within their lives, with at least some mention of feelings.

Example

Monday
Poor night's sleep
IBS (irritable bowel syndrome) not too bad
Told A that 3 things were bothering me, work, driving and him. Wondered about talking to him, but really not what I need at the moment, so I don't.

Tuesday
Slept OK, but woke early
IBS grumbling
Traffic not bad
Generally feeling pretty good
Reflect on talking about things. I have a lot on my plate over the next few weeks. I may put things off

Wednesday
Slept OK
IBS OK
Drive to school – weather bad, traffic bad, kids bad, drive home bad.
Totally fed up. Guts rough

This sort of writing, while short and to the point gives some material to work with and helps to make links between symptoms, events and emotions. It focused this very brusque teacher on what she was feeling, so that eventually she was clear about the link between her bowel symptoms and driving, particularly in bad conditions. It also made it clear to both of us how difficult she found it to talk about emotional issues, especially with her partner, and we were able to talk about these anxieties.

Other people may already make a link between their symptoms and what they are feeling, but the feelings they write about are all linked to their illness, which has become the central preoccupation of their lives, often displacing very painful issues on which they are unable focus.

Example

> Stomach gurgled a little, a little wind. Went up to the shops, walked up. Slight panic but pushed it away. Came back, went to the toilet, everything normal. Had to go to town. Went on the bus. I managed it all right without worrying. Walked around town OK, came back on the bus. One of the best days I've had with my stomach for ages.

This woman was aware of how much her anxiety could affect her bowel symptoms, and was working relatively effectively in a behavioural way to break the vicious circle and overcome the restrictions it was putting on her life. However, this exclusive focus on bodily pain is something that often seems to arise as an avoidance of emotional pain, so it is helpful if the therapy can be steered more into the emotional arena.

At the far end of the spectrum are those patients who turn the journal into their own therapeutic tool, which it can feel a privilege to share. The woman who wrote the previous example began to use the journal in this way later in therapy.

Example

> Stomach has been feeling quite calm, just a little shaky. I was watching TV. All the memories and the lonely feelings. I can't explain them. It's a feeling deep inside. As I'm writing this I can feel my stomach knotting up. I miss D so much.

She then went on to write three pages of vivid memories of her son who had been killed in an accident several years before, revisiting the pain that she had been unable to talk about until then.

Other clients will write reams and reams in a clearly very cathartic way.

Example

> One middle-aged, working-class woman whose symptoms were linked with severe physical and sexual abuse by both parents, turned her diary into an extensive and passionate letter to her parents, expressing some of her pain, outrage and self-loathing. That would clearly have been therapeutic for her in itself. However, it also served an important function within the therapy. The writings were so voluminous that we adopted the practice that she would leave the notebook with me to read before the next session, continuing her writings in a second book. It was much easier for her to commit things to writing initially than to express them to me. However, once I had read the journal and things were known between us we could talk about them and process them. At first she was worried that I might disbelieve or reject her, so my continued acceptance, encouragement and valuing of her writings became an important part of the therapeutic relationship.

Letters to important people in a client's life

Another useful and commonly used form of writing that can be very helpful in the context of therapy is that of 'unsent letters' to key people in the client's life, as a means of expressing difficult feelings that seem impossible to verbalise. The letter might be to someone who has died, particularly where mourning was incomplete or the client regretted things left unsaid. In other situations an unsent letter gives the client the freedom to fully explore the complexity of positive and negative feelings towards a significant person in their life without having to deal with real life reactions.

> **Example**
>
> H was a woman who had lost her father from cancer at the age of 7. Because of her youth she was not allowed to visit him in hospital or attend the funeral. Her physical symptoms started after the death of her mother many years later, which could not be talked about at the time either, because the doctors advised that the mother not be told she was dying. Her letter to her mother spoke of both these losses, expressing her anger with her mother as well as her own feelings of guilt, loss and love, and marked a key point in her therapy.

In other situations, unsent letters, through the catharsis and exploration of feelings they provide, can also enable the writer to think about how to communicate in reality with important people in their lives.

Writing to body parts or symptoms

Many of the people I worked with who had a strong psychosomatic tendency were very focused on their bodies. It can be helpful in that case to suggest they write to their symptoms or body parts if that seems like a way of expressing difficult emotions or understanding the emotional role their symptoms may play in their lives.

> **Example**
>
> One woman had a crippling loathing of her belly. I suggested she write to it, saying how she felt about it. She wrote a very angry diatribe telling her belly how it had let her down by becoming saggy, and how much she hated it. Somewhat dismayed I suggested she write an imagined reply, which she did. Her belly pointed out to her how it had grown her children, and how hard it was to be so hated and criticised. This raised many issues about her life and feelings about herself, allowing some healing of the damage caused by her own abusive childhood.

Similarly, letters from clients to their IBS, eczema or back pain, followed if it seems helpful by replies from the symptoms, can bring an understanding into therapy of their ambivalent feelings towards their illness. This may facilitate a recognition of the rewards, protection or companionship the illness may provide, alongside the problems, pain, frustrations and restrictions. Sometimes an unacknowledged aspect of their personality that has been split off into their symptoms can then start to be integrated.

Writing from conflicted parts of the personality

In cases where a person is trying to suppress particular emotions and feelings, it can be helpful to encourage them to give voice to that aspect of their personality.

> **Example**
>
> A woman in her thirties came for counselling with an obsessive and unfounded fear of sexually transmitted diseases. She was trying hard to be a committed wife and mother, devoting her life to her family. However, every so often she would get drunk and behave in an embarrassingly flirtatious way at parties, feeling huge guilt and shame afterwards. I suggested that she write about these two sides of herself, the dutiful mother and the flirty vamp, as if they were two different people, and imagine what each would think of the other. She wrote that the Dutiful Mum persona liked her life on the whole, and thought that Flirty Vamp was selfish and embarrassing, but realised that she envied her sexiness and bad-girl image. Flirty Vamp found Dutiful Mum rather bland and conventional but envied her security and stability. This enabled the client to think about ways that she might integrate these two aspects of her personality. She decided to indulge a long-held ambition by learning to play the saxophone, and joined a band where she could wear outrageous clothes and adopt a sexy, exhibitionist persona in a safe, enjoyable way.

Cheryl Moskowitz describes a more extended writing exercise she developed together with a woman suffering from leukaemia who wrote about her well and ill selves (Moskowitz 1998).

Writing by the therapist

Writing by the therapist can also augment and consolidate the therapeutic process. The author used a farewell letter similar to that used in cognitive analytic therapy (Ryle 1990 and Chapter 6) in a research study into IBS, as an integral part of a model of brief psychodynamic interpersonal therapy (Howlett and Guthrie 2001). It was used to reinforce the associations between physical symptoms and emotional factors discovered during the sessions, and to maintain the insight that clients with somatising tendencies often find it so hard to retain. It charted the progress made by clients in the course of therapy, and gave some indication of what they might need to continue working on after therapy ended. The draft letter was read aloud to the patient in the final session, with amendments and corrections, so that the final version they took away was one they felt happy with.

A follow-up study of patients' use of farewell letters indicated that for those who had responded well, the letter was an important adjunct to therapy, kept and reread, sometimes shared with important people in their life, used perhaps as a physical embodiment of the therapist to reinforce the messages of therapy, sustain them at times of difficulty and cope with the loss of therapy.

However, in the case of those therapies where outcome was poor, the farewell letter can be less beneficial, and possibly in some cases even detrimental, serving as a critical reminder of yet another failed attempt to relieve suffering, and raising the emotional issues the client is still avoiding.

The importance of ritual

Ritual can be particularly important for some people with psychosomatic tendencies, because of their literal way of experiencing life. Thinking with clients about what to do with completed writing can therefore be an important part of the therapeutic process. Different people may choose to keep the writing as a record of their progress, to leave it in the safekeeping of the therapist, to read it aloud in a place of special significance to them, to have a ceremonial burning, to rip it to shreds or even to flush it down the toilet. Any ritual they devise can be an important way of allowing them to achieve closure and move on.

Particular ways in which writing is helpful for clients with psychosomatic tendencies

Bearing in mind that the key therapeutic aim is to foster the ability to feel, express, communicate and deal with emotions for people who find this difficult, writing can be helpful in various ways:

- Focusing on emotions and bringing them into conscious awareness, so that they can be thought about, shared, normalised and made sense of, which is often a very new experience.
- Identifying and demonstrating links between symptoms and other aspects of the client's life, particularly emotional factors, which can then open the way to address those emotional factors.
- Writing is an individual act, allowing the private experience and expression of emotions and thoughts. This may be an essential first step for people who have always viewed emotions as bad, weak or taboo. Emotions that have been so long denied can feel overwhelmingly painful, dangerous and frightening. However, once this first step has been taken it becomes easier to share thoughts and feelings, both in therapy and in important interpersonal relationships. The writer is in control of how this is done and may choose to share the writing itself or the experiences and insights it has facilitated.

- Writing can play an important cathartic role, or function as a way of 'getting things out of my head', of fixing worries and feelings so that they can be put aside and thought about more productively rather than being endlessly ruminated on.
- Writing, as with any other aspect of the therapeutic interaction, provides a medium for the expression and identification of transference and counter-transference issues. This might be expressed in the content of the written material, or in the manner in which the client does or does not engage with writing assignments, their eagerness or reluctance to bring written material to sessions etc. With this client group, where there is often little psychological-mindedness, it can be difficult to reflect with them on the therapeutic process, and this manifestation of underlying processes provides an additional tangible means of doing this.
- With somatising clients there is often a bypassing of conscious awareness or understanding of emotions, which are evacuated immediately in a physical way, without an identification by the person of the emotions they are expressing. Such clients may suddenly find themselves sobbing or physically shaking, or experience a headache or lump in their throat without knowing why. The task in therapy is to identify the triggers and fill in the emotional links. The physical act of writing seems to have a similar mechanism. Often when writing in an uncensored, free-associating way, people find they are surprised at what emerges – almost as if they write things before they are conscious of them. Having fixed them on paper allows them then to think about and process feelings they didn't know they had. Writing can thus serve to bring emotions and connections from the unconscious into the realm of thought and understanding, helping the writer to start to symbolise their experiences.
- Writing assignments also encourage a more active engagement by the client, so that they continue to think about the issues between sessions. This is particularly important for this group, who can tend to banish therapy and emotional issues from their minds after the session, and find it hard to hold onto insights and understanding. Far from continuing to work on emotional issues between sessions, they are otherwise likely to revert to old patterns of 'not letting it get to me'.

When writing is not helpful

While writing can do much to augment, enrich and facilitate face-to-face therapeutic work, it is important for the therapist to use it judiciously, ensuring that it does indeed play this enhancing role.

Wright and Lowe (Chapters 1 and 2) refer to the need for caution in suggesting writing to clients suffering from chronic depression, who are highly disturbed, psychotic or suffering from post-traumatic stress disorder. Writing can be used to obstruct and divert from the therapeutic task. Some clients bring reams of writing which, if it were read by the therapist at the time would take up most of the session and avoid the possibility of engagement within the therapy room. It may also mean that all emotional expression takes place outside the sessions where it can be safely sealed off, rather than being shared and worked with.

In other cases there may be a passive compliance with writing assignments, which are then done 'for the therapist', and paradoxically absolve the client from taking an active role in engaging with their own issues.

It is always important for the therapist to be alert to potential pitfalls, and to find ways of addressing them or bringing them into the therapeutic dialogue.

Conclusion

Shakespeare's much-quoted injunction from Macbeth urges us to 'Give sorrow words. The grief that does not speak/Whispers the o'erfraught heart and bids it break'. This quotation has perhaps a more literal reality than is often perceived. In working with clients who express feelings in a physical way, it seems to be important for them not only to put words to their feelings, but also to give those words a physical reality by writing them down. Paradoxically, this external, written expression of emotions can often allow them to be taken back into the internal self, and truly experienced for the first time.

References

Bick, E. (1968) The experience of skin in early object relations, *International Journal of Psycho-Analysis*, 49: 484–6.

Bick, E. (1986) Further considerations on the function of the skin in early object relations, *British Journal of Psychotherapy*, 2: 292–9.

Freud, S. (1905) *Psychical (or mental) Treatment*, Standard Edition, 7: 283–302. London:Hogarth Press.

Howlett, S. and Guthrie, E. (2001) Use of farewell letters in the context of brief psychodynamic-interpersonal therapy with irritable bowel syndrome patients. *British Journal of Psychotherapy*, 18(1): 52–67.

McDougall, J. (1989) *Theatres of the Body*. London: Free Association Books.

Meltzer, D. (1974) Adhesive identification, in D. Meltzer, *Sincerity and Other Works: Collected Papers of Donald Meltzer*, (A. Hahn, ed.) London: Karnac, 1994, pp. 335–50.

Moskowitz, C. (1998) The self as source: creative writing generated from personal reflection, in C. Hunt and F. Sampson (eds) *The Self on the Page: Theory and Practice of Creative Writing in Personal Development*. London, Jessica Kingsley.

Nemiah, J. and Sifneos, P. (1970) Affect and fantasy in patients with psychosomatic disorders, in *Modern Trends in Psychosomatic Medicine*, vol. 2. London: Butterworth.

Ryle, A. (1990) *Cognitive Analytic Therapy: Active Participation in Change*. Chichester: Wiley.

Winnicott, D.W. (1960) The theory of the parent-infant relationship, in *The Maturational Processes and the Facilitating Environment*, pp. 37–55. London: Karnac Books, 1990.

Chapter 9

'When I write, I think': personal uses of writing by international students

Colin Lago

> He stopped the diary out of fear for his eyesight, and said that abandoning it was a form of death.
>
> (Tomalin 2002: xxxvii, 279)

> I always have to write something every day. A day when I write nothing is a desert.
>
> (Fowles 1998: 6)

Introduction

The phrase, 'When I write, I think' was proffered by a Chinese student, quite spontaneously, in a counselling interview several years ago. (Extraordinarily, the same phrase was expressed by another international student from quite another part of the world, in the survey described in this chapter.)

The two quotations used above (the first refers to Samuel Pepys, the seventeenth-century diarist) further underpin the very considerable existential value of writing for the writers themselves.

This chapter constitutes an attempt to synthesise the accounts offered by some international students at a British university on their 'personal' writing activities. In the UK, the majority of international students are between the ages of 18 and 30. They are a group (comprising approximately 100,000 students currently studying in the UK) who have ended up, for the purpose of pursuing higher education, living in a country other than their own for an extended period of time. This chapter therefore focuses upon their experiences of (and with) writing during their cross-cultural sojourn.

The following brief study highlights yet again the therapeutic and educational potential of 'personal writing' and also indicates the extent to which such writing might assist the writer in combating the many challenges to personal identity that are an inevitable and sometimes painful consequence of moving cultures.

The initial survey

> About writing . . . I do it all the time and more since I am away from home . . . the email is the lifeline of my existence now! I write just about everything . . . it helps me so much . . . introspection . . .
>
> (An international student interviewed for the following study)

Like most universities in the UK, the University of Sheffield has a considerable number of international students (approximately 3700 from 110 countries in 2002). Among the very wide range of educational and social opportunities afforded to such students by the university and the students union, there is an annual publication dedicated to articles written by international students reflecting on their experience in the UK. Entitled *SWIRL* (*So What's It Really Like?*), this publication not only offers the writers an opportunity to reflect through writing on their experience, but is also of great value to other students, who, as readers, may recognise aspects of their own experience in the articles and thus feel comforted.

This chapter offers an initial analysis of interviews conducted with international students by the author at the University of Sheffield. An email was circulated to all international students at the university and was written in the form of an invitation to those who naturally used 'writing as a personal resource' to be interviewed about this aspect of their behaviour. Four students were eventually interviewed. Despite the small number of interviewees, the following text provides some key themes and unique elements pertinent to personal writing, specifically in relation to the perspective of persons from a different cultural milieu to the UK.

The interviews lasted approximately one hour each, and following a brief introduction to the context by the author were essentially 'interviewee' directed in terms of content and depth of revelation. The interviewees were also reassured that their identities would remain confidential and personally identifying features would be eliminated or changed to preserve anonymity. The overall intention of this brief study was to attempt to gather a set of first-hand, phenomenological accounts of interviewees' experiences of personal writing. Only subsequent to the interviews were key themes identified by the author and these are detailed in the next paragraph.

Interestingly, all four interviewees talked in relation to their writing within the following core themes (as identified by the author):

- Biographical origins to their writing
- Challenges to and issues of personal identity
- Uses of language when writing and subsequent differences in experience
- Writing as therapeutic, 'working things through'.

The fourth theme was further subdivided into the following sub-themes:

1. Writing as a psychological 'container'
2. Writing as a personal route to understanding
3. Writing having an interpersonal value.

Several additional elements unique to the interviewees were also recorded and these are discussed later.

The core themes

Biographical origins to their writing

> I've always kept a diary or journal, since I was ten years old or maybe earlier.
>
> (Interviewee 1)

> I've kept a diary for at least ten years now, sometimes writing it every night, sometimes only once per month.
>
> (Interviewee 2)

> Since I was very little I had a little book in which I wrote down things, like little poems or funny things about my parents or God or my dolls . . . only my mum knew and she used to encourage me . . . my mother, sister and best friend have known I write since I was about five years old.
>
> (Interviewee 3)

> When I was eight or nine, I was entered for a district poetry competition – it had to be written 'on the spot' and as a consequence I was selected two months later for a national competition which I eventually won. Soon after that I started writing.
>
> (Interviewee 4)

Each of the interviewees referred, though only briefly, very early in their interviews, to their own beginnings as 'personal writers'. One participant had lived with her family within a communal setting during childhood where writing had clearly been used by the whole community as a way of generating an awareness of group needs, of drawing up agendas for discussion and of using lists as a way of memorising and ordering priorities.

Either through external influence (e.g. mother in the experience of Interviewee 3, or school for Interviewee 4) or from early internally driven experience, it is apparent that each of our participants had adapted personal writing as a significant means of self-expression from a very young age.

Daiute and Buteau (2002) cite several research studies that underpin the value of narrative writing for children. These include indications that narrative serves in identity development (Hermans and Hermans-Jansen 1995) and learning (Daiute and Griffin 1993). Children become acculturated through narrative (Nelson 1993). Because narrative writing is also a form of social positioning addressed to potential audiences and to oneself, children can use it to express their identities or reflect on them (Nystrand and Wiemelt 1993). These research findings support the hypothesis of how important writing can be in a child and young person's development and links to the values placed on it by the interviewees in this study.

Challenges to and issues of personal identity

> I seem to simultaneously experience three different people within me when I am here, first, who I am according to the culture, second, who I was before I came here and third my perception of my own culture after being here for two years now.
>
> (Interviewee 4)

The experience of living, either temporarily or permanently (whether chosen or not) in another country, inevitably confronts the individual's own sense of who they are. The overseas experience can be the first time when issues of selfhood and identity have so seriously to be confronted by the sojourner. Indeed, the challenge of life in another cultural milieu can prove so powerfully confronting to previously held beliefs, values, conventions and relationships that a full spectrum of reactive emotional responses can be evoked. This experience, often referred to as 'culture shock' or 'uprooting disorder' (Adler 1975; Golan 1980; Furnham and Bochner 1986; Fisher 1989) has been compared psychologically to other serious forms of human change and loss (e.g. loss of employment, amputation, loss of a loved one, etc.) and at worst may evoke a period of mental ill health:

> I had a very hard time when I first came here, I was homesick. Also, it was very hard to justify to my boyfriend that I needed time for this reflective activity [writing]. I eventually had to say to him I needed an hour every morning.
>
> (Interviewee 1)

Inevitably, each of these core themes that have been identified intersects, through the activity of writing, with others. The above quote already strongly relates to therapeutic usage, the writer identifying in herself a regular need to reflect on her daily experience, as a way of sorting it out and understanding it.

Having now been in the UK for two years, Interviewee 4, after much writing and reflection, was able to assert that 'these three points of reference definitely exist for me, they are not just simply divided by time, I am still evolving . . .' As an example of her use of writing to unpick and examine her various beliefs, she referred to her vegetarianism, which was linked to her cultural and religious origins:

> However, I am different to vegetarians here . . . during an Easter holiday in Europe I was faced with eating eggs; why not eat them? I thought . . . 'they come from chickens' . . . however simple this question may appear, it raised for consideration many of my cultural assumptions from home . . . so I wrote about it to understand it more.

Through writing, protagonists have access to a powerful medium for reflection on who they are within the world they find themselves in. In the case of a more public figure, the writer John Fowles expressed his relationship to writing as that of 'being' itself: 'I don't think of myself as giving up work to be a writer, I'm giving up work to, at last, be' (Fowles 1998: 7).

Though the groundbreaking work conducted by researchers such as Helms (1990) and Carter (1990) on racial and ethnic identity has been conducted within and applied to permanent residential communities, there is no doubt that those who live, even temporarily, in another country (for whatever reason) are also forced to reconfigure who it is they are in the face of their reactions to the new milieu and the resident community's reactions to them.

The impact of such cross-cultural experiences upon one's sense of self is very considerable indeed and it is not surprising, therefore, that the terms 'shock' and 'disorder' have found considerable recognition and acceptance among those impacted by such experiences. Adler (1975) however, also noted the positive potential in such experiences for personal growth and development. It would seem that, through employing the uses of personal writing, those undergoing and experiencing intercultural transition might benefit considerably in relation to their sense of security and their changing sense of self.

Uses of language when writing and subsequent differences in experience

> During the last few years my diary has been written entirely in English.
>
> (Interviewee 2)

The language that the interviewees chose to use for their writing proved of great interest. The term 'language' here is used to refer both to national language and to dialect usage. Obviously, for those students who hailed from a country where English was not their mother tongue, the language they ended up employing for their personal use, while here, had to be selected at some level of consciousness, though it was not always clear to the interviewees why they had written in one language rather than another:

> I first came to England six years ago for six months and in order to make best use of this experience I started to write in English . . . I came again three and a half years ago . . . I also met my boyfriend, who is Spanish, and so we had to use English as the common language. Somehow, one picks up this new language [English] as a child might, people speaking to you deliberately simply, trying to avoid technical or long words.
>
> (Interviewee 2)

For this interviewee, this deliberate and yet simplified acquisition of English somewhat reminded her of the differences between her own language, with its formal structures, in contrast to her 'very strong spoken dialect', which, in her country, was popularly perceived somewhat pejoratively: 'I like my dialect very much, it is very colourful, you can be two different persons in two languages [and dialects?]. One can also speak about different things in the two languages.' Similar to speaking, writing in one language as compared to another yielded different shades of meaning for the writers.

The three interviewees for whom English was not their mother tongue each stated that, when they were writing, they didn't mix the languages they were using within their texts. For example, if they started a piece in Japanese, then they continued with that language. This led the author to reflect on the neurological systems in the brain for storing languages and to wonder if these language stores are retained as separate repositories, which can, of course, be linked through the act of translation, but which do not switch easily while engaged in writing.

It is clear, from the above, however, that having a choice of language to use inevitably offers a wider spectrum for the expression of particular meanings, descriptions and reflections than is available to the monolinguistic person.

Writing as therapeutic: 'working things through'

Three separate sub-themes were identified in this theme. The testimonies indicated that, for each interviewee, writing seemed to hold therapeutic values within three different realms: that of (a) its value as a psychological 'container'; (b) as a source of enhancing personal understanding; and (c) as having an interpersonal value. These themes, among others, have been identified by authors such as Huizinga (1987, 1993) whose pioneering research work introducing the uses of writing to rheumatism sufferers was later adopted on a wider scale within the Netherlands. Examples are given below of each of these three sub-themes.

Writing as a psychological 'container'

> I write emails to myself and to friends and family but often choose not to send them, yet they are of great help to me.
>
> (Interviewee 4)

The writing itself becomes a container, a 'psychological holding station' as it were. Later reflection by the writer offers the possibility of either moving that writing on from the station to its destination or leaving it there. Psychologically, though, the writer can experience the relief that the thoughts and feelings have been expressed through the writing and therefore do not require either psychic energy spent in this subject's obsessive mulling over or avoidance and denial:

> Writing empties you and your mind onto the paper . . . you can go anywhere when your mind is free . . . but when not, you can paint yourself into a corner

> in your head into scenarios you cannot escape from . . . I often come away from my writing feeling cleansed . . . Also when you are looking down on it [the writing], it doesn't look so big as when you are thinking about it . . . it diminishes it.
>
> (Interviewee 1)

These aspects are even more explicit in this quote from Interviewee 1. In addition, the writer reports an increasing sense of distance from the concern, the experience having been de-intensified, with a resulting decrease in personal tension.

Writing as a personal route to understanding

> I can see better what it is about after I have written it . . . it offers a mechanism for seeing inside yourself.
>
> (Interviewee 3)

> I write to myself first because I can then see if I really have a problem and how much of one it is.
>
> (Interviewee 4)

These two quotations place the writer centrally, simultaneously and symbolically within the dual role of client and empathic responder (therapist). The writer's 'self', as depicted by the writing in this process, can come to be more understood and aware through the process of the 'reader's' empathic understanding (where both the writing and reading functions are housed within the one person).

Writing having an interpersonal value

> Writing helps me to work out what I'm feeling about someone or what I need to say to them . . . and these 'sample letters' then really help me work out what to say when I actually do write to them.
>
> (Interviewee 2)

This use of writing (i.e. sample letters) is often encouraged by creative writing practitioners. It has also become advice given in more recent years to those who communicate via email, as this medium seems particularly prone to provoking strong responses in readers who then, in their upset, can respond and retaliate instantly and feelingly to the original writer. Known as 'flaming', such 'knee-jerk' reactions, written and sent at moments of emotional upset, can then be forever regretted. Writing a trial communication first or expressing all the things you feel but without sending them can provide the essence for a more accurate and potentially less damaging communication to be composed:

> I have several friends whose own languages are different to mine and so we communicate using English. However, recently, a friend from Japan wrote to me in my mother tongue and I did appreciate it very much indeed, especially as he doesn't know it very well. I spent much longer in replying, doing it so carefully and, of course, doing several trial versions before composing the letter I sent.
>
> (Interviewee 2)

Not only did the interviewee, in this extract, experience the 'gift' of a piece of writing in her own mother tongue (which was different to their earlier correspondence) it is clear that through the mechanism of sample letters she wished to reciprocate with equal care, sensitivity and grace.

Some 'unique' experiences incurred through writing

The term 'unique' as used here refers specifically to particular themes shared with the author by only one of the interviewees. As each of the following themes was only introduced by one of the four and was not shared by the others, the term 'unique' seems most apt, but this does not infer that others in the world haven't, in some way, experienced what is described below!

Lists: an organising principle

Interviewee 1 cited the use and composition of lists as an organising principle. They could be used in a variety of ways but each offered her a mechanism for ordering her life, her priorities, her wishes and so on. This technique, of course, is one that is frequently used by many people (e.g. shopping lists, revision topics, lists of work projects, etc.). The value of lists, as described by this interviewee, however, was in the manner she could employ them to help her create some sense of order and priority between the many demands and obligations she faced.

A general criticism of lists (particularly within the realms of study skills) has been that they determine, by their very linear nature, a perception that is sequentially determined (i.e. that the first item leads to the second item and so on). This linear sequencing may thus determine or infer a hierarchy of importance of the subjects listed. 'Space diagrams' and 'brainstorms' were subsequently introduced into the 'enhancement of thinking' canon, to offer a mechanism for the conversion of (linear, sequential) lists into diagrams that could also be employed to assess priorities and relative locations.

It is clear from this interviewee's statement that it is this latter mechanism of clarifying and prioritising issues that she found so useful in compiling her lists.

On becoming a writer

The same interviewee also reported that her grandfather had been a writer and she aspired to this, though she believed that one had to confront one's demons honestly: 'You have to be open to where the writing takes you. It's a discipline; the contract with yourself is to absolute integrity.' She reported that it would be a dream combination for her to have both a place and the time to explore the possibility of such writing further.

Sound and music

> When I write something, I also sometimes have a sound in my head . . . it's not necessarily music but it can be. Sometimes hearing music also helps me to express, more spontaneously, and more accurately, what needs to be written and what I'm feeling.
>
> (Interviewee 3)

This interviewee not only acknowledges the stimulus of music to assist her writing experience (a frequent experience for people, and often acknowledged by students when studying), she also reports the experience of sensing sound(s) that accompanied the writing. It is as if her senses operated simultaneously and interconnectedly while engaged in writing. (Several other students have also reported this phenomenon to me over the years.)

Supporting others through sharing the values of writing

Interviewee 4 had been consulted by a younger and much troubled student and had obtained great satisfaction after learning that her suggestions of using writing (which she had used to help herself) had been tested and found to be most valuable by the troubled student.

Creating the 'legend'

Interviewee 3 had had a difficult educational experience in the UK. This had involving an involuntary transfer to another university for her research for reasons beyond her control. During a rest spell from writing up her research one summer, she commenced writing a long story, which she called 'The Legend'. Acknowledging its obvious autobiographical inspirations, this fictional account, she believed, could easily be read by others as a story, yet for her it had proved to be a project into which she had been able to pour three years of angry and aggressive feelings. The result, she considered, from an external perspective, was an interesting story. Yet for her, the exercise had proved immensely therapeutic.

Interestingly, the Dutch andragologist, Nijk, writes about the concept of 'story' in his article, 'The hermeneutic aspect of androgogy' (1982) He writes:

> A story can be an uninterested report, an expression of emotion: a form for daydreaming, an excuse or justification, an accusation directed towards oneself or towards other people, a supplication, and a kind of blackmail. All these movements in the story can be important and functional in a certain stage of the conversation. But the act of language that is the aim in an ultimate sense for the andragogical relationship is the 'act of commitment' that people accept for themselves, facing others. In this commitment one accepts the responsibility for one's own past and future behaviour.
>
> (Quoted in Huizinga, 1987: 6)

Conclusion

> Writing and thinking go hand in hand.

In concluding this chapter we have included, immediately above, a statement made by one of the interviewees in this study which links directly with the quotation (made by a different student entirely) included in the title to this chapter.

This brief exploration of the uses made of writing by international students proved to be most fascinating and this 'cross-cultural' area deserves further investigation. Not only are thinking and feeling enhanced through writing, but this chapter gives evidence of many other functions it serves for those who write.

As a medium for the exploration of identity and meaning – critical elements in the 'expatriate' experience – writing offers the opportunity to cope with loss and can be a spur to creativity. An introduction to and the encouragement of personal writing for international students could be a very useful adjunct to the student support programme in universities, particularly with its capacity to assist awareness and well-being.

The fourth student interviewed thought of writing as 'my best friend, I think'. This sentiment is reflected by the Spanish writer Ramón Sender (who was expatriated to the USA) who considered that without writing he would have gone mad (Penuelas 1970). Samuel Pepys, even while still living in his beloved London, viewed being unable to write his diary because of failing eyesight as a kind of death. By contrast, writing clearly offers the possibility of life, creativity and insight.

References

Adler, P.S. (1975) The transitional experience: an alternative view of culture shock, *Journal of Humanistic Psychology*, 15: 13–23.

Carter, R.T. (1990) The relationship between racism and racial identity among white Americans: an exploratory investigation, *Journal of Counselling and Development*, 69: 46–50.

Daiute, C. and Buteau, E. (2002) Writing for their lives: children's narrative supports for physical and psychological well-being, in S.J. Lepore and J.M. Smyth (eds) *The Writing Cure: How Expressive Writing Promotes Health and Emotional Well-Being*. Washington, DC: American Psychological Association.

Daiute, C. and Griffin, T.M. (1993) The social construction of written narrative, in C. Daiute (ed.) *The Development of Literacy Through Social Interaction*. San Francisco: Jossey-Bass.

Fisher, S. (1989) *Homesickness, Cognition and Health*. London: Lawrence Earlbaum Associates.

Fowles, J. (1998) *Wormholes: Essays and Occasional Writings*. London: Jonathan Cape.

Furnham, A. and Bochner, S. (1986) *Culture Shock: Psychological Reactions to Unfamiliar Environments*. London: Methuen.

Golan, N. (1980) *Passing Through Transitions: A Guide for Practitioners*. New York: Free Press.

Helms, J.E. (ed.) (1990) *Black and White Racial Identity: Theory, Research and Practice*. Westport, CT: Greenwood Press.

Hermans, H.J.M. and Hermans-Jansen, E. (1995) *Self Narratives: The Construction of Meaning in Psychotherapy*. New York: Guilford Press.

Huizinga, J.E. (1987) Helping clients to write about themselves. Research proposal paper, University of Amsterdam, July.

Huizinga, J.E. (1993) *Wat Reumapatienten Bezighoudt: Een Reumaleesboek*

Den Haag: Cip-Gegevens Koninklijke Bibliotheek.

Nelson, V.M. (1993) *Mayfield Crossing*. New York: Avon.

Nystrand, M. and Wiemelt, J. (1993) On the dialogic nature of discourse and learning. Paper presented at the annual meeting of the National Council of Teachers of English Research Assembly, Pittsburgh, PA.

Penuelas, M. (1970) *Conversaciones con R.J. Sender*. Madrid: Novelas y Cuentos.

Tomalin, C. (2002) *Samuel Pepys: The Unequalled Self*. London: Viking.

Chapter 10

'Every poem breaks a silence that had to be overcome': the therapeutic role of poetry writing

Gillie Bolton and John Latham

> The blood jet is poetry.
>
> (Plath 1981)

> Take that old, material utensil, language, found all about you, blank with familiarity, smeared with daily use, and make it into something that means more than it says. What poetry is made of is so old, so familiar, that it's easy to forget that it's not just the words, but polyrhythmic sounds, speech in its first endeavours (every poem breaks a silence that had to be overcome), prismatic meanings lit by each other's light, stained by each other's shadows.
>
> (Rich 1995: 84)

> Poems . . . profoundly alter the man or woman who wrote them
>
> (Abse 1998: 362)

Introduction

Poetry is an exploration of the most vital and intimate experiences, thoughts, feelings, ideas: distilled, pared to communicating succinctness and made music to the ear by lyricism. Poetry and healing have gone hand in hand since Apollo became the god of both: 'The use of and familiarity with the power of imagery and metaphor has always linked poets and artists to healers' (Flint 2002: vi).

In this chapter, Gillie Bolton explores the particular healing power of poetry writing, and the role of image and metaphor. John Latham offers a personal account of the ways he is able to make contact with what he needs to explore psychotherapeutically through poetry writing; he discusses the therapeutic insight and support thus gained concerning traumatic crises in his life, such as the death of his son, and alcoholism.

'Poems profoundly alter the man or woman who wrote them' because poetry can only be written from the otherwise most difficult to reach parts of oneself and one's world, in a process similar to the most effective therapy or analysis, or to the therapeutic use of the other arts (Flint 2002). Dannie Abse is poet, poetry tutor and medical practitioner: a combination with powerful precedence (Jones 1997).

Poetry writing within clinical psychology, therapy or counselling

Poetry writing can readily be a vital element of any practitioner's magic bag of healing strategies. Poetry does not need any specialist equipment, unlike art for example. Poetry uses the ordinary words we use every day, but gives them enhanced value and more flexible use. Practitioners need to overcome their natural anxiety that poetry writing is for special, gifted people, that it requires specialist knowledge of rules such as rhyme and metre, and that a great deal of time and energy is needed.

The therapeutic poetry writing experience is process (rather than product) based: thoughts of publication are inappropriate. Therapeutic poetry writing has a limited audience of the writers themselves and a few others close to and involved with them: 'One's written poems are primarily self-objects and secondarily word-objects' (Ihanus 1998: 90). The redrafting and editing stages involved in directing poetic material towards publication reduce its 'self-object' nature and increase its 'word-object' nature.

Interested practitioners can borrow the beginning processes of poetry writing to help patients or clients listen to, and make some sense of, the range of voices within them. The voices a client needs to listen to, such as John Latham's informing him about the alcoholism creeping up on him, are not ones we welcome, or wish to listen to. Poetry writing has the power to make them available and more acceptable, in a way similar to other therapeutic strategies (Bolton 1999).

Writing is often undertaken alone, away from the therapist. This can be a strength, extending the therapeutic hour, and giving the client work to do on their own. One of the most powerful factors of writing is that it is private, enabling the expression and exploration of vital areas, which the client can decide whether, or at what stage, to share with the practitioner or another reader. Here is a poem, the writing of which was a milestone in helping a client to begin to face the possibility of incest:

Mushrooms for Breakfast

Daddy knows
where fungi grow
mysterious in the night
Daddy knows which taste nice
a little girl mustn't go on her own

shut the door on the steam
of the kitchen, come
with Daddy, hold him
tight, in the whispers
of morning's half light

look with your touch
in the dew glint
growth
for the silk silver
tip

Daddy knows

Poetry writing is a staged process, each stage with its own therapeutic power. The first 'trawling' (see John Latham, p. 112) is followed by the later ones of sharing with a personal audience, and then redrafting and editing.

A beginning stage for poetry writing

The initial writing processes can be intuitive, intensely absorbing and almost trancelike. The writer allows the hand to write with no conscious mental direction: 'That willing suspension of disbelief for the moment, which constitutes poetic faith' (Coleridge 1817). Keats' opinion was that 'If poetry comes not as naturally as the leaves of a tree it had better not come at all' (1818). Winnie the Pooh clearly read Keats: '"It is the best way to write poetry, letting things come," explained Pooh' (Milne ([1928] 1958: 190). He'd also read Wordsworth: 'Poetry is the spontaneous overflow of powerful feelings; it takes its origin from emotion recollected in tranquillity; the emotion is contemplated till by a species of reaction the tranquillity gradually disappears' ([1802] 1992: 82).

Ted Hughes likened it to silent, still night watching for foxes: 'Till, with a sudden sharp hot stink of fox / It enters the dark hole of the head' (1967: 20). These are passive approaches which suggest that the writer has to be in a specific state of mind, and the inspiration will arrive.

Seamus Heaney used more active metaphors: 'Between my finger and my thumb / The squat pen rests. / I'll dig with it' (1980b: 11). And (along with such as Byron 1995 and Sansom 1994 who used the same metaphor):

> Usually you begin by dropping the bucket half way down the shaft and winding up a taking of air. You are missing the real thing until one day the chain draws unexpectedly tight and you have dipped into water that will continue to entice you back. You'll have broken the skin of the pool of yourself.
>
> (Heaney 1980a: 47)

Helene Cixous becomes a jewellery thief: 'These pearls, these diamonds, these signifiers that flash with a thousand meanings, I admit it, I have often filched them from my unconscious. The jewellery box . . . Furtively, I arrive, a little break-in, just once, I rummage, ah! The secrets!' (1991: 46).

This writing is sometimes called 'free associative'. A particular of the poetic imagination and ability with metaphor is that poets are willing, and brave enough, to allow themselves to enter that state of mind in which things can 'just come'.

Poetry writing is essentially private, and brings the writer into a near hypnagogic (awake dreaming) state: a process qualitatively different from any communication with another person, whether verbal or physical, and from thinking. The communication is with the *self*; but the communication is delayed until the writer chooses to reread. This can be never: writers can choose to destroy their writing unread – itself a therapeutic action. This delay of interlocution can help enable therapeutic catharsis.

The self is an appropriate and powerful interlocutor; but there is very little space given to private dialogues with the self in our culture. Interlocution – communication with another, whether verbal or in body language – is at the heart of the therapeutic relationship. But we have few channels which privilege private, individual reflection. The therapeutic relationship seeks to engender it, but it is readily viewed as self-indulgent. It is also often seen as scary: people say to me, 'What if it opens a can of worms which can't be dealt with solitarily?'

Poetry writing can enable just such an effective process of self-communication. It can feel dangerous, as John Latham points out below, just as any effective therapeutic process is experienced as teetering between the destructive and the healing. It is dangerous because, in order for this condition to be effective, writers have to enter into a liminal state where they lose some of their sense of habitual, rational, culturally-framed structures and ways of thinking, and are more open to whatever presents itself. It is a state in which the writer does not know.

Writers have used mind-altering drugs to induce this state (famously Coleridge and Aldous Huxley), but no clever or external form of dislocation is needed; these other worlds are there for the experiencing here and now: 'the kingdom of heaven is at hand'. Writers, who 'on honey-dew hath fed, / and drunk the milk of Paradise' (Coleridge [1798] 1969: 298), experience images and thoughts over which they have no control, and which can seem strange, disconnected, and to come from unknown sources. This seemingly disconnected state is healing, enabling connections to be made with a range of different voices that make up the 'self' and the world in which writers find themselves. The writer comes out of this experience a different person.

There is a degree of safety in using writing for such a shamanic exploration in search of healing: the writer only has to stop writing. I also always suggest a writer embarking on this kind of endeavour ensures there is a trusted friend reasonably easily available. My experience, over many years of facilitating this, is that writing is slow and gently paced, making it reasonably easy for the writer to perceive danger in time; but I would not recommend a deeply disturbed or psychotic patient undergoes it alone.

This type of writing is also physical. It is exhausting, as first-timers discover with surprise; and it seems to come from the body, bypassing usual mental awarenesses: 'I don't *begin* by *writing*: I don't write. Life becomes text starting out from my body. I am already text' (Cixous 1991: 52). The fact that 'the word was made flesh' and not speech is too easy to forget in our world of jabber-jabber mobile phones, PA systems, television and radio. Writers have to trust their bodies, through their writing hand, not only to tell them vital things about themselves and their place in society, but also to offer routes to connecting up and making whole. This is a holistic process, going some way to healing the Cartesian body/mind split.

Clinical staff have commented after workshops in which I have taken them into the shallows of this deep sea: 'I found it really surprising what came up', and 'it felt like forbidden luxury to let myself write anything at all'. It feels like a forbidden luxury because it is allowing oneself to dwell in the imagination – and to play there, like we used to play as children. The art of poetry provides a container for what is found there, a container which can be brought back, just as the shaman brings healing wisdom back from other worlds. The 'container' of poetry feels safe enough (Levine 1992); it can enable the pain which is encountered to be brought back in metaphorical and image form to be listened to, with more everyday ears. The images and metaphors can be reflected upon and understood slowly and gently, at whatever pace is required by the writer in the ensuing stages of writing.

Firm, 'luxurious' permission, from the self, and perhaps also from a facilitator, is required to enable people to enter this state. Trust is needed that this sort of writing not only works but is safe enough; faith in oneself that 'even I can use the same process as Heaney and benefit from it' and self-love are required to allow this 'luxury'. A practical guide to how to begin writing can be found in Chapter 19.

A middle stage for poetry writing

The insight and understanding engendered by such cathartic writing processes can be deepened and extended by the ensuing stages of writing. The first is the silent reading to the self. Although the initial 'trawling' is so intense as to be exhausting, the writer does not have time to *feel* the emotion: it is all being spent onto the page. On silent rereading, the writer thinks: 'Did I really do/think/feel that?' as the tears roll, just as they do after any intense therapeutic encounter, associated as it is with sudden depth of insight and understanding.

The writing might next be shared with a carefully chosen audience (such as a therapist, counsellor or clinical psychologist), or it might remain private to the writer. The reading to the self and the sharing with another can both be emotional stages. Sharing the writing, and therefore the intense memory, understanding, or emotion with another, is exposing that vulnerable inner self; it is also accepting: 'Yes, I *do* remember, think, feel that.' An audience can offer confirmation, support and advice, extending the therapeutic value.

Poetry on the page can relate back to its writer and other readers more intensely than prose. 'One reacts, not just to what is written but to what seems to hover around it unwritten' (Frampton 1986: 1594) on those suggestive white spaces which accompany a poem on the page. These white spaces are silences which contain elements of the explored images and metaphors which could not be written.

'Occasional poets' rarely venture beyond these first stages: to them the product of this trawl, the reading to the self, and the emotional sharing with another, is their 'poem'. Intense events may cause this, evidenced by the rash of 'poems' following the death of Diana, Princess of Wales, and 11 September 2001. Adolescence (Fuchel 1985; Atlas *et al.* 1992), falling in love, bereavement, and the approach of death (Frampton 1986; Sluder 1990) can be similarly stimulative to such writing.

End stages of poetry writing

The next stages of more conscious crafting of the writing can bring insight and consolidation. The redrafting of poetry is a powerful, deeply thoughtful process of attempting to capture the experience, emotion or memory as accurately as possible, in apt succinct words and images. Writing can be worked on in a way neither speech nor thought can, because it leaves footprints on the page; it stays there in the same state as when it was written. The etymological roots of the word 'record' are: *re-* meaning again, and *–cord* meaning heart (*OED*). These writings are records repeated again and from the heart. Redrafting is re-recording, getting closer to what is in the heart each time.

Redrafting, and eliciting support from another experienced writer in the redrafting, are stages which require a different frame of mind to the initial 'trawling'. It is a more cognitive process. Writers need to take this difference into account, and learn to recognise their frame of mind or need for what kind of writing to undertake.

Many poets use tightly controlled poetic forms, such as the sonnet: a discipline of having to find just the right word or image for just the right place. This creation of order out of the previously inchoate mass of emotions, thoughts and experiences, can enable not only clarity and succinctness of expression, but also understanding. It is also a controlling of the emotional impact of the situation: the memory or emotion is much more safely packaged up, having been turned into a work of art. 'Succinct' means to put a silk band round something (*OED*).

Poetry writing can assist clarity of thought and understanding, and offer discipline and a measure of control which can be stabilising (Lester and Terry 1992). An issue clarified into words, graphically visualised and controlled by poetic form is an issue on the way to being dealt with.

A conundrum here is that all this sounds so purposive, yet in order to work both poetically and therapeutically, poetry writing has to be undertaken in a pure spirit of enquiry: it must be process- rather than product-based. Writing in order either expressly to find answers to one's personal problems, or to get published will not create useful or communicative texts: 'The poetry does not matter' (Eliot [1936] 1974: 198). And the product is similarly open: 'poetry does not seek to prove anything at all.' (Ricoeur 1978: 13). Attempting the writing process in a purposive way would be as much use as practitioners deciding in advance what they wanted the client to tell them.

Here is poet John Latham explaining his first stage of writing, how he 'breaks the skin of the pool of himself' (Heaney 1980a).

Trawling the subconscious for poetry: John Latham

Trawling

The process of writing helps me to understand after a trauma in my life leaves me with unresolved issues (perhaps guilt, anguish, anger). With the understanding comes an acceptance, reconciliation, some degree of healing.

I've no guaranteed technique for creating the conditions under which it will happen. I can say only that it's more likely to occur when I'm isolated, when I can succeed in shutting out my external world, when I'm able to focus inwardly until I've achieved a state of readiness or receptivity.

At that point I'm quivering, unprejudiced, ignorant. I've no picture of what I want, I just know that I have a great need. I'm prepared to be patient. My pen or keyboard are close to hand. I am not in control of the situation.

Sometimes it doesn't happen. The period of waiting can be completely blank, or punctuated with false alarms in which a word or image may pop up to the surface but subside before it can be grasped.

Sometimes it does work. At first a slow seepage, a trickle of words, and then I know that a flood will happen if I let it; which so far I've always wanted to. This is the most exciting time, when I absolutely know that something powerful and unforseeable is about to occur, that I'm about to be swept away by it.

The thrill of the moment is heightened by the fact that I have the power to switch off the avalanche; a power I'll never use. Beyond that point all I can do is stay with the experience, write down whatever comes into my head, ignore all extraneous influences – it's quite clear that if I step away I can't come back.

For me, it's crucial to disconnect my brain. What is happening is between my subconscious and my fingers, without the involvement of the intellect. The words must be absolutely free to come. They are not to be shaped, or even noticed at the time.

Sometimes what comes is just a scattering of words. More often it's a paragraph or two, occasionally a couple of pages. They come quickly, as fast as I can write or type, but never faster than I can cope with. I'm totally absorbed, aware of nothing else.

After the trawl

I don't notice the cessation of the flow. I become suddenly self-conscious, aware of my surroundings, and then I realise that the words have stopped. I feel exhausted.

When I look at what I've written, I have no recollection of the words or images. I'll glance through them, on this first inspection, but only cursorily. It feels best to put them aside for a while.

If I'm writing something extensive, so that this process might make many contributions to the total work, I find it natural not to read any of it until I've finished.

It's strange to read page after page that I don't remember writing, but though the words are sometimes incomprehensible, they're always fresh and pertinent.

When this process is being employed in a long piece of writing, the exhaustion experienced at the end of each writing session tends to be cumulative, so that by the time of completion it can be total. In fact, it can be so severe that it can halt the writing before its natural end.

I find this process exciting, dangerous and irresistible. The danger comes from the fact that what is written is in some often chaotic way authentic, central and unresolved. As a consequence, it can be hard or even impossible to bear. I think I have an unconscious safety mechanism, which is that emotional exhaustion clicks in first, though only when I'm right on the brink. I think some people don't have this protection, which makes continuation more dangerous. Most of my most profound moments of revelation, and most of what I think of as my best writing, has come from finding the courage to swim out beyond my depth and relegate my safety to a secondary position.

The strongest personal benefit is the feeling that I've penetrated into the deepest recesses of myself and my relationship with the world. There is a simplicity there which is quite wonderful.

The next stages of writing

The sharing and redrafting stages can both have therapeutic value for me, though less powerfully than the trawling stage. In the former case, sharing a poem with someone I trust (or offering it for discussion with a group of trusted fellow writers) can enhance my own understanding of the experience which is the kernel of the poem. This relatively calm and dispassionate process, coupled with the receipt of different points of view, allows me to step back from the experience, see more clearly its totality, move closer to accepting it. Also, there can be comfort in the sharing. The trawling stage is necessarily solitary, I can feel terribly alone and vulnerable, and colleagues' readiness to empathise and accept some of the power and pain of the experience can assist me to feel more reconciled.

In the latter case, redrafting can again allow a helpful, more objective appraisal of the trauma. I have to be conscious, however, of the danger of possible conflict between remaining open and true to the experience and optimising the quality of the poem. These two goals can be incompatible, and I can be faced with an agonising choice. I can either write an inferior poem about a momentous episode in my life because absolute truth must prevail at all costs, or I can write the best poetry I am capable of – thus honouring the experience – yet in so doing engage in some degree of dishonesty. Either route has validity, though my own inclination is in the former direction. Fortunately, there are many occasions where the conflict can be eliminated. These, of course, generally produce the best poems.

About 'After Heavy Rain' and 'Encounter'

The two short poems which follow have both been through the complete sequence of stages outlined by Gillie earlier in the chapter, starting with trawling and terminating with redrafting. Each stage produced significant changes, hopefully improvements, although my experience is that redrafting can sometimes be excessive, excising inadvertently the magic which, if one is lucky, is created in the first stage – only in the first – and constitutes the primary strength of the poem.

Both poems are prompted by experience of heavy drinking. The first, 'After Heavy Rain', touches on the way in which an altered mind-state, which can for example result from drink or drugs or fever, can provoke the recognition of a truth which has proved elusive up to this point. The truth here is the presence of suppressed anger which is contrasted with – and thus revealed by – the moon's acceptance of the fact that it is drowning: an observation a sober person is unlikely to make. The quiet moon is a metaphor for the person the man subconsciously wants to be, but cannot until he opens the valve which releases his fury.

'Encounter' is connected with more common, negative accompaniments to drunkenness: the perverse mixture of narcissism and self-hatred; exacerbation of fear and loneliness; the desire to appear ridiculous and be humiliated – which Dostoievsky writes about so powerfully. And as the drunk starts to sober up in the final five lines, the sometimes convenient feeling of hopelessness.

After Heavy Rain

What surprised him most, the night
he saved the moon from drowning,
was how it seemed reconciled,
at peace below the surface,
its ebbing light just strong enough
to pick out lichen pools, craters
giddy with the smell of bitumen,
the astonishing absence of fish.

He knelt, cradled it, lurched off
towards the dawn. He could feel it
aching in the sky's dark pull.
Its cool heat thawed him, and before
it climbed away, years of rancid anger
trickled through his fingers to the ground.

Encounter

This man in the mirror is not well.
Hiccupping, eyes lurching
in and out out of focus,
he looks silly, though he's trying

to seem dignified and poised
and I can tell from the grimace
in the corner of his mouth
that he's afraid of drowning,
seeks the comfort of warm arms.
I smile at him, inviting,
but his lips droop to a howl
so thin and pale it cannot stop.
I begin to wonder if he's drunk.
I wink to show I love him,
but he can't wink back,
his bloodshot eye just twitches
as if it's a butterfly
pinned onto a board
sensing the sweet scent of ether.
(John Latham)

Poetry and mental ill-health

Poetry has probably always been used by poets to deal with depression and anxiety. Here is *Webster*'s dictionary:

> Only thin lines separate poetry, prophecy, and madness. We don't know if that's generally true, but it is in the case of "vatic:" The adjective derives directly from the Latin word "vates," meaning "seer" or "prophet." But that Latin root is in turn distantly related to an Old English word for "poetry," an Old High German word for "madness," and an Old Irish word for "seer" or "poet."
>
> (*Merriam-Webster* 2002)

Kay Redfield Jamieson's (1993) study found that poets are 30 times more likely to undergo a depressive illness than the rest of the population, and 20 times more likely to be committed to an asylum. Felix Post found that writers have far more psychiatric problems and illnesses than the rest of the population, but that poets suffered least of all writers (Post 1994, 1996). This, he suggests, might be the psychotherapeutic effect of 'putting into harmonious and rhythmical language one's own inner sufferings and distress in the concentrated form of the lyric poem' (1997: 13). It is beyond the scope of this chapter to address whether this means that poetry drives us insane, or that a very large number of mentally ill people turn to poetry writing; but I incline towards the latter.

Ann Kelley runs poetry workshops at a drop-in centre for people with mental health problems (see also Kelley 1999). She gave them an exercise encouraging them to write about what they might have lost or found in their lives, starting by reading one of her poems which had been very helpful to her to write. Here is her poem, one by a participant, and her reflection:

Recurring Dream

I am with a small boy – you.
I show you my childhood –
beach, funfair, quiet streets, sun.
Then you are not there.
I search for you.
Heaped dirty snow
on the darkening estuary beach
and the tide flooding fast.
(Ann Kelley)

Heather Ashworth responded with this:

Lost

Lost
All my possessions.
Freedom
All left behind.
Found
A bright blue sky
And a summer's day
In Cornwall.
I have nothing
But a bag of clothes
And a broken radio
But I am happy here.
(Heather Ashworth)

For Heather, writing this was cathartic. She had perhaps been concentrating in her mind on what she had lost as a result of her mental health problems. Writing the poem helped her realise that she had in fact moved on from loss, made a new life for herself and admitted to herself at last – 'I am happy'.

> I had a similar experience after the final drafting and publishing of 'Recurring Dream'. (However, reading it out loud to an audience still makes me emotional.) I do still have anxiety dreams but I seem to have purged myself of that particular nightmare. The very act of writing down the emotions of anxiety or sorrow, or even a bad dream, and then crafting it into a form, perhaps a poem, helps us to bring order to chaos, and allows us to get on with life.
>
> (Ann Kelley)

The role of image and metaphor

Poetry relies upon image and metaphor to explicate and convey complex experiential, emotional and mental happenings, elements which would otherwise be difficult or impossible to communicate. Such images are also significantly more memorable than descriptions.

It is not only poetry which relies upon metaphor, but 'our ordinary conceptual system, in terms of which we both think and act, is fundamentally metaphorical in nature . . . human *thought processes* are largely metaphorical' (Lakoff and Johnson 1980: 6, original emphasis). There is barely anything we can think or say without it having some metaphorical content or reference. For example, our language makes heavy everyday use of metaphorical *up* and *down*: 'that child is really high'; 'she is very low'. Metaphors enable us to paint pictures, create symphonies, banquets, perfumes, silk – in words: they enable us to make use of all our five senses in creatively grasping an issue as fully as possible. A poetic example is Robert Burns' 'O my Luve's like a red, red rose'. In Aristotle's words:

> Metaphor is the application of a word that belongs to another thing: either from genus to species, species to genus, species to species, or by analogy. I call "by analogy" cases . . . like Empedocles, call old age "the evening of life", or "life's sunset".
>
> (Aristotle 1995: 105–7).

Susan Sontag adds: 'Saying a thing is or is like something-it-is-not is a mental operation as old as philosophy and poetry, and the spawning ground of most kinds of understanding, including scientific understanding and expressiveness' (1991: 91) and the philosopher Ricoeur (1978: 7, original emphasis):

> Metaphor is the rhetorical process by which discourse unleashes the power that certain fictions have to redescribe reality . . . The metaphorical *is* at once signifies both *is not* and *is like*. If this is really so we are allowed to speak of metaphorical truth.

Metaphor can allow us to grasp the ungraspable. For example, we really don't understand what happens when anaesthetic has been administered: the metaphor of swimming, of going *under* water is invaluable (Shafer 1995). Jacqueline Brown used an extended metaphor in her poetry sequence about childlessness, *Thinking Egg* (1993). It includes this chilling image of a woman at her marriage: 'she cannot foresee the moment / when she will be cracked and eaten'. John Latham uses the image of 'drowning' when writing about being drunk in his two poems above.

Metaphor, with its power of 'metaphorical truth' is not merely a poetic device, but an essential aspect of our mental and physical furniture, prior to thought; it is the 'open sesame' to memories. It is the way of linking up the disparate elements of ourselves and our world; a way of enabling the voices of these elements – normally clamouring silently – to speak and be heard. Audrey Shafer (1995: 1332) said: 'metaphor is the "aha!" process itself'. And Arnold Modell, a psychiatrist, believes that:

> metaphor [is] the currency of mind, a fundamental and indispensable structure of human understanding. It is by means of metaphor that we generate new perceptions of the world; it is through metaphor that we organise and make sense out of experience . . . The locus of metaphor is now recognised to be in the mind and not in language . . . metaphors have their origin in the body. There is a privileged connection between affects and metaphor. As feelings are to some degree beyond our control, translating such feelings into metaphors provides us with some degree of organisation and control. Through the use of metaphor we are able to organise otherwise inchoate experiences, so it is not surprising that somatic experiences, such as affects, are transformed into metaphors . . . Cognitive metaphors form bridges between the past and the present; metaphor allows us to find the familiar in the unfamiliar. This means affective memories are enclosed as potential categories; we remember categories of experience evoked by metaphoric correspondence with current perceptual inputs. We can think of ourselves as owning a library of categorical memories of pleasurable and painful experiences, all of which at certain points in our life will be activated by means of metaphoric correspondence with current inputs.
>
> (Modell 1997: 219–21)

Encouraging patients or clients to play with metaphor in poetry writing harnesses the innate power of metaphor to connect with those memories and experiences which are unretrievable in other ways. People too often feel they have no authority to write poetry, and think only clever people know how to use metaphors. I once asked a group of medical undergraduates if any of them could give an example of metaphor. They looked blank and rather scared (I could see them thinking 'we're scientists'). One responded: 'I can't think of any, my mind's a blank sheet.' We use metaphors all the time, entirely unaware that that's what they are.

If clients are encouraged to experiment *playfully* with words – *doodle* with metaphors – they can find they've 'absent mindedly' found a way into all sorts of areas of experience of life, as well as into those categories of memory as described by Modell above. Metaphor works partly because it does not come at these elements head on; it sidles up without coming too close. Writers might even not understand their own metaphors at first (as dreams are frequently not understood); when they do, it's the indrawn breath of 'aha'. It can often seem these effective metaphors are created by accident. It only seems like accident because we are so used to the Cartesian understanding of the self: 'I think, therefore I am.' Such powerful images occur once we have the courage to be 'absent minded' or to pay attention to absent mindedness (as Freud suggested about parapraxes).

Metaphors are much used in psychology, therapy, counselling and medicine, and nursing – both consciously and unconsciously – and their use has recently come under scrutiny (e.g. Caster 1983; Marston 1986; Fainsilber and Ortony 1987; Martin *et al.* 1992; Shafer 1995; Mabeck and Oleson 1997; Modell 1997; Holmes and Gregory 1998; Bayne and Thompson 2000; Spall *et al.* 2001). The work undertaken between therapist and client lies somewhere between normal discussion and a dual creation of poetry.

The power of image

William Carlos Williams said: 'no ideas but in things' (1951: 231). In effective writing, 'things' (such as events, experiences, memories) carry or infer 'ideas' and emotions, rather than these abstract elements being expressed directly. T.S. Eliot used longer words than Williams, and coined the expression 'objective correlative' (1951: 145). An idea, emotion, feeling or thought is not presented in the abstract but as a concrete, graspable entity. The power of poetry lies partly in this, both to the writer and the reader:

> The only way of expressing emotion in the form of art is by finding an 'objective correlative'; in other words, a set of objects, a situation, a chain of events which shall be the formula of that *particular* emotion; such that when the external facts, which must terminate in sensory experience, are given, the emotion is immediately evoked . . . The artistic 'inevitability' lies in this complete adequacy of the external to the emotion.
>
> (Eliot [1920] 1996: 100)

Sappho (1992) must have been one of the earliest writers to use image in writing for therapeutic benefit. A wealth of loneliness is carried in:

> The moon has set
> and the stars have faded
> midnight has gone,
> long hours pass by, pass by;
> I sleep alone

Conclusion

'Every poem breaks a silence that had to be overcome' because poetry trawls a communicating channel into those areas where things seethe hitherto uncommunicated. The use of metaphor can facilitate that channel, as Modell (1997) suggests. Poetry writing is the most effective vehicle for creating such communicating metaphors as well as vital supporting description – Ricoeur's 'redescription of reality' (1978).

Poetry writing uses words as an artistic medium. It lifts language out of its condition of being an everyday 'material utensil . . . blank with familiarity, smeared with daily use' (Rich 1995: 84), moulds it like clay or paint (Flint 2002), until it gains 'prismatic meanings lit by each other's light, stained by each other's shadows' (Rich 1995). Prose writing, with its rules of grammar, syntax and form, is less effective for this endeavour. Handwriting can further dissociate language from these constraints, as well as ensuring the physicality of the writing act.

Poetry writing breaks that 'silence that had to be overcome' (Rich 1995: 84), allowing memories, thoughts and reflections on experience to be explored and expressed. But poetry writing, in most of its stages, is itself nearly silent. The quiet of the *trawling* stage is facilitative: halfway between the silence of Heaney's deep 'pool' (1980a) and the noise and chatter of the world. Hitherto silent voices can be enabled to speak through the quiet whisper of the pencil. 'The blood jet' (Plath 1981) can run free through the veins.

Bibliography

Abse, D. (1998) More than a green placebo, *The Lancet*, 351 (9099): 362–4.

Aristotle (1995) *Poetics*, trans S. Halliwell, pp. 105–7.

Atlas, J.A., Smith, P. and Sessoms, L. (1992) Art and poetry in brief therapy of hospitalised adolescents, *The Arts in Psychotherapy*, 19: 279–83.

Bayne, R. and Thompson, K. (2000) Counsellor response to clients' metaphors: an evaluation and refinement of Strong's model, *Counselling Psychology Quarterly*, 13(1): 37–49.

Bolton, G. (1999) *The Therapeutic Potential of Creative Writing: Writing Myself*. London: Jessica Kingsley.

Brown, J. (1993) *Thinking Egg*. Todmorden, Littlewood Arc: Lancs.

Byron, C. (1995) in S. Thomas *Creative Writing: A Handbook for Workshop Leaders*. Nottingham: Nottingham University.

Caster, J.H. (1983) Metaphor in medicine, *Journal of the American Medical Association*, 250(14): 1841.

Cixous, H. (1991) *Coming to Writing and other Essays*, ed. D. Jonson. Cambridge, MA: Harvard University Press.

Coleridge, S.T. ([1798] 1969) *Poetical Works.*, ed. E.H. Coleridge, p. 298. Oxford: Oxford University Press.

Coleridge, S.T. (1817) *Biographia Literaria*, Ch 14.

Eliot, T.S. ([1920] 1996) *The Sacred Wood: Essays on Poetry and Criticism*. London: Methuen.

Eliot, T.S. [1936] 1974) *Collected Poems*. London: Faber & Faber.

Eliot, T.S. (1951) *Selected Essays*. London: Faber & Faber.

Fainsilber, L. and Ortony, A. (1987) Metaphorical uses of language in the expression of emotions, *Metaphor and Symbolic Activity*, 2(4): 239–50.

Flint, R. (2002) Fragile space: therapeutic relationship and the word, *Writing in Education*, 26: ii–viii.

Frampton, D.R. (1986) Restoring creativity to the dying patient, *British Medical Journal*, 93: 1593–5.

Fuchel, J.C. (1985) Writing poetry can enhance the psychotherapeutic process, *The Arts in Psychotherapy*, 12: 89–93.

Heaney, S. (1980a) *Selected Prose 1968–1978*. London: Faber & Faber.

Heaney, S. (1980b) *Selected Poems*. London: Faber & Faber.

Holmes, V. and Gregory, D. (1998) Writing poetry: a way of knowing nurses, *Journal of Advanced Nursing*, 28(6) 1191–4.

Hughes, T. (1967) *Poetry in the Making*. London: Faber & Faber.

Ihanus, J. (1998) Dancing with words: transference and countertransference in biblio/poetry therapy, *Journal of Poetry Therapy*, 12(2): 85–93.

Jamieson, K.R. (1993) *Touched with Fire: Manic-depressive Illness and the Artistic Temperament*. New York: Free Press.

Jones, H.A. (1997) Literature and medicine: physician-poets, *The Lancet*, 349: 275–8.

Keats, J. (1818) Letter to John Taylor, 27 February.

Kelley, A. (1999) *The Poetry Remedy*. Newmill: Hypatia Trust & Patten Press.

Lakoff, G. and Johnson, M. (1980) *Metaphors we Live By*. Chicago: University of Chicago Press.

Lester, D. and Terry, R. (1992) The use of poetry therapy: lessons from the life of Anne Sexton, *The Arts in Psychotherapy*, 19: 47–52.

Levine, (1992) *Poesis: The Language of Psychology and the Speech of the Soul*. Toronto: Palmerston Press.

Mabeck, C.E. and Oleson, F. (1997) Metaphorically transmitted diseases: how do patients embody medical explanations? *Family Practice*, 14(4): 271–8.

Marston, J. (1986) Metaphorical language and terminal illness: reflections upon images of death, *Literature and Medicine*, 5: 109–21.

Martin, J., Cummings, A.L. and Hallberg, E.T. (1992) Therapists' intentional use of metaphor: memorability, clinical impact, and possible epistemic/motivational functions, *Journal of Consulting and Clinical Psychology*, 60(1): 143–5.

Merriam-Webster Dictionary (2002) Word for the Day: 24 October, http://www.Merriam-Webster.com.

Milne, A.A. ([1928] 1958) *The World of Pooh*. London: Methuen.

Modell, A.H. (1997) Reflections on metaphor and affects, *Annals of Psychoanalysis*, 25: 219–33.

Plath, S. (1981) *Collected Poems*. London: Faber & Faber.

Post, F. (1994) Creativity and psychopathology, a study of 291 world famous men, *British Journal of Psychiatry*, 165: 22–34.

Post, F. (1996) Verbal creativity, depression and alcoholism, an investigation of one hundred American and British writers, *British Journal of Psychiatry*, 168(54): 545–55.

Post, F. (1997) Preface, in K. Smith and M. Sweeney (eds) *Beyond Bedlam: Poems Written out of Mental Distress*, pp. 13–18. London: Anvil.

Rich, A. (1995) *What is Found There: Notebooks on Poetry and Politics*. London: Virago.

Ricoeur, P. (1978) *The Rule of Metaphor: Multi-disciplinary Studies in the Creation of Meaning of Language*, trans R. Czerny. London: Routledge & Kegan Paul.

Sansom, P. (1994) *Writing Poems*. Newcastle upon Tyne: Bloodaxe.

Sappho (1992) *Poems and Fragments*, ed. J. Balmer. Newcastle upon Tyne: Bloodaxe.

Shafer, A. (1995) Metaphor and anesthesia, *Anesthesiology*, 83(6): 1331–42.

Sluder, H. (1990) The write way: using poetry for self-disclosure, *Journal of Psychosocial Nursing*, 28(7): 26–8.

Sontag, S. (1991) *Illness as Metaphor; Aids and its Metaphors*. London: Penguin.

Spall, B., Read, S. and Chantry, D. (2001) Metaphor: exploring its origins and therapeutic

use in death, dying and bereavement, *International Journal of Palliative Nursing*, 7(7): 345–53.
Williams, W.C. (1951) *Selected Poems*. London: Penguin.
Wordsworth, W. ([1802] 1992) *The Lyrical Ballads: Preface*. London: Longman.

Chapter 11

On the road to recovery: writing as a therapy for people in recovery from addiction

Claire Williamson

Introduction

As a writer, I have worked in the field of addiction recovery for over three years, facilitating groups which focus on the sharing of autobiographical written work, produced by clients in residential treatment centres.

Writing autobiographically is not alien to the addiction recovery setting. Many treatment centres ask clients to write their 'life story' to read to their peers within the first weeks of arrival. Autobiographical writing in an addiction recovery setting is a powerful tool. Autobiography is different from creative writing because it emphasises a quest for personal truth: 'AUTOBIOGRAPHY: . . . literary work, novel, poem, philosophical treatise, etc., whose author intended, secretly or admittedly, to recount his life, to expose his thoughts or to describe his feelings' (Lejeune 1989: 123).

The consequence of writing autobiography is an increased sense of self: 'It is through the act [of writing] that the self and the life . . . take on a certain form, assume a particular shape and image, and endlessly reflect back and forth between themselves as between two mirrors' (Olney 1980: 22). This chapter looks at my experience of working in a multi-disciplinary team. It also offers background, rationale and a case study.

Setting the scene

I worked with Secondary Addiction Recovery Centres, which ran residential rehabilitation programmes for people addicted to drugs, alcohol or food. The centres were counselling based, with daily groups and weekly one-to-one sessions with clients. Numbers of residents varied from 2 to 17. Ages ranged from 17 to 60. A broad social spectrum was covered.

Clients were often poly-drug users. The majority of people in the centre had not used any mood-altering chemicals for at least six weeks before they arrived. This is important to a writing group, because while clients are withdrawing from active addiction they are often bombarded with emotions and too raw to focus on the past or present:

> Loss of the drug causes overwhelming feelings similar to those in bereavement, as well as physical withdrawal symptoms. It is during this period after a decision has been made to give up the drug that the person is at his/her most vulnerable.
>
> (Waller and Mahony 1999: 3)

Writers are well aware that perspective is required in order to gain understanding: 'For the present when backed by the past is a thousand times deeper than the present when it presses so close that you can feel nothing else' (Woolf 1976: 98). R.W. Moore's review of substance abuse literature concluded that there were certain addictive personality traits. These included loneliness, low self-esteem, helplessness, an inability to communicate in a genuine way and the loss or lack of a sense of control (Waller and Mahony 1999: 8).

Clients are resident at the centre for three months to a year. This critical time in their lives enables them to make significant personal changes, which can mean the difference between life and death. The requirement to write autobiographically invites clients to make an immediate examination of their experiences, which directly tackles an inability to communicate in a genuine way. One group member commented, 'In writing you are with yourself and there are no boundaries or walls.' Another client remarked, 'It's about allowing your real self to be seen', much like the Narcotics and Alcoholics Anonymous phrase, 'Keep it real'.

Helplessness and a loss or lack of sense of control is frequently experienced because of the overwhelming prospect of coming to terms with years of active addiction and the guilt and shame accompanying it. By focusing on short writing assignments, each issue can be tackled in bite-sized chunks, echoing the recovery phrase 'Just for today'. It is empowering to finish a piece of prose or poetry which embodies difficult feelings. This mirrors the experience of Virginia Woolf who described the tortuous feelings she experienced in relation to her father:

> Until I wrote it out, I would feel my lips moving; I would be arguing with him; raging against him; saying to myself all that I never said to him. How deep they drove themselves into me, the things it was impossible to say aloud.
>
> (Woolf 1976: 149).

The things that are impossible to say aloud isolate people. Writing naturally combats loneliness because the act of writing creates an 'implied reader' (Iser 1974): as the Narcotics Anonymous phrase goes, 'Never alone'. By taking the risk of reading work aloud to the group, clients discover a real audience. One client said, 'It's reassuring when people can relate to things I've written about.' Another commented, 'It challenged my fear of intimacy and trust.'

The low self-esteem of recovering addicts is given a lift by the increased sense of self, experienced through writing autobiography. Alan Ball, screenwriter of *American Beauty* writes, 'Writing teaches me what I believe and what my values are' (Ball 2002: 173). Likewise, one client commented, 'I began to see a wider picture of myself and that I have many sides.' Another client said writing 'massively increased' his confidence.

The writing group

The group is closed and a compulsory part of the clients' recovery programme. The main aim is to encourage clients to create autobiographical written work, connecting them with their feelings. The expected outcomes are increased self-awareness, self-esteem, understanding of other group members and an ability to share feelings. Clients also practise listening skills and experience writing as a tool for self-expression, which they can go on to utilise outside the requirements of the group.

Today, six clients are seated in a circle. I introduce the new male member, Ishty, to the writing group, saying that I am a writer who facilitates a weekly 'personal writing' group which is compulsory for all residents. I am an advocate that writing is therapeutic and can help individuals understand themselves and their lives. Each week I will give Ishty a title to write around for the following week's group. Writing quality, including spelling, is not the purpose of the group, instead honest writing and sharing are paramount. He is welcome to use images or metaphors if it helps to describe his feelings. The idea in being given titles is to encourage him to explore areas pertinent to his recovery, which he would not necessarily choose himself. Each new title will lead from the previous group, so by the end of his time at the centre Ishty will have a 'journey of personal writing' to keep for future reference.

Today, he does not have to share any work, but I encourage him to give feedback on the work he hears and participate in the opening round, which is called 'How are you feeling today?' Each member takes up to two minutes to describe their feelings. Maria is angry. She has had a telephone argument with her ex-husband, Joe. She wants to discuss the issue more, but we need to move on to the written assignments. I begin with Charles, who is a senior group member. He says he was unhappy about doing the piece at first, but once he got into it he started to realise it was useful. He reads the piece entitled 'Things I need to take responsibility for'. He describes wanting to be part of his children's lives. He hasn't seen them for three years and he misses them. He wants to take responsibility for not drinking, and for his own feelings and actions. The group is silent while he reads; I make notes.

Feedback begins in a circle. People encourage Charles to make the effort with his children. Then Billy says if Charles wants to be more responsible, he should start around the resident's house. Charles is angry. He wants to break the feedback circle to confront the challenge. I say that we must listen to everyone before he speaks. The feedback is completed and Charles asks Billy what he meant. Billy says that Charles is lazy with the house duties. I ask Billy to be specific. He says Charles never empties the kitchen bin. Charles agrees that Billy is right about the bin, but if he had a problem he should have said something before. Billy acknowledges this.

We move on. Maria is the next to read 'Things I enjoy'. She reads about long lost interests. Her previous anger subsides and tears roll down her cheeks. She says she doesn't know why she is crying; she felt fine when she wrote the piece. Feedback consists of how nice it is to hear what Maria likes and how she should go for walks and make clothes more often. Maria says she feels sad because she has forgotten herself in 20 years of using, but it is good to have remembered what she enjoyed.

Billy is next. With a sigh, he unfolds a piece of paper he has had in his jeans pocket. He stares at it. He says he doesn't want to read it out. It is the first piece he has prepared: 'This is who I am'. There are encouraging noises from his peers, who say it is worth the risk. Billy reluctantly begins. He describes himself as a loser, a bastard, a liar and a thief. When he finishes he screws up the paper and throws it on the floor. His peers feedback that the person he described is not who they have been living with for two weeks and that he is being hard on himself. The new client, Ishty, admits being worthy of the same labels and that he is trying to see himself as a recovering addict, not a loser. I suggest to Billy that he is angry. He says he is bloody angry.

Sally reads next. Her piece is 'Goodbye Mum'. She has written a letter to her mother who died while Sally was in active addiction. She did not attend the funeral. She says that she cried while writing the piece and the loss feels real for the first time. It begins 'Dear Mum, I'm sorry to have let you down' and ends 'I really love you and hope that you can see me now and be proud.' The room is full of sadness. Feedback shows that people are thinking of loved ones they miss. Sally is crying. Maria suggests that Sally visits her mum's grave to lay some flowers.

Janet is the last to read. It is her final creative writing group before she moves on from the centre. The piece is entitled 'Goodbye'. Janet has addressed each of the clients by name, mentioning how they have influenced her recovery. She uses a metaphor of the garden blossoming into summer to describe the growth she has experienced. She says how she used to hate the writing group and how valuable it has become to her. She can express herself without being interrupted or having to justify her feelings, or feeling she is being judged, or dismissed. I read out my notes from when she wrote her first piece, 'This is who I am'. The group discuss how Janet has changed in the six months she has been a resident.

It is time to give everyone titles for the following week. I give Billy 'A conversation in my head', so he can explore his negativity towards himself and begin to understand what makes him angry and why. He says he'd rather do something else. I suggest he give the title a try and if he's struggling, to ask his counsellor to suggest an alternative. I give Maria 'Letting go of Joe' to allow her to explore the end of her marriage. I give Charles 'Letter to [name of his children]'. I give Sally 'My week' so she can explore her feelings of grief. I give Ishty 'This is who I am'.

I ask if there are any questions. Sally asks if I want her to do a diary. I say she should do whatever feels right for her. We stand, join hands, and say the serenity prayer. I leave to process the group with the counselling team.

Case study

Carolyn, a single mum, who was away from her daughter in the recovery centre, wrote the following poem in response to the title 'Letter to [daughter's name].' This title followed 'An anger list', where Carolyn described her guilt, fear, rage and inconsolable pain, alongside the consolation that her daughter was in the world.

Between the Lines

You're so special to me, my sweet-pea
There's nobody more special than you and me.
I love you way up to the sky
I love you this high.

When I feel sad,
Because I know that I miss you,
I think of your smile and
I just want to kiss you.

I think of your day
How you just want to play
And I know it's just how it should be;
Everything about you is special to me.

When we talk on the phone
I feel so warm,
It tells me that
You've come to no harm.

We talk gobbledegook
I hear a boop
And we giggle
And then we laugh
(naughty elephant)

And I'm thinking of you
When we went to the Zoo.
How you loved that tall giraffe.

Listen Moo,
What I want to tell you,
It's something you mustn't forget,
When you're feeling sad
When things look bad
And all your colours are black.
Think of me and remember,
Mummy always comes back.

Six months later Carolyn reflected on her poem:

> It helped me to accept the fact that she [her daughter] wasn't with me. I was passing the three-month mark and I didn't seem to be getting anywhere. It was about facing the separation myself, exploring the idea of doing recovery for me and not for her. I had previously had her with me in recovery and it was very easy to focus on her and not myself. The language in the poem is very personal to our relationship. The line 'Mummy always comes back' dealt with my own detachment issues as well as detaching from her. It helped me to face a lot of guilt and denial, with me focusing on monthly visits and not the bits in between. It's about the long-term good of recovery, coming out to be a better parent had always been just words, now it is a reality.

Working within a multi-disciplinary team

The prospect of incorporating a writer in an addiction-recovery environment can be daunting for both the counsellors and the writer, as artists have traditionally been viewed as 'pushing boundaries' and recovery centres need to be well-boundaried. A knowledge of addiction recovery and a certificate in counselling skills can be valuable precursors for the writer. I found learning the 'house rules' to be important, so the writing groups were facilitated under similar conditions to counsellor-led groups (e.g. no hats, gum or sweets). It is useful if the team understand the nature of the work and that a visiting writer is not a counsellor. The format of my group was overt and counsellors were encouraged to input suggestions, as I found the support of the counselling team was vital for the success of the writing group. I learned that detailed handovers were essential before each session, so that I had a current 'picture' of each client and that a post-group handover was equally important, so that I could pass on the work of the group. I photocopied my notes for the counselling team, so any counsellors who were not present at the handover could be informed of their clients' work.

The counsellors monitored work for appropriateness and had the power to veto a title, if they felt it distracted from current work with clients. One counsellor commented, 'Creative writing is complementary to group therapy and engages the clients at a very profound level, enabling them to make significant connections and therefore lead them to a deeper understanding of themselves.' Another counsellor remarked, 'I have been impressed by the ability to reach the clients and offer them opportunities to express themselves, build confidence and self-esteem.'

Conclusion

In an addiction recovery setting where providing an effective short-term recovery programme is the goal, autobiographical writing is an effective tool, which directly challenges the characteristic traits of clients in early recovery from addiction. Loneliness is immediately addressed by the experience of writing with the presence of the 'implied reader'. The sharing of personal work in a group and a subsequent increased sense of trust and intimacy further dissipates isolation. Because people are being heard and understood, self-esteem is increased, along with a greater sense of self, which comes from the reflection of oneself on the page and through feedback from peers.

By completing a coherent piece of writing which examines difficult issues, a sense of control is restored to clients. Genuine communication is achieved as group members begin to drop masks and labels to show themselves and their emotions. As Margaret Atwood says, 'Possibly, then, writing has to do with darkness, and a desire or perhaps a compulsion to enter it, and, with luck, to illuminate it, and to bring something back out to the light' (2002: xxiv).

References

Atwood, M. (2002) *Negotiating with the Dead*. Cambridge: Cambridge University Press.

Ball, A. (2002) Alan Ball, in J. Engel (ed.) *Oscar Winning Screenwriters on Screenwriting*. New York: Hyperion.

Iser, W. (1974) *The Implied Reader*. Baltimore, MD: Johns Hopkins University Press.

Lejeune, P. (1989) *On Autobiography*. Minneapolis, MN: The University of Minnesota Press.

Olney, J. (1980) *Autobiography: Essays Theoretical and Critical*. Princeton, NJ: Princeton University Press.

Waller, D. and Mahony, J. (1999) *Treatment of Addiction*. London: Routledge.

Woolf, V. (1976) *Moments of Being*. London: Sussex University Press.

Part III

Writing online

Chapter 12

Therapy online – the therapeutic relationship in typed text

Kate Anthony

Introduction

The impact of the internet on our social and business lives meant that the use of typed text surged before much sense could be made of how or when it was appropriate. The need to meet face-to-face or make a telephone call was replaced with the speed and ease of sending an email. In addition, the use of mobile phone short message services ('texting') has also meant that the spoken word has found a back seat in our interaction with one another. The implications for the future of communication within society in the light of these technological developments is not the remit of this chapter, but it is worth noting how this has demanded a rush in development of electronic mental health provision and therapy in particular. The essential point is that the widespread use of text communication in internet therapy provision has happened *despite* concern with and lack of evidence about its appropriateness or efficacy.

As early as 1966, Joseph Weizenbaum developed a programme called ELIZA[1] to emulate a Rogerian therapist, using a basic natural language engine that recognised keywords and could reply in hard-coded stored sentences. This was done to show how a computer could convincingly be considered to be an actual person, in this case a therapist. ELIZA's communication was very basic, and yet an interesting result emerged as its users developed meaningful relationships with the program, sharing sensitive information and considering the exchange to be therapeutic, even after becoming aware that they were interacting with a piece of software (O'Dell and Dickson 1984). The first attempt to use internet communication to deliver therapy dates back to 1972, between computers at Stanford and UCLA. Fee-based 'mental health advice', usually one-off question and answer sessions, started to appear in the early 1990s. By 1995, ongoing helping therapeutic relationships were being used through what is now considered therapy via email and internet relay chat.

In early 1999, I started researching internet therapy in response to my own use of email and chat rooms as a therapeutic tool. Already familiar with the social use

[1] Online version available at <http://www-ai.ijs.si/eliza/eliza.html> (accessed 30 May 2002)

of these two methods of communication through my internet service provider America On-Line (AOL, which is strongly community based), an accident left me incapacitated and incarcerated in my office at home, with little more than an internet connection to amuse me for two months. It was at this point that I noticed how my online friends and colleagues across the world, whom I had never met, spoken to or seen photographs of, were prepared to interrupt their own lives in order to help me through the boredom and pain I was experiencing. These relationships were every bit as 'real' to me as the friends and colleagues I interacted with face to face, and seemed more intimate and open relationships in many cases. What is important for the reader to understand here is that the shift from my use of the spoken word to text happened without my noticing. I had seldom used text and writing solely as a communication tool previously, and yet it was now second nature for me to choose it over and above spoken communication. As this became evident to me, I noted that clients of mental health services were doing exactly the same thing.

Some anecdotal research

At this point in my research into internet communication for mental health, it was apparent that the counselling and psychotherapy profession seemed unwilling to accept this new phenomenon as a viable method of therapy, in the general belief that the lack of bodily presence was too great an obstacle for a therapeutic relationship to be able to be nourished and developed as it is in face-to-face therapy. However, despite this professional reserve, it was obvious that clients were choosing such opportunities and I believed the whole area deserved greater examination and scrutiny. At the time of writing (September 2002), we are only able to cite a few small research studies into the efficacy of the method (see e.g. Cohen and Kerr 1998; Celio *et al.* 2000; Klein and Richards 2001) but anecdotal evidence is widespread about the usefulness to clients of using text over the internet as a way of accessing and benefiting from therapy.

One criticism of online therapy centered on the question and challenge of transferring face-to-face interaction to the computer. This resulted in statements such as 'therapeutic interactions may be reduced to mere advice giving when face to face interactions are translated to the electronic medium' (Pelling and Reynard 2000: 71). In challenging internet communication, Pelling and Reynard, among others, felt that the basic therapeutic skills were unable to be translated to online work, or that it required a greater 'level of skill or degree of effort'. This is indeed my experience of online therapy, although whether this would be the case for a therapist more familiar with using writing cures in general is debatable.

Suler (1997a) proposed that for some people, 'Sights and sounds are but extraneous noise that clogs the pure expression of mind and soul'. The therapeutic potential of an electronic setting without the possible physical bias or limited access that exists in the world of face-to-face therapy is huge. In removing the physical aspect of the therapy, the 'pure expression of mind and soul' may be communicated effectively, bypassing the defences of therapist and client. Clarkson (1990) cites Guntrip (1961) as believing that only when the therapist and client have bypassed each other's defences does true psychotherapy happen. In the light of my own experience of online relationships, I recognise that having communicated over the internet I have an actual memory of a conversation with a person, not a piece of text. Acknowledgement of this means that Suler's 'sights and sounds' do exist over the internet – the important point being that they are a visual and auditory recollection created by the person experiencing the communication. This is supported by Brice (2000), who identified the use of 'speech words' in order to describe the contact within email (e.g. 'when you *told* me that, I felt . . .'; 'when you *said* that, I could see that . . .').

Studies of online therapy show that new methods of communicating emotion (in the face of no bodily presence) are essential within internet therapy, and we shall visit these later in the chapter. This relates to the client indicating their emotional state via the written word, instead of relying on the other person being able to see the facial and bodily indications. Suler (1997b) demonstrates the importance of being more expressive, subtle, organised and creative in communicating via text. Mitchell and Murphy (1998) also note the importance of developing compensatory skills in the absence of the physical presence. My own experience of elements of how people communicate in cyberspace – such as talking in shorthand and using symbols to indicate emotion – has shown that it is important to understand what works for the client. Grohol (1999) indicated that 'a person [should] be adept and relatively comfortable with reading and writing, and that the participants be able to communicate at similar levels of comprehension'. An ability to picture the client's experiences may demand a similar level of cultural experience, and this factor is discussed in Chapter 16 on ethical considerations. Laslow *et al.* (1999) identify that research into internet therapy is indeed based on face-to-face theory – that is, trying to translate face-to-face therapeutic methods to the computer screen. This is an assumption of needing to *transfer* offline skills as opposed to *developing* or *extending* them, which the existence of netiquette (a truncation of internet etiquette) conventions defy.

The British Association for Counselling and Psychotherapy (BACP) published a special report into the opportunities and risks of counselling clients via the internet (Lewis 1999), which gave definitions and a snapshot of the state of the art at that time. The second BACP document was *Guidelines for Online Counselling and Psychotherapy* (Goss *et al.* 2001), which I co-authored and which was also circulated for comment before publication to a wide international consultative group, including members of the International Society of Mental Health Online (ISMHO) (see www.ismho.org).

How the therapeutic relationship exists

The rapport between therapist and client in cyberspace is developed not by reacting to another person's physical presence and spoken word to interpret a person's state of mind, but by entering the client's mental constructs via the written word and responding in a like manner. The client who is chaotic does not need a chaotic therapist, but by recognising chaos in the choice of and jumble of words, the therapist can see how the world looks to the client and empathise, for example. The rapport between therapist and client grows with the work as it progresses, as it does in face-to-face work. In this way, and importantly, the consistency or dissonance of the client's communication can indicate vital changes or aberrations in the client's mental state, replicating interpretation in the face-to-face encounter of, for example, a client telling you that he is 'OK' while looking distressed. From the perspective of the client, the consistency and congruence of the therapist's communication is also vital to give evidence of the mutual journey that they have embarked upon. In speaking, tone of voice and pacing is considered. In the written word, and particularly within IRC (internet relay chat), it is the spacing, pauses and descriptive words used. This intentional way of looking at and responding to the written material allows the therapist to empathise and respond in an appropriate manner. This gives the client a sense of support, being understood, and not being alone in a situation where they have been unable to seek (or gain) face-to-face help. In the I-Thou relationship (Buber 1970 cited in Clarkson 1990) it is this mutual existence that facilitates the recovery of the client, and this can be just as effectively communicated online (Anthony 2000).

The rapport between client and therapist within the electronic I-Thou relationship is facilitated by the sense of presence (sometimes called co-presence, or telepresence). This is a concept examined by Lombard and Ditton (1997). For them, presence is 'the perceptual illusion of non-mediation'. In taking this concept, the media used (in this case the computer and keyboard) becomes secondary and you are interacting with another person in a virtual separate space during synchronous communication. Using the internet, this is called cyberspace ('we are together'). In the case of email intervention, the concept of presence becomes 'you are here'.

The interaction with another person through a keyboard is a social action, which can take the form of a letter in the case of email, or a conversation in the case of synchronous communication. Putting this into a counselling context, we can see that the therapist's action can be perceived as a therapeutic interaction for the client, as it is when a client enters the therapist's consulting room and the conversation starts. With respect to the mutuality of the electronic I-Thou relationship, it may even be more beneficial as the two people travel together to a place where the power balance is more equal – the internet is seen as a neutral common ground and is client determined, rather than the therapist's physical consulting room which is therapist determined.

This interaction, particularly in the case of synchronous therapy, applies not only at the time but also in retrospect. The actuality of the client-therapist communication online is experienced and remembered as having taken place in 'real time' with the notion of a physical presence, despite knowing very little about the other person.

Communication online creates an experience which is much more 'open' than communication offline. This not only facilitates the mutuality of the relationship, but also makes for the work to be an honest representation of the client's situation; whereas face to face a client's guilt or shame may prevent them from being able to communicate openly and effectively. This factor hastens the therapeutic process and is probably best explained by the client:

> because you're not in the same room it's hard to read body language, which is why I feel I can be so much more open and honest than if I am in the same room, because hey . . . I can be in my pyjamas and he won't know, I can have my dinner, or a drink, or something next to me that I can be sipping on, I can get up and pace . . . in other words, I can be as comfortable as I want to be.

The client also points out that the more open the therapist is about him/herself, the more she or he is open to share. This activity of self-revelation online works to aid the visual representation, and therefore the presence, of the person you are in communication with (the client), and is also important in demonstrating the congruence and genuineness of the therapist. This openness is considered by the participants to be an advantage of online counselling as a therapeutic factor, as it allows the client to be honest with their feelings without being ashamed or embarrassed and speeds the therapeutic process within the electronic I-Thou relationship, known as the 'online disinhibition effect' (Suler 2001). The level of self-revelation also compensates for the lack of a bodily presence because it allows the participant's imaginations to represent it.

As well as being able to read and write, synchronous communication requires a certain typing ability, although this need not necessarily be the case with email. Having an adequate standard of written communication is important, along with certain knowledge of how clients use the internet in general (for instance, do they conduct cyberaffairs or take part in multi user dungeon games (or MUDs)?). This is facilitated by having more time to tune in to the other person's construction of the world and consider the response, particularly in the case of email. A lyrical narrative individual style, reflecting the personality, is essential for the concept of presence of the therapist, as well as providing a stimulating therapeutic forum for the client's feelings. It is also the basis for being able to reflect and emulate the client's world, creating a forum for the rapport, and therefore the therapeutic process, to take place.

The therapist has to reflect his or her genuineness in the written word. Writing to conceal an aspect of the therapist's self (e.g. suppressing a sense of humour at an appropriate moment) does not facilitate the rapport or the condition of presence, and as internet communication is for the most part silent, knowledge of what is appropriate netiquette is important. Within a counselling context, this is less extreme than in a straightforward chatroom environment, but the smiley **:o)** is used by both therapist and client to indicate a smile, and typing in capital letters is still seen as

SHOUTING. Other net shorthand is defined by client preference, and includes the ubiquitous LOL (laugh out loud). A client puts it thus: 'if I am upset about something, it would show on my face and if we were sitting in the same room you could see it, but online I'd have to do something like **:o(** or **<<sigh>>** or **<<crying>>**'.

An awareness of 'lag' within IRC, the time taken for the words to cross the internet (usually a few seconds after the send icon is clicked), should be acknowledged as this can make for responses overlapping. Not allowing for this can be compared to not allowing the client to develop his or her thoughts and continue a theme face-to-face by allowing a period of silence. This period of lag also gives the luxury of having more time to consider the appropriate response or consider the meaning of the client's words. The use of dots can define a continuing sentence, such as this fictional example:

Client: When I came back from France he'd taken a new job . . .

Client: . . . and so he left me anyway <<sigh>>.

Without the use of the dots, the therapist would be halfway through a response before realising that a second, important piece of information was being sent that could change the appropriate response required. These conventions of internet communication require the new counselling skill of working with text to be learnt by the therapist if the typed intervention is to be considered therapeutic.

Thinking about what you are writing and reshaping it to reflect exactly what you mean to say is a luxury that online therapists and clients have. This is also true for reflecting upon what the correspondent has written, and therefore being able to tune into the meaning behind the words considering what is known about the person's mindset. This is a case of reacting purely to meaning and not being distracted by possibly misleading visual clues (e.g. the client laughing while imparting a devastating experience). For the client, this is also a passage to understanding the self, seeking the truth about their feelings when presented with them in black and white on the screen.

The ease and speed of the communication method (as opposed to other forms of working with text) also helps the client at the moment of crisis to share it with his or her therapist and for the therapist to help the client without waiting for the weekly face-to-face session. Boundaries and the therapeutic contract should be considered here to avoid intrusive emails from both parties. This also helps face-to-face clients to feel contained and supported between sessions, and makes room for the time in a face-to-face session to be better utilised.

The client has time to process the work, to consider what has been said and the impact that this will have on them. In a face-to-face session, this may be blurred by the tone of voice or mannerisms of the therapist, and also by the initial reactions of the client, such as anger. When working with the written word, there is time to ponder over the meaning and consider what impact it has had or might have. The therapist also has a verbatim record of what has been said, and is able to return to it, reconsider what happened, and gain a better insight into its meaning. This process may also be cathartic for the client, allowing them to keep a journal in the form of emails, and sometimes answering their own questions about their lives and thoughts having seen them in writing.

There are methods of looking at the client's material differently when it is before you on the screen or on paper. The use of punctuation by a client is a consistent personal style, similar to mode of speech or phraseology. By paying attention to this style, and any inconsistencies within it, a better picture of the client's state of mind is available. Inconsistencies within the client's typing and also their choice of substitute words (Freudian slips occurring through the fingers) may also be utilised as an indication of thought processes. These unconscious indications again aid the online therapist in understanding the process and the client's representation of the world.

A visual, auditory and kinaesthetic representation system of the client compensates for the absence of the physical body within online counselling by creating a physical body image in the client's mind. The visual and auditory experience of the therapist and client exists in the person's imagination, but the client may attribute meaning to their experience of it in a way that allows them to accept the therapeutic intervention more readily than in a face-to-face situation. The lack of bodily presence or tone of voice means that the recollection of the session has a nuance that would not have been apparent in a face-to-face session, because it is the client's perception of the words that fit their ideal of the therapist. The client creates this in accordance with the same constructs of the world that facilitate rapport. The attribution of a fantasy of the other person can mean that the therapy can move beyond such factors as 'first impressions' or bias about a therapist. The client can picture and hear the therapist in whatever way suits him or her best for their therapeutic growth, a fantasy that can be modified to contain any material the therapist chooses to share about him or herself.

The internet offers a valuable service for people who, for various reasons, feel unable to meet a therapist face to face. An awareness of this, and the specifics of the significant reason(s) for not seeking face-to-face counselling can be considered as significant by the online therapist. A client whose sense of shame prevents him or her facing a therapist will have quite different reasons for seeking online counselling from those of a wheelchair user, for example. For many, entry into face-to-face counselling develops from having online counselling.

Conclusion

We have seen the ways and techniques in which typed text can be used to create a meaningful therapeutic relationship between two people when working over the internet. The ethical stance we must take and the considerations in ensuring client safety and confidentiality in offering these services are covered in Chapter 16, and there is a wealth of further research that needs to be done with regard to the use of text not only for individual and group therapy, but also for counselling training and supervision. Technology moves quickly, and the profession must keep up with it with regard to research if such writing cures can be considered a good way forward for the profession. But with the technology and improved communication facilities, such as broadband, already developed enough for us to use the internet for face-to-face therapy through the use of videoconferencing, we must consider that our clients often prefer not to sit with us and therefore choose text-based therapy, and as such it seems likely that it will always have a place within the profession.

References

Anthony, K. (2000) Counselling in cyberspace, *Counselling Journal*, 11(10): 625–7.

Brice, A. (2000) Therapeutic support using e-mail: a case study, *Counselling*, 12(2): 100–1.

Celio, A.A., Winzelberg, A.J., Wilfley, D.E., Eppstein-Herald, D., Springer, E.A., Dev, P. and Taylor, C.B. (2000) Reducing risk factors for eating disorders: comparison of an internet and a classroom-delivered psychoeducational program, *Journal of Consulting & Clinical Psychology*, 68: 650–7.

Clarkson, P. (1990) A multiplicity of psychotherapeutic relationships, *British Journal of Psychotherapy*, 7(2): 148–63.

Cohen, G.E. and Kerr, A.B. (1998) Computer-mediated counseling: an empirical study of a new mental health treatment, *Computers in Human Service*, 15(4): 13–27.

Goss, S., Anthony, K., Palmer, S. and Jamieson, A. (2001) *Guidelines for Online Counselling and Psychotherapy*. Rugby: BACP.

Grohol, J. (1999) *Best Practices in E-Therapy*, http://psychcentral.com/best/best3.htm, accessed 9 March 2000.

Klein, B. and Richards, J.C. (2001) A brief internet-based treatment for panic disorder, *Behavioural & Cognitive Psychology*, 29: 113–17.

Laslow, J., Esterman, G. and Zabko, S. (1999) Therapy over the internet? Theory, research & finances, *CyberPsychology & Behavior*, 2(4): 293–307, http://www.geocities.com/HotSprings/Resort/7579/internet.htm, accessed 25 April 2000.

Lewis, K. (1999) The view of the British Association for Counselling: counselling online – opportunities and risks in counselling clients via the internet, *BAC Special Report*, September.

Lombard, M. and Ditton, T. (1997) At the heart of it all: the concept of presence, *Journal of Computer Mediated Communication*, 3(2), http://www.ascusc.org/jcmc/vol3/issue2/lombard.html, accessed 11 August 2000.

Mitchell, D. and Murphy, L (1998) Confronting the challenges of therapy online: a pilot project. *Proceedings of the Seventh National and Fifth International Conference on Information Technology and Community Health; Victoria, Canada*, http://itch.uvic.ca/itch98/papers/ftp/toc.htm, accessed 14 April 2000.

O'Dell, J.W. and Dickson, J. (1984) ELIZA as a therapeutic tool, *Journal of Clinical Psychology*, 40: 942–5.

Pelling, N. and Reynard, D. (2000) Counselling via the internet – can it be done well? *The Psychotherapy Review*, 2(2): 68–72.

Suler, J. (1997a) *Psychological Dynamics of Online Synchronous Conversations in Text-Driven Chat Environments*, http://www.rider.edu/users/psycyber/texttalk.html, accessed 25 April 2000.

Suler, J. (1997b) *The Final Showdown Between In-Person and Cyberspace Relationships*, http:www.rider.edu/users/suler/psycyber/showdown.html, accessed 25 April 2000.

Suler, J. (2001) *The Online Disinhibition Effect*, http:www.rider.edu/users/suler/psycyber/disinhibit.html, accessed 29 August 2001.

Chapter 13

Developing online, text-based counselling in the workplace

Jeannie K. Wright

This chapter will be out of date before it is word-processed. The speed of development in electronic communications means that attempts to describe and illustrate the present position in online counselling (e.g. the usage of asynchronous email to seek and offer counselling support) risk missing out major changes by the time they are published.

Some recent developments are, however, worth pinning down on the basis that, first, they are consumer driven: clients are sending us emails and asking for help. What is the evidence that we can offer a therapeutic relationship online? Second, some of the fundamental concerns raised by practitioners will be under discussion long after we've moved from text-based (typed) computer-mediated correspondence with clients to voice-activated correspondence and beyond. For example:

- Is it counselling?
- Can we guarantee confidentiality?
- Is it cheaper for providers and clients than face-to-face counselling?
- What are the advantages and disadvantages of a text-based 'virtual' relationship for counsellors and clients?
- What is the evidence for the efficacy of this form of helping?

In this chapter I will briefly explore some of these questions and provide some indicative 'evidence' based on a review of current research. I will also draw upon the experience of setting up an online service for staff at Sheffield University. To ensure anonymity, I will refer only to fictionalised case material, made up of a composite of those clients who have used the online service at Sheffield.

Why set up online counselling?

Research into the effectiveness of online counselling has lagged behind experimental practice (Oravec 2000). Online counselling is in its infancy and as the British Association for Counselling and Psychotherapy (BACP) *Guidelines* (Goss *et al.* 2001: 8) emphasise, practitioners using this 'innovative and under-researched means of service delivery' should proceed with caution. Much more research is needed. However, our rationale for offering asynchronous email counselling to staff at Sheffield University was based on the following factors:

- The connection between 'writing therapy' and online, text-based counselling is clear (see Lange *et al.* 2001; Wright 2002). In particular, research with university staff as participants, showing links between writing about stressful experiences and stress prevention and reduction at work (Francis and Pennebaker 1992) seemed worth pursuing.
- Client choice and the possibility of extending client access to counselling from home/office at any time (Collie *et al.* 2000; Murphy and Mitchell 1998).
- Reducing barriers for the disabled (Griffiths 2000) and those at some distance from the counselling service premises or who cannot access them (Page 2000).
- Reducing the continuing stigma about accessing counselling, especially pronounced in workplace counselling services (Cheesman 1996; Kurioka *et al.* 2001).
- Reducing inhibition about disclosing distressing experiences (Pennebaker 1995) using the relatively private and anonymous medium of email (Walther 1996; Joinson, 1998).
- Greater client control over the experience of seeking help using email when compared with face-to-face counselling (Cohen and Kerr 1998).
- The potential for text-based consultation and supervision is extended and the client has a permanent record of the online counselling relationship (Murphy and Mitchell 1998; Lange *et al.* 2001).

Is it counselling?

Some North American exponents of online therapy explicitly exclude those in need of crisis counselling from lists of those for whom 'e-therapy' is appropriate (Ainsworth 1999). Some also agree that this is not 'therapy' but argue that an online counselling relationship can be therapeutic (Suler 2001).

Online counselling using email, like any other form of text-based, computer mediated therapy may sound professionally and ethically radical. However, in terms of using confessional and creative writing or keeping a reflective journal, it has its roots, like much older and more traditional forms of correspondence therapy, in creative writing itself (Abbs 1998; Bolton 1999; De Salvo 1999). A significant amount of empirical evidence has shown the efficacy of expressive writing for reducing stress and for general improvements in mental and physical health. Reviews and meta-analyses of randomised controlled trials (e.g. Smyth 1998; Esterling *et al.* 1999) have mostly concentrated on North American research. However, Pennebaker's initial paradigm (Pennebaker and Beall 1986) for the emotional processing of naturally occurring traumatic or stressful experiences through writing has now been replicated and extended internationally and across populations (Lepore and Smyth 2002). Chapters 1 and 2 review this research.

The experiment referred to above, involving 41 staff in an American university (Francis and Pennebaker 1992) found that writing about difficult experiences for 20 minutes once a week for four weeks resulted in significant improvements in emotional well-being, physiological functioning and absenteeism.

Most of the experimental studies and randomised controlled trials into using email for therapeutic purposes carried out by the Amsterdam Writing Group (Lange *et al.* 2001) have used students as participants. The age range of the sample group is limited in terms of generalising the encouraging results of 'interapy' to a broader population. A study carried out in a workplace setting in Japan however (Kurioka *et al.* 2001) refers to 'health counselling' and confirms the suggestion that younger employees (aged 20–30) are more likely to use email for this kind of support.

The BACP *Guidelines* (Goss *et al.* 2001) use the terms 'counselling' and 'psychotherapy' interchangeably in the context of online work, a bold decision in this still contentious area. As in an earlier article, however (Goss *et al.* 1999), the conclusion is for practitioners to remain cautious: 'publication of these Guidelines should not be taken as any endorsement of online therapy per se' (Goss *et al.* 2001).

Caution appears to be less characteristic of the UK client group than of practitioners (Parker 1999). Certainly the online clients who presented themselves in Sheffield did not seem to question what the service was called. It seemed to me that what I was offering as an additional medium of access to our service was a kind of supported writing therapy, using email for convenience. Certainly some clients reported finding this support therapeutic.

Is it cheaper for providers and clients than traditional face-to-face counselling?

Common sense tells us that some of the overheads associated with being in private practice, for instance, office space, heating and reception cover will be reduced if not completely obviated by working online. For clients there are also obvious savings in travel time, costs and convenience (Cullen 2000).

The financial implications of providing mental health and other services by email ('telehealth') have been analysed and evaluated (Laszlo *et al.* 1999) in the USA where relatively dispersed populations and immense geographical distances have made telehealth an important new development.

Our experience at Sheffield indicated that as much time in responding to client emails was required as in meeting face-to-face, and therefore there was no saving in terms of 'therapy hours'.

Can we guarantee confidentiality?

The short answer is 'no'. The need to communicate clearly to potential online clients the limitations of any computer-mediated service is underlined in all the recently published research (Lange *et al.* 2001). At Sheffield we were fortunate in having a member of the online counselling group who was both a therapist and a manager in the corporate information and computing services. His assessment of the risks of loss of privacy in using email for counselling (McAuley 2001) was offered to potential clients in full. Both this assessment and our messages to online clients emphasised the need to encrypt messages and, even with that safeguard, pointed out the remaining risks of using email provided by 'the employer'. However, we also indicated that, when compared with face-to-face practice, such risks might seem less significant. As a practitioner, I was concerned about every word of the communication between online clients and me being open to a different kind of exposure than in conventional therapeutic relationships. The following comments on this anxiety are extracts from a diary I kept during the pilot project: 'I feel paralysed if I allow myself to think too deeply about the potential for breakdown of confidentiality in this work. When clients "forget" to encrypt or seem not to want to be bothered with encryption, there is nothing I can do – no way I can "shut the counselling room door".' Ethical issues for online counsellors are undoubtedly complex and are dealt with in more detail in Chapter 16.

Disadvantages of online counselling

- The risk of technological breakdown (and human error in using that technology) seems to me to be one of the major limitations of email counselling. In another extract from the diary, I said: 'Well, here's a good reason not to do online counselling at all. I've just spent an hour refining a response to Z who emailed this morning only to lose the whole thing once I sent it as an attachment. One split second – clicked on the wrong button and that's it. Couldn't retrieve it and Z emailed to say she couldn't open it.'
- One client made a mistake with her password used to encrypt our emails during online counselling and lost a long and very important message she had written to me. It proved impossible for her to retrieve or rewrite the email and she was very distressed and demotivated by the loss.
- Loss of visual and other sensory cues (Lago 1996). Online counselling has been at times an impoverished experience. I have missed the colours, gestures, voices – the *presence* of the client in the room.
- Loss of confirmation of true identity, emotional state, sobriety, real-time focus on the communication.
- Potential for misunderstandings of meaning (BACP 1999; Griffiths 2000). Communication may also appear colder and more impersonal than the author intended.
- Lack of control when the client is not in the room with the counsellor, when online clients choose not to take up strong recommendations to encrypt their messages, for example.
- Confidentiality and crisis intervention in cases of threatened or actual harm to others or self.

First online client

The first member of staff to use the online counselling service emailed me out of the blue. A group of colleagues and I had been working on the idea of offering counselling by asynchronous email for over a year but were progressing with extreme caution and had not yet circulated any publicity. A (the client) was based at a campus some distance from the university counselling offices and said she would prefer to write about what was troubling her, as she'd feel too embarrassed to talk to someone about it face to face.

We already had a code of ethics in place, relating to online work and based mostly on American Counseling Association materials as the BACP *Guidelines* were still under discussion. We had also devised some information sheets for online clients, including a 'contract' mirroring the one we offer to face-to-face clients. I pointed out to A that she had the choice and could come into the office for face-to-face counselling if she changed her mind at any time. She was very eager to start and pre-empted a lot of the careful planning we had been doing about negotiating with online clients regarding confidentiality, encryption and all the detailed process of registration. 'I've read all that – I just want to get on with getting better', was her reply.

A. was in her early twenties and had been 'sent' to see a counsellor as a teenager when her older brother was killed in an accident. She had not found that experience helpful and said several times in her email messages that she could write things she would never be able to talk about face to face. A did not mention her brother's death until the middle of our online work, which lasted over several months, sometimes with gaps of three or four weeks between messages from A. This was frustrating at times, but I had contracted to reply once on a regular day of the week to A's messages.

Some of what was worrying A were physical symptoms. She had consulted the doctor and had all sorts of tests. Nothing at all serious was diagnosed but her anxiety continued. She wrote in detail about what was happening to her body, in her life and, like a lot of clients, asked what she could do to start feeling more like 'my old self'. Most of my responses to that first message were 'empathic following'. But the anxiety around 'getting it wrong' meant that replying to A took much more time and agonising over the wording of particular responses than I had anticipated. Given over two pages of A's typed words, where should I intervene? How could I start to build a therapeutic relationship based solely on contact via a computer?

Reflecting on that experience some weeks later, I wrote 'This is like becoming a novice, an apprentice all over again.' The lack of confidence and anxiety I had felt on starting with my first counselling client years before was at times overwhelming. I took some comfort from Rogers (1993: 105):

> What gave me courage to offer expressive arts to clients was my strong foundation in client-centered counseling. I knew that the client is our best

teacher. I knew that if I offered something to a client as an experiment and continued asking for feedback, we could evolve a process that would be meaningful to her.

Hopes, fears and expectations: a summary

We were concerned about how staff would feel about the confidentiality of a service offered via the university network. We 'mirrored' the face-to-face service for staff at Sheffield University as far as possible in asking online clients to register in the usual way with the service. Although ethically sound, we were aware that this lack of anonymity would deter some users, anonymity being a stated advantage over traditional face-to-face counselling.

There was also the uncomfortable knowledge that some staff would not have access to the university network. Staff counselling in the face-to-face tradition has reached a wide cross-section of the university staff including cleaners and porters. These people, unfortunately, would be excluded from the pilot project unless they had access to personal computers and the internet at home.

At Sheffield we hoped that we would attract some clients who otherwise would not choose to or not be able to access the counselling service (Murphy and Mitchell 1998). The opportunity to access support via email would provide clients with the possibility of externalising their thoughts and feelings, possibly for the first time, in a relatively non-threatening situation using their keyboard, whether at work or at home. That disclosure of hitherto undisclosed experiences or feelings might result in negative mood states in the short term (Esterling *et al.* 1999) as the original stressor was restimulated. However, in learning from the 'writing therapy' research, we were careful to point out this potential 'side-effect' to online clients. We also emphasised that the research findings consistently indicated that various health benefits would result in the longer term. Access to email from home or from work could mean that immediate feelings and thoughts could be expressed at the time and could then be reflected upon before deciding whether or not to send them to the counsellor in an email message. Coupled with the well-documented relative lack of inhibition, specifically of negative emotional expression in online communication (Walther 1996; Cummings 2002), we hoped that some clients would find the medium both liberating and in their control. Although we were unable to carry out the evaluation of the pilot project as we had initially hoped, a number of clients commented on this relative freedom:

> I am able to say things this way that I would never be able to be open about if we met face-to-face – especially about those nasty feelings. I do tend to bottle things up.

> I do feel a lot of it is out of my head now. I thought I was paranoid about it all and had kept so much to myself for a long time. It was good to share it.

We were frustrated by the lack of research based on online counselling practice in the UK and hoped we would be able to fill a very small part of that gap. We also talked about the possibility of widening the online service if this pilot proved successful. The idea of extending the nightline service to an online peer support service for students might also be a future possibility.

Conclusions and implications for research and practice

Counsellors in workplace settings are often familiar with telephone counselling and can see the similarities between online work and using the telephone, which has become 'normalised' as a medium for 'counselling at a distance' (Tait 1999). Email is somewhere between speaking and writing: it is more informal than letter writing and more immediate. A recent study (Day and Schneider 2002) compared face-to-face therapy and video and audio treatment with promising outcomes for using distance technology with a range of clients. Such studies are now urgently needed to compare text-based, online and face-to-face counselling and psychotherapy.

One direction for future research would be to analyse how many online clients move into face-to-face therapy and why. Another would be to continue the work begun into the client and counsellor experience of the relationship online (e.g. Anthony 2000; Brice 2000; Cullen 2000). There is a lot to be learned from the substantial body of research already available to us about the benefits of therapeutic writing. Some of this learning can be adapted to writing on the screen, rather than on paper.

References

Abbs, P. (1998) The creative word and the created life: the cultural context for deep autobiography, in C. Hunt and F. Sampson (eds) *The Self on the Page: Theory and Practice of Creative Writing in Personal Development*. London: Jessica Kingsley.

Ainsworth, M. (1999) Is this therapy? www.metanoia.org/imhs/alliance.htm. Last accessed 12.10.03.

Anthony, K. (2000) Counselling in cyberspace, *Counselling*, 11(10): 625–7.

BACP (1999) *Counselling Online – Opportunities and Risks in Counselling Clients via The Internet*. Rugby: BACP.

Bolton, G. (1999) *The Therapeutic Potential of Creative Writing – Writing Myself.* London: Jessica Kingsley.

Brice, A. (2000) Therapeutic support using email: a case study, *Counselling*, 11(2): 100–2.

Cheesman, M.J. (1996) Is staff counselling an effective intervention into employee distress?: an investigation of two employee counselling services in the NHS. Unpublished PhD thesis, University of Sheffield.

Cohen, G. and Kerr, B. (1998) Computer-mediated counseling: an empirical study of a new mental health treatment, *Computers in Human Services*, 15: 13–26.

Collie, K.R., Mitchell, D. and Murphy, L. (2000) Skills for online counseling: maximum impact at minimum bandwidth, in J.W. Bloom and G.R. Walz (eds) *Cybercounseling and Cyberlearning: Strategies and Resources for the Millennium*. Alexandria, VA: American Counseling Association, ERIC/CASS.

Cullen, D. (2000) A byte size study of online counselling: who is doing it and what is it like? Unpublished MSc dissertation, University of Bristol.

Cummings, P. (2002) Cybervision: virtual peer group counselling supervision – hindrance or help? *Counselling and Psychotherapy Research*, 2(4): 223–9.

Day, S.X. and Schneider, P.L. (2002) Psychotherapy using distance technology: a comparison of face-to-face, video and audio treatment, *Journal of Counseling Psychology*, 49(4): 499–503.

De Salvo, L. (1999) *Writing as a Way of Healing*. London: The Women's Press.

Esterling, B.A., L'Abate, L., Murray, E.J. and Pennebaker, J.W. (1999) Empirical foundations for writing in prevention and psychotherapy: mental and physical health outcomes, *Clinical Psychology Review*, 19(1): 79–96.

Francis, M.E. and Pennebaker, J.W. (1992) Putting stress into words: the impact of writing on physiological, absentee, and self-reported emotional well-being measures, *American Journal of Health Promotion*, 6(4): 280–7.

Goss, S., Robson, D., Pelling, N.J. and Renard, D.E. (1999) The challenge of the Internet, *Counselling*, 10(1): 37–43.

Goss, S., Anthony, K., Jamieson, A. and Palmer, S. (2001) *Guidelines for Online Counselling and Psychotherapy*. Rugby: BACP.

Graham, C. (2000) Psychotherapy by computer: a postal survey of responders to a teletext article, *Psychiatric Bulletin*, 24: 331–2.

Griffiths, L. (2000) Communicating therapeutically via the internet. Unpublished MA dissertation, Sheffield Hallam University.

Joinson, A. (1998) Causes and implications of disinhibited behaviour on the internet, in J. Gackenbach (ed.) *Psychology and the Internet: Intrapersonal, Interpersonal and Transpersonal Implications*. San Diego, CA: Academic Press.

Kurioka, S., Muto, T. and Tarumi, K. (2001) Characteristics of health counselling in the workplace via email, *Occupational Medicine*, 51(7): 327–32.

Lago, C. (1996) Computer therapeutics: a new challenge for counsellors and psychotherapists, *Counselling*, 7: 287–9.

Lange, A., Van De Ven, J.P., Schrieken, B. and Emmelkamp, P.M.G. (2001) Interapy: treatment of posttraumatic stress through the Internet: a controlled trial, *Journal of Behavior Therapy and Experimental Psychiatry*, 32(2): 73–90.

Laszlo, J.V., Esterman, G. and Zabko, S. (1999) Therapy over the internet? Theory, research and finances, *CyberPsychology and Behaviour*, 2(4): 293–307.

Lepore, S.J. and Smyth, J.M. (eds) (2002) *The Writing Cure: How Expressive Writing Promotes Health and Emotional Well-Being*. Washington, DC: American Psychological Association.

McAuley, J. (2001) Risk assessment of loss of privacy by using email for counselling. Unpublished paper, University of Sheffield.

Murphy, L. and Mitchell, D. (1998) When writing helps to heal: email as therapy, *British Journal of Guidance and Counselling*, 26(1): 21–32.

Oravec, J.A. (2000) Online counselling and the internet: perspectives for mental health care supervision and education, *Journal of Mental Health*, 9(2): 121–35.

Page, S. (2000) Counselling by e-mail, *Counselling*,11(3): 162–4.

Parker, L.(1999) *Counselling Online: Survey on the Extent of, and Attitudes to, Online Counselling Amongst 425 BAC Members*. Rugby: BACP.

Pennebaker, J.W. (ed.) (1995) *Emotion, Disclosure and Health.* Washington, DC: American Psychological Association.

Pennebaker, J.W. and Beall, S.K. (1986) Confronting a traumatic event: toward an understanding of inhibition and disease, *Journal of Abnormal Psychology*, 93(3): 274–81.

Rogers, N. (1993) *The Creative Connection – Expressive Arts as Healing*. Palo Alto: Science & Behavior Books (reprinted Ross-on-Wye: PCCS Books 2000).

Smyth, J.M. (1998) Written emotional expression: effect size, outcome types and moderating variables, *Journal of Consulting and Clinical Psychology*, 66(1): 174–84.

Suler, J. (2001) The online clinical case study group: an email model. *CyberPsychology and Behaviour*, 4: 711–22.

Tait, A. (1999) Face-to-face and at a distance: the mediation of guidance and counselling through the new technologies, *British Journal of Guidance and Counselling*, 27(1): 113–23.

Walther, J.B. (1996) Computer-mediated communication: impersonal, interpersonal and hyperpersonal interaction, *Communication Research*, 23(1): 3–43.

Wright, J.K. (2002) Online counselling: learning from writing therapy, *British Journal of Guidance and Counselling*, 30(3): 285–98.

Chapter 14

Electronic text-based communication – assumptions and illusions created by the transference phenomena

Lin Griffiths

Introduction

Each person who regularly communicates using electronic text communication paints a picture of themselves in words and simultaneously creates a picture of the recipient. The words are received, interpreted and reacted upon as if the 'real' person were physically present. The image is constructed by the assimilation of shared factual data and the assumptions and illusions that come from information drawn on by the individual to make sense of reality.

Assumptions and illusions on a daily basis help us anticipate the world. They form our personal constructs (Kelly 1963) and our interpersonal relationships are often maintained by criteria we have absorbed throughout life (Jacobs 1985). However, we may need to acknowledge that there is an art and many skills necessary to communicate effectively online. The forum of text communication to give meaning to reactions, responses and behaviour has potential and opportunity and 'concepts that we have inherited from years of writing on paper to begin to dissolve' (Price and Price 2002).

Trainers, counsellors, therapists and coaches may need to consider new theoretical frameworks within which to operate and will need to start by acknowledging the fundamental principles that govern the 'decoding' between transmitter and receiver in this type of communication and therapeutic relationship. Without the clues and cues of facial expression, body language and tone of voice, individuals have little choice but to fill in the blanks. Making sense and anticipating reactions, responses and meaning can only be achieved from data collected in life experiences.

Many of us are now completely reliant on text-based communication via the internet with no formal training. This has resulted in adapted and adopted modes of using text with haphazard patterns of shorthand and abbreviations. The technology of recent years has catapulted even the most cautious of technophobes (Brosnan 1998) into some sort of use of the computer and the positive and negative outcomes that go with it.

It was as a result of working as a relationship counsellor and trainer of counsellors that the therapeutic elements of using text, and particularly electronic text, became apparent. My work online developed from the research needed for my masters degree (Griffiths 2000) where I was able, with permission, to use two case studies with transcripts.

Since then I have been involved in setting up a service online to help couples address difficulties in their relationships. In my face-to-face counselling practice I use a mixture of emails and face-to-face contact with some clients – usually those who find it difficult to keep regular appointments, those with baby-sitting difficulties, travel tensions, in far-flung venues and those who find the use of email and text communication a preferred medium.

The anonymity of typing onto a screen and pressing a send button which transmits thoughts and feelings expressed in text zooming into cyberspace has led people to pour out their innermost feelings in a deep way: 'the Internet appears to have a profound capacity to function either as a vehicle for insularity and disconnection or as a vehicle for increasing relatedness' (Civin 2000: 59). So how does the relatedness occur? When we communicate with another via the internet do we automatically become engaged with the other person? Are there some anonymous people who after one or two exchanges of text we no longer care to continue relating to? What of those we do relate to? What is it that keeps us interested in continuing to communicate with some and not others? Price and Price (2002) suggest that we have to work hard to become a human being when using the internet to communicate and that we struggle to break through the artificiality of the experience. The idea that we adopt a persona for each person we communicate with may not be unique to electronic text communication, although the option of *time* to consider responses and envisage a satisfactory outcome can certainly be an advantage over face-to-face spoken dialogue.

Can text create the sort of reactions and responses that we are familiar with in interpersonal relationships and be in any way referred to as 'transference'? The transference phenomenon plays an important part in the therapeutic alliance for some therapists; for others its very existence is dismissed. In general, 'transference' suggests that we respond to every new relationship and situation according to patterns from the past. In therapy a client may perceive through their experience of the therapist a sense that the therapist represents a significant person from their childhood and therefore 'it is a substitute for a true relationship' (Mattinson 1975). The *experience* of the here and now is informed by assumptions and triggers and can lead to reactions and responses that form the basis of the relationship between client and therapist: 'The understanding of transference must include everything that is brought into the therapeutic relationship . . . how they convey aspects of their inner world built up from infancy . . . often beyond the use of words' (Joseph 1985: 447–54).

Those who support the existence of transference (Freud and Brewer 1950; Klein 1952; Balint 1993) maintain that we transfer feelings and attitudes developed in earlier, similar experiences, and apply them to the present, especially when there are no clues available as to how to react. Does this suggest therefore that if text is the *only* clue then the potential for transference is heightened?

Within casework

After working with a male client in face-to-face counselling for four weeks his company suddenly asked him to work at their southern office for a contracted time. Faced with the dilemma of halting the counselling contract I suggested we keep the continuity by maintaining a weekly email communication. The first email came from my client giving me information about his new workplace and accommodation. I received it, reflected, and assessed that this could be the basis of a news bulletin of events and circumstances and might not progress the work we had started. My response was to acknowledge his change of context in the work setting and highlight the change of context in our therapeutic setting. I invited the client to write about what that meant for him: how did he think it would change the way we were working and communicating together? What did he want to explore at this stage in writing and what did it remind him of?

His response was long; his words flowed like thoughts without punctuation or paragraphs. There was no order and no obvious sense or meaning. The final sentence of this second email stated: 'I do not want to go back and spell check or change what I have written. My words have been spontaneous and it feels good to have got all that off my chest. It reminds me of when I was eleven years old and kept a diary for a while. Hope you can cope with all of this.'

In this example it is clear that the therapeutic benefit was in cathartic terms and the transference issue lies in the here and now, although the experience temporarily took the client to the past experience of the 11-year-old boy he had been. Interestingly, the final sentence refers to the relationship that I had with him in the present, and appeared to question my capacity to manage his 'story' that he sensed could be overwhelming. It could also have been the 'other' 'parent' or 'transference' link (Malan 1979) for the boy who committed his thoughts and feelings to a diary because at that time he felt that no one could manage or be trusted with such information.

Most of us can be triggered by circumstances or situations in this way, although often the transference moment is very short, even seconds. Any one of the senses available to the individual may take our minds to that time and place. Smells are a good example – school milk, boiled cabbage, semolina, certain fruit and flowers. For an instant (and it often is only an instant) we can mentally transport ourselves back to earlier moments and capture the nuances of those times. Even the sound of someone's voice over the telephone can conjure a picture of the caller (Rosenfield 1997). It is possible for the voice to remind us of a person from the distant past with either a positive sense of knowing or a negative one.

Text as a personal construct

With the absence of visual clues, therefore, we can easily create illusions based on our memory or the way we have constructed our inner world and the sense we have made of it. Our assumptions are therefore built on the ability to draw on information we have collected that helps us manage the circumstances before us.

Trauma occurs when we do not have any information to draw on. We make sense of the world by way of anticipation (Kelly 1963). The more we have experienced, witnessed and can make sense of, the more we can anticipate reactions and responses to the environment around us.

Our 'programming' (the way we have taken in information) becomes essential to our output (the way we think, feel and behave) in much the same way as the information put into a computer is essential to the feedback that is derived from it. There seems a logical conclusion therefore that the sight of text may trigger more than the actual words we see. By the time we are adult, most of us will have added to our experience of written text to include newspapers, magazines, hoardings, signposts, advertising and all kinds of printed ephemera. Without realising it we will have built up an association with the sight and meaning of the written word as surely as we have built up reactions to the spoken word.

The shape, style and context of words may trigger us momentarily to past moments when similar sightings held a memory or formed part of the personal construct of our inner world. Our attitude to certain words can be held in our early approaches to those words. We generally read text in our heads; we are inventing our own tones, inclinations, emphasis and sounds within our internal world and minds. We can only do this by using the way we have constructed and built our reactions to the stimuli of the text in front of us. These reactions and responses are spontaneous. They may trigger responses that can include joy, anger, shame, blame, ambivalence, confusion, anxiety, intrigue, etc. and can promote reactions that include various forms of defence and attack, withdrawal and engagement.

A female client engaged in a chat exchange over a period of two to three weeks. She engaged at high levels of text emotion using expletives to emphasise her feelings. I responded to her disclosures of domestic violence as follows:

> < you cannot stop him hitting you, but you can stop being hit by not being in the firing line >

She chose to completely ignore this response but later, when talking more about herself and not her partner, she wrote:

> < for the most part I've always been the 'fixer' and pretty much keep upbeat but lately it's hard and I feel myself sinking>

Realising my desperate wish to 'fix' it for her I responded:

> <ok, Roosevelt said 'when you get to the end of the rope, tie a knot in it and hold on'>

Her response:

> <I have a lot of knots on my rope Lin>

The analogy had found its mark and we went on to explore her strengths and her resources for surviving life thus far. In the follow-up questionnaire her final comments were:

> < upset to think that I've had such a shitty life . . . I see some correlation. Thank you so much for your interest, who would ever think this could help this way, but it has>

I might be tempted to believe that my responses were just what she needed, however I realistically believe that they were only a small part of the 'therapy'. The opportunity for innermost thoughts and feelings to be expressed and responded to in the here and now anonymously, with a limited time boundary, in a supportive way and without prejudice may well have increased coping resources that were depleted and needed recharging.

When we meet someone face to face for the first time the communication is taking place verbally (the spoken word) and non-verbally (face and body behaviour and mannerisms). The known (conscious) information is being absorbed by the individuals at the same time as the unknown (unconscious) processes occur. A lot is conveyed by the dialogue which checks out assumptions – for example, 'this person reminds me of my brother, but is not responding as my brother would' (known). Alternatively, 'this person reminds me of my brother and I am relating to him as if he were my brother' (unknown). If we consider online communication in a similar way, there are no clues to inform us verbally and the non-verbal communication is restricted to text and timing. How much greater is the potential for filling in the gaps with any data that either suits us or makes sense for us, because of lack of information.

Text as stimuli to reactions and responses

Object relations theorists would argue that we project or externalise some positive and negative attributes of ourselves. We do this to protect ourselves in the main and choose the projections according to how we anticipate the responses and reactions if we were to express those parts of ourselves. Clearly then, when communicating via electronic text we have all the components to express ourselves in a transitional manner. We can test the world outside of ourselves to see if different ways of expression receive positive or negative feedback and thereby relearn ways of perception. Faber (1984) suggests that the computer is a substitute object, a replacement for the maternal object that could not be controlled perfectly. Instead of seeing the maternal object as one that could meet our needs on the one hand and deny our needs on the other, rendering ourselves powerless, Faber sees the computer as having the potential for meeting or denying our needs while all functions remain within our power. Thus the instrument that transmits or delivers the text-based communication is something we have power over and we can exercise that power with the simple touch of a key!

A young woman described to me how an online relationship developed with the sharing of information over a short period of time. She told me how she sensed very early on that she was the dominant one of the pairing. All her remarks were the leading ones (e.g. her thoughts and feelings about a catastrophic event were mirrored without giving any indication of the man's own thinking). His desire to please and be agreeable gave no measure of any original thinking. The limited vocabulary and the spelling errors in his email exchanges started to engage feelings of insurmountable differences for this young woman. She had been pleased at first by his agreeable nature but found it frustrating and boring not be challenged and stimulated in the way that she had experienced other men in her family and life. The man, on the other hand, had spent his entire life trying to please his mother and without clues on how to do this in text he had mirrored many of the statements received and gave no indication of any depth or identity to relate to. The relationship petered out as it became circular and had no potential for growth.

My work with a young man who became a social phobic after recovering from a bad 'E' drug at a disco, started out with him addressing me without name or title. After several interactions via email and one emotional exchange he started to use my first name. This was a significant moment in the therapeutic alliance. Noticeably the disclosures were deeper and the text communications longer. He started to use his own typed words to make sense of his thoughts and feelings with only minimal prompts from me:

> <Dad always said we could go and live with him but I don't think he ever meant it. He got Sophie to move in pretty quick and they got a good life. He says he's interested in us but he doesn't listen, asks the same questions every time we see him. He thinks I'm still working, he couldn't handle all the aggro, complains that I don't talk to him, then tells me what to do when I do. Is that it Lin, can't please my Dad and can't please my Mum, who can I bloody get it right for?>

The intervention that had brought him to this point was the classic 'me-too' which in general social interaction prevents the 'talker' from going any further. Part of my response to this client was to include the fact that it had taken me most of my life to realise that the only person I had to 'get it right for' was myself!

In this instance the intervention provided some basis of connection and was clearly perceived as understanding and supportive. Craig Childress (1998) explains this well by saying, 'When another person responds with a story about a similar experience, their self-disclosure breaks through the technological void and provides us with an experience of being united with humanity.'

Some of the transference issues can be checked out when an individual finds himself or herself reacting to words like 'you must', 'you should', or 'you ought'. The authoritative 'critical parent' (Berne 1961) is perceived by the recipient and the response may well come back as defensive, submissive or rejecting. The need to resurrect and maintain the adult/adult relationship may take another two or three emails. John Suler (1998) suggests that even under the best of circumstances, there is often some aspect of our mental image of the other person that is based more on our own expectations and needs than on the reality of the other person. If the relationship we have with our computer becomes a substitute for mother, father, husband, wife, lover or friend then our reactions to the text that the computer delivers could be similar to reactions we have when communicating within 'real' relationships, whether past or present. An online client suggested that I sounded just like her mother at one point and it became a real breakthrough in her understanding about taking responsibility. Understanding in this case was mutual when I realised that I responded to her as if I *were* her mother!

Words that are originated from within ourselves and received by the computer without contest or contempt may produce the feelings that tell us we are being accommodated. Is this denial of reality or is it the individual's unique reality upon which he or she has managed to create a tool for expression and containment? Relating in this way it could enable the reclamation of projected parts of 'self' by way of introjections and therefore serve to help the individual with whole relatedness.

There are many advantages to consider in electronic text communication. We can take time (when using email or text messaging) to consider the content we will be sharing. Time also to consider our reactions and therefore our responses. We can take risks by sharing more personal information if there is a degree of anonymity and we can share that information more quickly than we might do face to face. We can make contact at a time to suit ourselves and not in an intrusive way, such as a telephone call for example.

There are of course many disadvantages, not least that using text to communicate as part of a therapeutic relationship may not be appropriate, helpful or safe. The therapist cannot exercise some of the ethical boundaries that are commonplace in face-to-face work. The issue of the client harming themselves or others is a concern to therapists, organisations and their insurers. Contracting is as necessary online as in any other setting. Responses are not always spontaneous and leave the person waiting for a response in anticipation, regret or paranoid reflection of their own 'sent' comments. The 'delete' and 'end' of a relationship is as sudden and abrupt as some deaths can be and could easily trigger the feelings and trauma associated with loss. I have endeavoured to let online clients know of holidays or breaks well in advance yet have still experienced a client's distress when a response was delayed.

Humour is not an international language: many stand-up comedians have tripped up when a joke told in one country does not even receive a titter in another. Developments in online communication have included 'emoticons' – small pictorial symbols and faces to indicate mood and expressions. They remain a poor substitute for conveying the shrug of the shoulder, the grimace, the sly smile and all the subtleties of face-to-face communication.

When an online client who did not have English as a first language told me that he had spent a good evening relaxing and drinking red wine, I responded in an encouraging (or so I thought) way, by typing 'just what the doctor ordered'. He was enraged at what he thought was both sarcasm and criticism. It took a paragraph to explain the 'encouraging' remark in a non-defensive manner and stay with the possibility that my sentence had triggered something quite important for him that led to his confusion and the notion that I was being either sarcastic or critical or both. He associated my words and their perceived meaning with his father, who he felt had not shown humour with any facial expression whatsoever, leaving him confused and often rebellious as a result. He remembered trying to work out whether his father meant what he said or whether there were any signs facially or otherwise that could make his statement(s) have a different meaning. In the absence of being sure, my client had always taken the remarks as critical and his own reactions generally brought about further critical reactions and responses in their turn. He had responded to my comment exactly as he would have done when there were no other clues available to him.

Most of the disadvantages of using the internet to communicate can be resolved with time and understanding. The relationship or alliance that develops via text communication will undoubtedly develop a style of using text that is unique and this will involve checking out meanings: 'When we relate to others we often play complicated games, checking out whether we can trust the other to understand enough to get a little closer to them and at the same time withdrawing again to a safe enough place that leaves us relating in a more conservative manner' (Van Deurzen 1998).

When a therapist checks out with a client information given to them verbally, the intervention can be swift and spontaneous; a reflection, a paraphrase, an open question. Language can match the client's own, can elaborate, emphasise according to visual response and the level of empathy, tone, use of creative adjectives, etc., be adjusted to the here and now experience. In text, the client is more likely to react or respond spontaneously according to the picture or image they have created of the therapist and the therapist is often left deliberating and weighing up the anticipated reactions and responses of the client that they have created. On the one hand these images may struggle together as the process develops and on the other they may have greater capacity for healing as both the therapist and client work harder to establish a connection. In their mutual endeavours to relate to each other and be 'heard' and 'understood' the cyberspace between them creates a transitional time warp where the past and present have a chance to achieve ultimate clarity.

References

Balint, E. (1993) Unconscious communications, in S. Ruszczynski (ed.) *Psychotherapy with Couples*. London: Karnac.

Berne, E. (1961) *Transactional Analysis in Psychotherapy*. New York: Grove Press.

Brosnan, M. (1998) *Technophobia – The Psychological Impact of Information Technology*. London: Routledge.

Childress, C. (1998) *Potential Risks and Benefits of online Psychotherapeutic Interventions*, www. ismho.org. Accessed 4/6/00.

Civin, M. (2000) *Male Female Email: The Struggle for Relatedness in a Paranoid Society*. New York: Other Press.

Faber, M.D. (1984) The computer, the technological order and psychoanalysis: the preliminary remarks. *Psychoanalytic Review*, 71(2): 263–77.

Freud, S. and Breuer, J. (1950) Studies on hysteria, in *Standard Edition of the Complete Psychological Works of Sigmund Freud*, vol. 2. London: Hogarth Press.

Griffiths, L. (2000) Communicating therapeutically via the Internet. Unpublished masters thesis, Sheffield Hallam University.

Jacobs, M. (1985) *The Presenting Past*. London: Harper & Row.

Joseph, B. (1985) Transference: the total situation, *International Journal of Pyscho-Analysis*, 66: 447–54, reprinted in E. Bott and M. Feldman (eds) *Psychic Equilibrium and Psychic Change: Selected Papers of Betty Joseph*, pp. 156–67. London: Tavistock/Routledge, 1989.

Kelly, G.A. (1963) *Theory of Personality: The Psychology of Personal Constructs*. New York: Norton.

Klein, M. (1952) The origins of transference, *International Journal of Psycho-Analysis*, 33: 433–8.

Malan, D.H. (1979) *Individual Psychotherapy and the Science of Psychodynamics*. London: Butterworth.

Mattinson, J. (1975) *The Reflection Process in Casework Supervision*. London: Tavistock.

Price, J. and Price, L. (2002) *Hot Text: Web Writing That Works*. Indianapolis, IN: New Riders.

Rosenfield, M. (1997) *Counselling by Telephone*. London: Sage.

Suler, J. (1998) *E-Mail Transference: Seeing the Other Clearly*. Online self-help and psychology magazine, shpm.com. Accessed 9/4/00.

Van Deurzen, E. (1998) *Paradox and Passion in Psychotherapy – An Existential Approach to Therapy and Counseling*. Chichester: Wiley.

Chapter 15

Messages to Jo – the Samaritans' experience of email befriending

Stephanie Howlett and Robert Langdon

Introduction

> Can anyone tell me some painless ways that I could commit suicide?
>
> I've been thinking, but . . . even though I open my arms regularly with razor blades I hate pain. Thank God I can't feel it. I've really tried too.
>
> E-mail me please!!![1]

A message like this is stark and shocking, but is not atypical of the 64,000 email contacts received by the Samaritans in 2001 (Samaritans 2002). With a rapidly expanding email befriending service that has been up and running since 1994, the Samaritans have perhaps the greatest body of experience and expertise in offering therapeutic email work of any organisation in the UK. While they are clear that what they offer, as in their longer-established telephone and face-to-face work, is befriending and not therapy, it is certainly therapeutic, and they have a solid body of experience that can prove very valuable for others entering the field of online therapy.

Background

The original initiative to establish an email service came from a Samaritans volunteer working in their Cheltenham branch. He was struck by the use that people were already making of chat rooms and websites to express some of their deepest emotions, feelings of despair, of not coping, and thoughts about suicide. Via the internet they were able to express these feelings and get a response of some kind, and clearly this was meeting a real need. He encouraged the Samaritans to consider using email as an additional medium through which people could access support, and a pilot scheme was set up in July 1994.

[1] The Samaritans never disclose details about individuals who call them. Quotes are used strictly with permission and they do not use the contents of any calls to the Samaritans. The examples of emails used in this chapter are fictional exchanges typical of those received in reality.

The branch received 37 messages in the first 24 hours, and by the end of that first week the percentage of people writing about their suicidal feelings had reached 46 per cent, twice the rate for those using the telephone and face-to-face contact. It was apparent that email befriending was there to stay as a fundamental and much-needed part of the service. The next branch came online in 1996, and since then other centres have joined at a steady rate. By the end of 2001 there were 61 branches online, between them receiving 64,000 emails during the year (Samaritans 2002). This rapid growth has occurred despite the Samaritans taking a relatively cautious approach to publicity. They are very aware that the potentially worldwide access to their service via the internet could bring a deluge of calls that they would be unable to handle, and are keen to establish the service on sound foundations, maintaining their aim of responding to emails by the next day.

The Samaritans saw the potential of the new service to extend access to some vulnerable people who would have been hard to reach by their existing approaches. Suicide attempts by young men have almost tripled over the last 20 years, and they felt that depressed, isolated young men might be more able to reach out via email than by telephone. It would also improve accessibility for people who were disabled (particularly in terms of their speech or hearing), for people who did not have private access to a telephone and those who were geographically remote. The additional degree of anonymity made contact easier for some people.

Guiding principles

The Samaritans have set email befriending firmly within the regular work of the service. It is an additional means of fulfilling the Samaritans' mission of providing confidential emotional support, available at any hour of the day or night, to people experiencing distress and despair and at risk of dying by suicide. They aim for the email service to mirror their existing befriending service, following all its key principles and practices, so that email is merely an additional vehicle for the service, allowing for the differences occasioned by the medium.

The Samaritans' current strategy for email states that:

> E-mail befriending is offered to callers in a manner consistent with all other methods of contact (i.e. telephone, letter and face to face). Callers that choose to contact The Samaritans by e-mail will receive a response that is caring and compassionate and in accordance with Samaritans' policies.

The Samaritans have been keen to avoid email work being possibly seen as the preserve of an elite group, detached from the rest of the service. They have thus chosen to locate the work not within a centralised call centre, but within their local branches. The computers are located in the central operations room alongside the telephones, not tucked away somewhere separate. The email work is done by existing, experienced volunteers who, at different branches, may take on an additional email shift in addition to their regular telephone work, or may respond to email callers as part of their ordinary shift.

Branches apply to join the email scheme, but will only be accepted if early briefing meetings indicate that the majority of volunteers are supportive. All volunteers in the branch will then be expected to attend an initial training providing a basic awareness of email support and how it is integrated into the work of the branch. Email work will thereafter be included in the initial training for any new volunteers joining the branch. There is then a further five hours of training for those who will be directly involved in downloading messages and drafting replies.

Responsibility for email work is shared within the branch: volunteers downloading messages and drafting replies, supported by others talking through possible responses and proofreading replies. The system demands that all replies should be overseen by another volunteer before they are sent. At present about 4000 volunteers nationally are estimated to be involved in email work in some capacity.

How is the service operated?

The email service is run in an integrated way by all Samaritans UK online branches, and two branches in Hong Kong and Perth, Australia, united under the umbrella organisation, Befrienders International.

All emails are routed through one email address (jo@samaritans.org). Emails go onto a global list and the next branch to log on will deal with the email at the top of the list, so that any email can go to any branch. This remains the case if the sender makes a second, third or fourth contact, so that one sender may be dealt with over time by several different branches. To ensure the coherence of replies the history of all the exchanges in one 'episode' is attached to the emails, so that the volunteer taking the email can look back at all the previous messages and responses to help them gauge how to respond.

This framework means that there is no establishment of any ongoing relationship between particular 'callers' and particular volunteers. All the email volunteers use the relatively gender-neutral pseudonym 'Jo', and callers are made aware of this in a standard footnote. In fact, it is part of Samaritans policy positively to discourage any kind of ongoing relationship between individuals as this can foster an unhelpful dependency in both directions. The relationship is always between the caller and the organisation, rather than the caller and an individual befriender.

There are exceptions to this random allocation, however. Branches have a responsibility to judge whether it might be beneficial for a particular caller to be assigned permanently to one branch. This enables the branch to manage the caller care for that person, and consider the type of support offered, imposing restrictions on the service offered if necessary. This helps to avoid the danger of the service being used as a chat line. Even then they try to ensure the emails are not handled by a single volunteer.

Who is contacting by email?

An email service offers great potential for anonymity. Statistics can be compiled only on the basis of what callers choose to disclose. The evidence that is available suggests that the typical email sender profile is not as initially anticipated. While there are contacts from the isolated young men of the original target group, of the 64,000 emails in 2001, 56 per cent came from females, 26 per cent from males and 18 per cent from individuals of undisclosed gender. This compares with the Samaritans overall figures for the same year of 53 per cent of calls from men and 44 per cent from women (Samaritans 2002). Volunteers are reporting contacts from disabled people and also from professionals with email access at work, who make contact when alone at the end of the working day.

How is email work different?

Emails differ from other contacts. For example, 50 per cent of emails are from people expressing suicidal thoughts, compared with 26 per cent of telephone calls. Email callers are much more likely to express difficult feelings; messages are also more direct, raw and intense. The discussion of feelings and suicidal thoughts in telephone contact is often edged towards gradually, whereas emails are much more likely to open with something such as, 'I'm going to kill myself tonight, there's nothing you can say is there?' (Armson 1997).

The possible reasons for this reflect in a reciprocal way both the nature of the medium and those using it:

- The caller is not obliged to build any sort of relationship with the volunteer. While the personal nature of the telephone can be very important for some callers, this might deter suicidal people, who are often very withdrawn.
- Many people, particularly men, find it very hard to expose emotions; they can become embarrassed if they cry during telephone calls. Paradoxically, email can enable the sharing of emotions with someone else with no personal witness to emotional reactions. Email callers are more in control of what they share, and so they are able to make contact and to share more.
- In email the element of distance frees people from the normal rules of conversation and the need to exchange pleasantries. There is no awareness of or response to the reactions of someone else, so the real reason for calling can be plunged into with no preamble.
- An email is composed in private. People can compose their message in a careful and considered way. The moment of sharing and commitment only comes when they push the 'send' button.

This belies the theory suggested by some web experts that people use email for brief or trivial messages and face-to-face encounters are preferable for important issues, with telephone contact coming somewhere in between. Many counsellors and psychotherapists would also put forward this hierarchy in therapeutic work. Face-to-face work with clients, and the personal therapeutic alliance this entails, is seen as the most effective; telephone work, with its loss of direct contact and visual clues is seen as rather inferior; and email work with its asynchronicity, anonymity and the complete loss of non-verbal communication is viewed as something hardly counting as therapy at all. The experience of the Samaritans is that email is the least threatening medium for callers to express their feelings, telephone next, and face to face the most threatening.

How effective is it?

In all the befriending work of the Samaritans, contact is fleeting and volunteers rarely know what happens to callers afterwards. Email work is no exception, making evaluation and comparisons between the different forms of work difficult.

What feedback the Samaritans do receive is positive and tends to confirm the advantages outlined above for some callers. For example:

> I've been using your email service for a few months and really don't know how I would have carried on without it. It really helps me to express how I'm feeling and because I only have to type, not speak, it means that if I get upset it doesn't matter . . . THANKYOU!
>
> (Anonymous comment sent via feedback page on the website)

> I think it's really useful that you can email people because all the other help-lines just have phone numbers which is difficult if you don't want anyone to hear or if you can't get to a phone.
>
> (Comment from 17-year-old student)

Samaritans' email training

The Samaritans have developed a comprehensive experiential training package for volunteers in befriending by writing. This draws on their now considerable experience in this work.

Email work requires the use of particular skills and approaches. In a telephone call there is an immediacy of response, a gradual unfolding of communication and an almost constant interaction and responsiveness, using both verbal and non-verbal means (e.g. tone of voice, silences, crying, sighs). With email there are no non-verbal clues, and the communication comes in larger chunks separated by substantial time lapses. This means that both caller and volunteer have time to consider what they are reading and writing. Responses are 'fixed' in writing so that callers can save, print off, study and reread them, possibly increasing their usefulness and prolonging their effect. This also means that choice of words, clarity and unambiguousness are very important.

The use of direct, simple everyday language, avoiding long-winded phrases-in-phrases, is stressed. Care needs to be taken with the use of personal pronouns. The use of 'I' can introduce an element of personal connection, but if overused can put more emphasis on the sender's thoughts than the recipient's feelings. Similarly 'we' can suggest togetherness and support, but may feel contrived and over-familiar. It is important to make sure that there is no ambiguity between 'we' meaning 'you and me' and 'we' meaning the Samaritans.

Email callers may sometimes use a lot of jargon and email text symbols. Volunteers are advised not to attempt to respond in kind, but to stick to simple language and ask about feelings.

In email work it is necessary to find new ways of building trust and demonstrating listening and responsiveness. How is it possible to show in a written message that the caller is really being 'listened to'? Ways suggested are:

- By concentrating on the caller's feelings whether expressed or implied.
- By mentioning key points or specific issues from the caller's message. This might sometimes entail quoting parts of the caller's message in the reply. Having access to the entire history of emails and replies, so that these can be referred to, is also part of that responsiveness.

Wording needs to be non-judgemental without inadvertently implying either criticism or approval of specific actions or opinions. It is doubly important that the wording cannot be construed as advice: phrasing that might be used in a telephone call could easily be construed as advice in printed form (e.g. 'I wonder if you have ever thought of leaving him'). Misunderstandings from ambiguity cannot be picked up and corrected as they might in a telephone call.

The mode of starting and ending emails also needs to be considered. Samaritans are advised to reflect the mode of address used by the caller, responding to 'Hi' with 'Hi' and 'Dear Jo' with 'Dear Mary', unless the caller has used a derogatory pseudonym for themselves. The caller's name should only be used if the caller has used it themselves in the body of the email, not just in the address (it might be somebody else's name). It is advised that volunteers sign off in a way that is neither impersonal ('Yours faithfully/sincerely') nor over-familiar. Possibilities suggested are 'Take care', 'Go safely' or simply 'Jo'.

Sometimes the emails sent by callers are very long and complex. The following guidelines for drafting a response are given:

- read the whole message through, focusing on details as well as the general scenario;
- highlight the main feelings in the message;
- acknowledge the feelings that the message generates in the reader;
- write the reply in one go, drawing on the original message but responding to the three or four main points only;
- treat each general area as a paragraph;

- the first, well thought-out response is often the best and most natural, but it is good to talk it through with someone else;
- at each stage it is important to bear in mind the caller's main stated feelings; feelings/events that are implied but not stated; feelings/events that are vague and not clearly expressed; questions to ask the caller.

The key issue for the Samaritans is to enable the caller to express their most closed-in and hurtful feelings, especially feelings about suicide. It is therefore crucial to find a way of asking about feelings that enables the caller to find expression for difficult emotions honestly. Asking directly about suicide and exploring the nature of suicidal feelings where this seems appropriate is fundamental, as in all Samaritans' work.

A typical initial email and the sort of exchange that might follow is given below.

From: Sarah232@hotmail.com
Reply-To: Sarah232@hotmail.com
Subject: Re: I need help

PLEASE HELP ME!!!

I REALLY NEED SOMEONE TO TALK TO. I am so drowning in misery.
I am getting so weak I can hardly function. How can I be a mother
like this?
What do I do? All I want to do is just DIE
I am soon going to quit thinking and just do it . . . Help . . .
Sarah

To: Sarah232@hotmail.com
Subject: Re: HELP

Dear Sarah

I'm glad you felt able to contact us and sorry that you are
'drowning in misery'. What is it that is making you feel so
miserable and so down that you want to die?
When you say, 'you are getting so weak you can hardly function' do
you mean that you are ill?

You mentioned that you are a mother – looking after children is a very
energy sapping occupation.

If you feel it helps to contact us we are here for you while times are so bad.

Take care

Jo

From: Sarah232@hotmail.com
Subject: Re: HELP

I am ill I am anorexic. I am tired of the daily fight within myself I am lost in a sea of darkness and depression. Every day is a battle to get up and feed my kids and take care of them. I am a terrible mother, these days. doctor has made me go see him every day this week to make sure I'm ok
I AM NOT!!!
I am afraid to tell him I'm suicidal for fear of going to the hospital.
I hate it there.
Life just seems pretty dam hopeless

Sarah

To: Sarah232@hotmail.com
Subject: Re: HELP

Dear Sarah

Thank you for contacting us again, you sound as if you are in a very desperate situation. I hope it helps a little to talk to us about the anorexia and how it makes you feel. Perhaps you might be able to see us as a sort of life-line in that sea of darkness and depression?

It mentions that you have been in hospital before and did not like the experience. Would it help if you told us about the things there that you hate?

Anorexia and depression are both terrible illnesses, is it possible to separate them any more, or do you feel that they combine to drain you?

Children are so demanding and must take a lot of energy to care for, are you able to get any help with them so that you have some energy left over to care for yourself?

You say that you are scared to tell your doctor that you are suicidal. Do you want to die, or is that you want to end the way you are feeling?

Remember we're here to support you while you are going through these difficult times.

Take care

Jo

The experiences of volunteers

The intensity and rawness of many email messages means that answering them can be intensely emotionally demanding work. One volunteer said, 'In a telephone conversation you build up the picture gradually, but in an email you get all the information at once. It knocks you back, almost gives you indigestion. It's a big shock each time.'

The immediacy of telephone contact allows volunteers to pick up some sense of the caller's response by the end of the call, and they can also ask the caller for more detail. In email work, by contrast, the volunteers see only the pain of the original desperate message. They have no way of knowing how the caller may have been helped either by the act of sending the message or the response they receive. Often they are aware that a very distressed caller has had to wait a long time before receiving a reply, and this can also generate anxiety.

Another daunting aspect of this work for volunteers is that their replies are much more public, recorded in black and white and available for the whole branch, and potentially other email branches, to read. Once sent they are fixed and unchangeable: ' In a telephone call you can correct nuances. In an email, once it's gone it's gone. You have this vision of it being printed off and carried around with them.' It is understandably easy for volunteers to have doubts about replies.

It is recognised that email volunteers may need a lot of support. This needs to be provided by other volunteers on duty, or the shift leader being available to discuss messages, sound out possible replies and talk through the feelings generated. For some volunteers the sense of sharing and teamwork is seen as a very positive aspect of the work. No one person takes sole responsibility for the response.

There seems to be general agreement that the email work is in many ways more demanding, but volunteers do not seem to find it any less satisfying:

> I find it more rewarding. I joined the Samaritans to support people who are suicidal. A higher proportion of email callers are suicidal, so there is more reward; a greater sense of being there for the right reasons.

> We are tapping into a different audience. We get a lot of calls from young girls who are self-harming or have eating disorders. A lot of them are in counselling, but it's not helping, they don't feel heard. That makes the email work feel more valuable.

Although there is no continuing contact between the caller and an individual Samaritan, volunteers describe a greater sense of continuity with the email work, in that they see the whole history of calls and replies. This rather public sharing of work, though daunting, also helps with a sense of building up competence: 'It's a good thing about emails. You can read other people's nice turns of phrase and steal them. Also you get feedback from the organisation.'

Future developments

The Samaritans are continuing to develop the potential of the internet to expand their work, particularly in reaching out to young people. They have set up a dedicated website for teenagers experiencing emotional distress at exam results time. Developments such as video links, low-cost internet connections and the ability to access the internet via a mobile phone will all have an impact on the demand for the service. Additionally, given the government's aim that all schoolchildren be given their own access to email, it is possible that email will increasingly become the preferred method of communication.

The Samaritans have recently agreed a three-year partnership with a major international bank who are providing funds to develop and expand the email service further. The launch of this partnership will enable the Samaritans to promote and publicise the email service with increased vigour. It is envisaged that by the end of 2004 over 120 branches will be online, and all by the end of 2112.

Conclusion

The Samaritans have used the potential of new technology to extend their work completely congruently with their existing aims, ideology and structure. Their email work is an extension of a very solid base of existing expertise. They have demonstrated the potential of the medium for reaching out to the very distressed and young people who have difficulty in accessing other forms of help. Their experience of establishing and running such a service, and the thorough training package they have developed, provide a solid foundation of knowledge upon which other organisations can usefully build.

References

Armson, S. (1997) Suicide and cyberspace – Befriending by email, *Crisis*, 18(3).
Samaritans (2002) *Information and Resource Pack 2002*. Ewell, Surrey: The Samaritans.

Chapter 16

Ethical and practical dimensions of online writing cures

Stephen Goss and Kate Anthony

Introduction

The new and developing field of online therapeutic work presents exciting new possibilities and challenges to practitioners. Yet, given the ever-changing nature of communication technology, it seems likely that definitive descriptions of the method will elude us. Hardware and software continue to become ever more sophisticated and new information technology solutions to communication barriers continually emerge. Along with exciting challenges and possibilities comes the potential for new and increased risk for clients, not to mention pitfalls for practitioners. It is a seriously under-researched field even at the time of writing in October 2003, although small-scale studies continue to emerge. Yet it seems that, despite the appropriate caution shown by the counselling and psychotherapy profession, increasing numbers of clients are willing to embrace this new method of communication for gaining psychological assistance, a phenomenon which seems likely to increase as future generations become more at ease with technology being part of their everyday lives.

Online counselling and therapy services already exist; it is therefore incumbent on the profession to keep up with the phenomena and examine this emerging field with a view to establishing its effectiveness and, if effective, how it can best be utilised. To this end, the British Association for Counselling and Psychotherapy (BACP) published an initial discussion document (Lago *et al.* 1999) and more formal guidelines (Goss *et al.* 2001). The latter document set out to provide the most thorough and precise guidance that could be offered to practitioners and users of online services that could be produced at the time, and was written in consultation with international experts in the field, including representatives of a number of professional bodies around the world. This chapter is partly based on these BACP documents and highlights a number of ethical and practical aspects of therapeutic communication via the exchange of emails between practitioner and client (asynchronous therapy), and the use of internet relay chat (IRC, synchronous therapy), both using the written (typed) word.

The values, principles, ethical considerations and the general skills and competencies needed to be a therapist in any modality are taken automatically to apply to the therapist who wishes to practise online. However, additional ethical and practical considerations apply if working online with text. In the absence of definitive research in this field, as with any innovative mode of therapy provision, practitioners are urged to consider the issues involved carefully before embarking upon this as yet unproven method. Their prime concern, as with any innovative practice, must be to ensure that the potential for harm to their clients is clearly outweighed by the additional benefits online work can offer in comparison with, say, referral to sources of more 'traditional' methods.

Basic competence

The therapist wishing to work online should hold appropriate qualifications (which may vary widely from country to country) and conform to professional standards to support their practice just as they would with any other form of therapy provision. Extensive experience of post-qualification face-to-face work is also appropriate, as it is widely acknowledged that converting from face-to-face work to working with text within a new environment such as the internet is not to be recommended for novice practitioners. In short, a practitioner who is not competent to work offline should never consider themselves competent online.

Courses exist that encompass the essential elements that need to be examined in transferring skills to the internet, and these are becoming more available as the research body grows. It is even arguable that the training course should take place over the internet, in keeping with the method. Familiarity with email and IRC for personal or business use does not qualify a practitioner for being an online therapist, although this has not always been fully appreciated. First, there is a degree of technical and computer knowledge required, although fast and accurate typing skills are only essential when using IRC. Second, the online practitioner must have a thorough knowledge of the communication skills, possibilities and norms when using the internet ('netiquette'). The niceties of internet communication are an important facet of online mental health provision and have become an interesting focus of research where they are used between therapist and client (Stofle 2001). Third, there are important differences from more traditional methods of therapeutic intervention (such as coping with thc lack of body language) that indicate a need for further training to avoid client or practitioner damage (Anthony 2000) from a theoretical, practical and ethical point of view.

Information technology has meant that access to the growing body of research and other literature is easier than ever before. Practitioners need to be in a position to make informed judgments as to whether their theoretical orientation and clinical skills are able to make the jump into working with text without the usual benefits of a face-to-face relationship. Some theoretical orientations rely too much on reading body language or using practical tools in physical space that become untenable when working in a virtual environment. If the transfer to working online is to take place, practitioners must reflect on what adaptations they will have to make to their usual methods. They may find that integrating online skills and theory into their orientation is not a straightforward matter and may even prompt changes in their face-to-face working practices.

The global market-place and cultural issues

Issues of ethical practice are especially acute where clients and therapists make use of the opportunity offered by the internet to operate on a global scale across national boundaries. One of the internet's great strengths, the opportunity for people from all over the world to be in contact with each other, also creates some of the greatest challenges by creating relationships that must then cope with what may be vast cultural and psychological, as well as physical, distances.

The most important difficulty from a therapeutic point of view is the differences of perception and use of language in different cultures. The role of 'counsellor' in the UK may be fulfilled by very different activities in other cultures (Lee and Bond 2002). The very titles that practitioners use to describe themselves may, even if translated, either have little meaning or be understood differently. Counselling is a term that indicates different things in the UK and USA in comparison with much of, say, Eastern Europe or sub-Saharan Africa. Explanations of the services on offer must therefore be extremely carefully phrased to account for the quite different readings that might be put upon them. Even where services are welcomed when introduced to cultures radically different from those in which they were developed, expectations can vary wildly.

Merely offering some services (such as those relating to abortion or marital relations) may be culturally taboo or otherwise unacceptable in some parts of the world. It has never been the case that practitioners are ethically required to steer clear of crossing cultural boundaries nor that they should necessarily avoid being unpopular or out of step with received social mores. However, a sufficient degree of cultural sensitivity is most certainly requisite, and in general practitioners are well advised to only offer their services to clients in countries in which they can demonstrably meet the local professional requirements and practice in a manner that does not clash directly with any local imperatives or cultural expectations. This implies that the possibility of therapy services with a truly global reach is likely to be limited in practice by the extent to which those services are truly transferable to other cultures.

The global market-place and issues of jurisdiction

Issues of international professional jurisdiction, such as in relation to regulation, complaints procedures and redress in instances of malpractice, have proved difficult to map as yet. The problem can be summarised by one question: where is the therapy taking place? When client and practitioner are working remotely from each other, it can be argued that the therapeutic work is at the client's computer, the practitioner's, or indeed in the space between them within the internet – commonly known as cyberspace.

It is quite possible that clients could attempt to complain about, or even sue their therapist, in their own country. What effect this might have for the practitioner, should they decide not to cooperate by attending voluntarily, would depend on the legal agreements between their own country and that of the client. Reciprocal arrangements on these matters vary widely and it is a complex and evolving area of law. For example, despite close cultural and diplomatic ties, there is no extradition treaty between the UK and the USA. If, say, an action were successfully brought by a client in the USA against a practitioner in the UK (or vice versa) the only necessary and inevitable practical result might be that the practitioner could not easily travel to their client's country. Even this, however, is not certain and the practitioner's ethical obligations might be thought to override legal ones in many such situations. Practitioners should be cautious, especially given the variation in legal definitions and the implications of issues such as working with 'young people'. Who is defined as a minor, and the requirements for obtaining informed consent, vary widely from country to country. Practitioners can reduce the level of risk, but not eliminate it, by stating explicitly in the pre-therapy contracting information what is to be the applicable legal structure. Deliberate choice of which country will have legal jurisdiction over a contractual arrangement is supported by the Rome and Brussels Conventions. The European Union and the UK have signed up to these conventions but other countries have not, and practitioners should still proceed with caution and get their own expert legal advice on all the relevant legal issues.

The BACP recommendation is that 'regardless of the location of their client, practitioners should always consider themselves bound to maintain *at least* the standards of practice required by their own professional organisation' (Goss *et al.* 2001: 5, original emphasis). That is, no service should ever be offered of a lower standard or with lesser quality controls and right of redress than if the client lived in the practitioner's own country. Thus, a practitioner would be considered to be bound to accept that the client had the right to complain about them to the practitioner's own professional body even if that were not an absolute required of them by the usual complaints procedures.

Furthermore, the BACP guidance goes on to state that where differences in standards exist, such as the necessary level of qualification and experience required to practise or licensure and accreditation requirements, practitioners should assume that *both* sets of requirements apply. Thus, if I wish to offer services to clients in Maryland, USA, I should ensure that I meet the requirements of that state *as well as my own* country. Conversely, if I seek therapy from outside my own country, I should be able to expect the practitioner to measure up to the standards that I would expect if seeing a therapist in my own town.

The practical difficulties of ensuring that this is adhered to for services offered to all parts of the globe are another reason that practitioners may prefer to consider the reach of their online services to be limited – at least to those countries with which they are sure of being sufficiently familiar.

Practical and technical considerations

The importance of clear, explicit contracting becomes highlighted in online work, since clients often mouse click a box stating that they have read, understood and accepted the conditions of the service without necessarily having done so. Therefore, there is a strong argument for reiterating all terms and conditions of the contract within the main body of an email in addition to information posted on a website. The range of ways of delivering an internet service to client groups is vast, but the following considerations should be a basis for discussion when planning what services could or should be offered.

Time boundaries make up a big part of using the internet to deliver written therapy. The time taken to respond to each email must not only be practicable for the practitioner, but also provide a good service to the client, who will be waiting for an objective and caring response to often sensitive material. Sending such material from one computer to another can involve a 'black hole' effect, where the absence of an expected email response can create anxieties and insecurities about where the original sent communication went or where the expected communication has got to (Suler 1997). The time spent reading and composing emails also needs consideration as the 'therapeutic hour' can be stretched in the case of both emails and IRC.

With emails, this can involve the ability to split the hour to enable time to reflect upon the writing (and adjust as necessary) to ensure a coherent and appropriate response has been composed. With IRC, the length of the sessions may need to be reviewed in the light of the time lag between responses as the communication travels across cyberspace, taking up valuable moments of the therapeutic hour. Also important is whether interim messages between sessions should be accommodated, either for administration of appointments, 'homework' or to impart information pertinent to the work (to save time when an important event needs a long description and would interrupt the flow of a session, for example). The definition of what comprises a 'session' should be assessed and explicitly stated (for instance, one exchange of emails), as should a suitable length of contract. International time zones may also need consideration. Finally, taking breaks from the computer screen every hour is a health and safety issue that may impinge on the work.

The length of emails is a personal choice, but explicit guidelines as to suitable length can be given in pre-therapy information. Commonplace literary, as opposed to verbal, techniques are often valuable, such as using regular paragraph breaks to avoid the client feeling overwhelmed by large chunks of sensitive written material. In an IRC session, it takes time to adjust to the client's style of writing. They may include sequences of several short sentences (which can become confusing when trying to respond to each without interrupting), or tend to write in longer sentences that take more time to arrive because of the amount of typing involved to convey the meaning. These styles of communication are often quickly adapted to, but guidelines for the client as to how the practitioner intends to indicate they have more to write can be given before the sessions start.

Procedures should be in place to ensure good care of client and practitioner in the case of unplanned termination of the contract by the client. Email accounts can be set up and disbanded with a few clicks and are less permanent than a postal address should the need arise to address client safety in the event of non-attendance at a session. There is an argument for additional contact details being available to the practitioner with emergency procedures for client and practitioner well-being, including care of clients in the event of illness or the consideration of death.

Deciding fees and the fee structure is another wide-ranging issue. Some examples of how therapists charge are per email, per block of emails, per IRC session or per block of IRC sessions. This also varies by definition of what constitutes a 'session' (some websites have charged per minute of online time). Payment over the internet may also be more complex than in face-to-face contexts, requiring consideration of issues such as international exchange procedures and secure online payment facilities. Clients may also need to be warned to allow for additional internet service provider costs and telephone charges.

Confidentiality and its limitations in online practice require particularly careful consideration, as do data protection issues, not least due to the heightened possibility of third-person intervention. Practitioners are encouraged to use three separate email addresses for personal, business and client use to maintain boundaries around the possibility of confusing client emails with other received and sent mail within one inbox.

Practitioners should consider what levels of security should be implemented, such as use of firewalls, encryption, password procedures, service provider access, and the client's environment (e.g. when they are using a public method of internet access or a shared family computer). Clients should be made aware of their responsibilities for the storage of both printed and electronic records of all sessions and communications. Practitioners have a duty of care to online clients in discussing with them within the assessment the likelihood of a third party having a vested interest in accessing the material. A clinical example of this has been in the case of a marriage where the abusive spouse was able to guess the other party's password to access the therapeutic emails and threaten both client (physically) and therapist (electronically).

The sending of attachments involves two aspects. On the plus side, it is a useful way of sending diaries and other instances of writing. On the minus side, both client and practitioner need to be aware of the importance of virus checking, and have strict boundaries in place as to how attachments are used and for what purpose. In general, other technical requirements are optimum hardware specifications, agreement on what software (both word processing and communication) are to be used, and what to do in the case of technical breakdown (another reason for ensuring that alternative means of communication are available).

Assessment and intake considerations

'Impression management' is, to some degree, a factor in all human interactions, including therapy (Paulhaus 1986; McLeod 2000). In online therapy, however, it is far easier and can be taken to much greater degrees, including outright impersonation. It is possible, and can sometimes be unproblematic, for clients to present themselves under the guise of any identity they wish (although it would be ethically unacceptable for practitioners, of course). While doing so may hide potentially important issues, the ability to explore and express aspects of the self that may otherwise remain less prominent has been seen as a positive benefit of distance therapy provision, especially when via text-based media. However, there are some circumstances when a therapist may wish to take steps to verify a client's identity. These may include, but are not restricted to, the following:

- where the therapist has reason to believe there is risk of harm to the client or others (e.g. through homicide, through sexual, physical or mental abuse or through self-harm);
- where the therapist has information about apparent illegal activities;
- where the therapist has reason to believe that the client requires referral, perhaps involuntarily, to other services such as to in-patient psychiatric care.

Assessment procedures over the internet are difficult to define. Of course, it is important to make them as robust as possible, but there is a fine line between making absolutely sure the client is suitable for online work and the assessment procedure impacting negatively on the delicate nature of the work. However, in general, it is probably more difficult to assess whether a person is suffering from a psychiatric disorder or is liable to display risky behaviour when assessing their state of mind via text. As a baseline, practitioners should use in the first instance an online application form requesting details of information such as medication, history of depression and violent behaviour, reason for seeking help, etc. From this, an initial intake session (email or IRC) should generally be offered free of charge to gain an understanding of the client and whether referral is appropriate, and procedures will need to be in place for this, particularly when working across global boundaries.

The need for research

As has been noted above, online therapy of all types remains, at the time of writing, a drastically under-researched area. The important potential of research in this area has been recognised by the Economic and Social Research Council, among others, who have committed £6.5 million through their 'e-society' funding programme.

First and foremost, there is an urgent need to establish the effectiveness and safety of online provision. Counselling and psychotherapy are evidence-based professional activities and it could be argued that those who are prepared to offer services to the public ahead of definitive research are acting prematurely. Thus far, most research has been limited to relatively small-scale enquiries rarely even attempting to address such issues. New research need not necessarily be expensive or large scale, although there is also a clear need for major randomised controlled trials too.

Further research is also required to identify which client groups are most, and least, likely to benefit from online therapeutic provision. Many groups have been proposed as particularly unsuitable – such as those who are suicidal, underage or personality disordered. Conversely, for most such groups it is also arguable that online services may be especially appropriate. For example, although not counselling or therapy provision *per se*, the Samaritans offer an email service explicitly targeted at the suicidal. Elsewhere, it is often thought difficult to ensure that access to young people, many of whom are likely to be more at home with online communication than their elders, is conducted and offered with proper ethical consideration as to their suitability. The difficulty of defining who is suitable, or otherwise, for online therapy is exemplified by the conflict between the sensible caution regarding international service provision noted above, and the immense opportunity offered by the internet to render mental health services far more equitably accessible by cultural and national groups who are otherwise routinely under-represented among our clients.

Despite the increasing body of theoretical and anecdotal literature on the subject, many aspects of online provision are yet to have any definitive empirical basis. The vast amount of work that remains to be done should be a strong stimulus to research activity of all kinds and, at least in some areas of importance, studies are already under way. However, we will have to wait for convergent findings to create an empirically supported evidence base before we attempt less speculative, and more definitive, comment than that which has been offered here.

Conclusion

Any statements about the ethics of therapy online have a very short shelf life. New considerations are appearing every day with more experience of the method being developed and examined worldwide. But international standards for regulation of online services are required, and international consultation also takes time. Technological change occurs during such processes, and keeping up with it is difficult.

However, this is a field that, apparently, offers immense potential. At this early stage in its development, like any innovation in the psychological therapies, every expression of hope must always be tinged with caution. Much work remains to be done to establish the characteristics of online work, its boundaries, limitations and opportunities. Whether practitioners can develop online therapies while responding positively to the challenges working online also presents, rendering the pitfalls acceptably small, will determine whether this is an area that, in time, becomes mainstream and is accepted by the profession as a whole. There is already clear reason to be optimistic about the future of online therapy. Now we must get to grips with the research and generate the evidence on which all new developments must, ultimately, rest.

References

Anthony, K. (2000) Counselling in cyberspace, *Counselling Journal*, 11(10): 625–7.

Goss, S.P., Anthony, K., Palmer, S. and Jamieson, A. (2001) *BACP Guidelines for Online Counselling and Psychotherapy*. Rugby: BACP.

Lago, C., Baughan, R., Copinger-Binns, P., Brice, A., Caleb, R., Goss, S.P. and Lindeman, P. (1999) *Counselling Online: Opportunities and Risks in Counselling Clients via the Internet*. Rugby: BACP.

Lee, C. and Bond, T. (2002) An investigation of counselling activity in selected countries. Paper presented at the 8th annual BACP Counselling Research Conference, London, May 2000.

McLeod, J. (2000) The contribution of qualitative research, in N. Rowland and S. Goss (eds) *Evidence-Based Counselling and Psychological Therapies Research and Applications*. London: Routledge.

Paulhaus, D.L. (1986) Self-deception and impression management in test responses, in A. Angleitner and J.S. Wiggins (eds) *Personality Assessment via Questionnaires: Current Issues in Theory and Measurement*. Berlin: Springer-Verlag.

Stofle, G. (2001) *Choosing an Online Therapist*. Harrisburg, PA: White Hat Communications.

Suler, J. (1997) *Psychological Dynamics of Online Synchronous Conversations in Text-Driven Chat Environments*, http://www.rider.edu/users/psycyber/texttalk.html, accessed 25 April 2000.

Part IV

Reflective practice

Chapter 17

Reflective and therapeutic writing in counsellor training

Jaquie Daniels and Colin Feltham

Introduction

In this chapter, we attempt to define personal development within counselling training and to explain its importance. Results of a small survey are used to illustrate issues arising from writing journals in this context. Difficulties are outlined and suggestions for addressing them made, with the expanded use of personal development writing being commended for counselling trainees.

Personal development in the counselling training context

It is a long-standing tradition in counselling training that trainees are required to write a personal journal as part of their personal development. Practice varies between courses, so that some trainees may keep their journal entirely private, while others may have to submit it, or parts or a summary of it, to be formally assessed. Trainees are sensitised to the challenging personal nature of counselling training from the interview stage onwards, and many course components, such as skill development modules, require trainees to share, reflect on and work with their own life experiences and issues (Mearns 1997). It is also traditional on a majority of training courses that participation in personal development groups (PDGs) is required, and intensive residential components are common. The British Association for Counselling and Psychotherapy (BACP) requires accredited courses to include a personal development component. Many courses also, or alternatively, require trainees to undergo their own counselling or psychotherapy. It is perhaps surprising then that a clear definition or understanding of what personal development means is often lacking.

Most agree that counsellors and psychotherapists need to be highly self-aware, non-defensive, familiar with the experience of the client role and committed to personal development in order to be effective practitioners (Johns 1996; Wilkins 1997; Wosket 1999). Many assert that it is an advantage to be a 'wounded healer', to have experienced difficulties and to have come through them, especially with the aid of therapy. In particular, Page (1999) points to the importance of bringing some unconscious processes into the light in order to work in more self-aware, flexible and creative ways with clients. However, John Norcross suggests that the subject of therapists' own problems and own therapy is far from clear cut (Dryden 1991). Mackaskill (1999), reviewing evidence for the effectiveness of trainees' personal therapy, comes to fairly negative conclusions. Irving and Williams (1999) draw attention to the semantic and conceptual confusion associated with the terms 'personal growth' and 'personal development'. It is important, therefore, to attempt to be clear about what we mean by the concept of personal development, the reasons for its requirement, and the ways in which it is believed to be facilitated by reflective and therapeutic writing.

Personal development is, broadly, the consciously applied intention to change aspects of one's own life. Change implies improvement but this may be highly idiosyncratic to each person and should be determined without coercion from others. One may develop in a wide range of ways, including reducing negatives and boosting positives. For example, conscious of unhealthy habits, you may decide to develop healthier ones by first eliminating smoking, addressing overeating and an over-sedentary lifestyle. Conversely, change could mean simply developing further self-awareness or self-acceptance. The need for self-acceptance may be precipitated through failing at familiar self-defined goals like those listed above. Less obviously, on realising how anxious certain situations seem to make you, you may decide to take more risks, to foster spontaneity. More positively and ambitiously, you may decide to explore the neglected spiritual aspects of your nature.

Typically, this process entails a sequence of relative ignorance, awareness, investigation, willingness, action, meeting obstacles, reflexive learning and re-commitment. A useful illustrative model is Prochaska and DiClemente's (1986) well known stages or cycles of change: pre-contemplation, contemplation, action, maintenance and relapse. This model realistically acknowledges the common resistances to personal change, even when we set our own agenda for change. Relapse does not imply failure but setback and 're-start'. In every personal development endeavour there is some notion of difficulty, defence mechanism, resistance, stuckness and so on. There are divided opinions among different theoretical and clinical orientations about the importance of outcomes. For some, increased insight may be enough, others value heightened emotionality, some more rational thought processes and productive behaviour. Table 17.1 shows the main areas for personal development. The BACP has argued that trainees' personal development, like all course components, should ideally reflect the particular theoretical orientation of the course. It is not possible, however, to demand a definitive level of self-awareness or personal growth, since these will vary widely between individuals.

Table 17.1 Areas for personal development

Behaviour, will, motivation	What do I avoid or do to excess? What do I want or need to change, e.g. in work and relationships?
Feelings and sensations	What are my most typical, valuable or troublesome feelings and bodily sensations? What changes could I make? How?
Imagery	How aware am I of creative or intrusive images, metaphors, dreams, nightmares? How can I explore, understand and change these?
Cognition	What part does rationality (or irrationality), analysis and intellectual development, play in my life? What changes can I make?
Somatic (bodily) awareness	How aware am I of health issues (diet, nutrition, fitness), the place of sport, dance, appearance, etc.?
Interpersonal	How sociable or solitary am I? Am I satisfied with the quality of my relationships? Do I have 'unfinished business' from childhood or other relationships? Do I want to increase my social skills? How?
Practical-technical	What strengths and problems do I have in negotiating the everyday world? Do I want to change anything? How?
Sexuality	Am I happy with my sex life and sexual orientation? To what extent am I fulfilled? Are there any changes I can make or want to make?
Sociopolitical	How aware and involved am I in 'personal politics'/my local community/macro-politics? Do I want to be more active?
Spiritual-existential	What is my attitude to the 'big questions' of life? Am I engaged in any meditation, prayer, search for meaning, etc.? Do I want to be?
Untapped potential	Have I ignored or downplayed aspects of myself? Do I have 'wasted' musical or other talents? How might I develop these?
Self-esteem	To what extent do I have low self-esteem? Can I accept myself regardless of how much I achieve (or not) of my self-defined aims for personal development?

Trainees' views on the use of journals for personal development

Trainees on our Diploma in Counselling course vary in their approach to writing their journal. A purpose-designed questionnaire on 'Writing related to personal development' was distributed and 17 out of 32 were returned and collated, all from trainees completing a journal as part of the personal development component of the Diploma course. The journals are confidential and the assessment requires a summary of individual learning from a combination of the personal development group experience, themes addressed in maintaining the journal and reading over the year.

When asked for the advantages and disadvantages of writing compared to counselling face-to-face and personal development groups as an effective means towards personal development, interestingly most of the responses echoed those of clients in counselling. Key words used included: time/space, reflection, a means of clarifying thinking, expressing and identifying feelings, confidential, honest, freedom of expression: 'When you write you can be as free as you choose, sometimes it can be painful and that is often easier to deal with in private.' Links were also made with the counselling process: 'Understanding myself and being reflective helps me to be more congruent in counselling and in personal development groups.' Indeed, the individual writing process has been advocated as a method by numerous self-help books (Hay 1984; Bass and Davis 1988; Jeffers 1991), some of which are aligned with particular theoretical orientations, and which propose free writing as well as specific, focused exercises as a means to achieve further self-awareness and self-acceptance. Also, trainees identified writing as a unique means of expression: 'Writing enables me to articulate in a non-vocal way material that I wouldn't dare express in any other way.'

When asked about the benefits of journal writing itself, without comparison to other approaches to personal development, even though some trainees were sceptical to start with, all found great value in it, as demonstrated in the following quotations:

> Seeing them [my feelings] on paper also helps me to understand them.
>
> Looking back and seeing how I've grown.
>
> Insight and understanding.
>
> Reading back all of it was really beneficial, made me realise how busy I am etc.
>
> . . . gives me personal satisfaction, without the need to necessarily prove myself to others by having work published or read by others for approval.
>
> It gives you the chance to have a rational debate with yourself, often enabling you to correctly put issues into focus, perhaps for the first time.

Few disadvantages were identified and these were concerned mainly with the lack of available feedback and challenge, and also with fears around the permanency of the writing: 'I can't take it away or forget what is written.' Difficulties expressed were identified in terms of time, including setting aside sufficient time, and the vulnerability of self-disclosure. For example, 'If someone else were to read my journal they may not understand or be upset by something that I have written which may have been necessary for me to write at that time', and 'opening up so much on paper and putting stuff into words'. Trainees were also worried about losing focus: 'Sometimes I don't have an issue to explore and I waffle about nothing.' Although stream of consciousness works effectively as a format, it is also useful to have the periodic reminder of potential areas for personal development as listed in Table 17.1.

The structure of personal journals

There is some debate about how much structure should be provided. Trainees on the Diploma tended towards preferring a guide rather than a specific format or structure. For example, 'would welcome some ideas'; 'a little would be helpful but very loosely based'; 'I guess it would allow you to focus on more specific things, but I don't really mind because I can usually write about anything'. A specific structure was seen as a definite disadvantage by some: 'I've been put off by writing a journal that has a structure [Egan model]. I found that I was censoring what I wrote. The beauty for me is the fact that it isn't structured, I can write when I want, how I want'; 'Prefer not to have a structure but to produce the journal in my own way'. It becomes clear that trainees need to choose their structure according to individual preferences combined with the theoretical orientation in which they are immersed.

The predominant formats used by trainees on the Diploma course were stream of consciousness, dreams, unsent letters and poems. Also, non-written expression was identified as popular, including doodles and drawing/painting, and reference material in the form of images/pictures. Trainees also referred to specific exercises and reflections on particular aspects of the course and organised these, for example, as a skills log, evaluation or supervision notes. A mixture of formats was common among all trainees: 'I just write how I feel and about significant events in a reflective and creative way'; 'Stream of consciousness and skills log running side by side and learning from experiences'. As an example of a prescribed structure, Progoff (1992) offers a well known Jungian-inspired approach to 'personal renewal' that includes meditation, a daily log, a 'stepping-stones' procedure and dialogue between parts of oneself and aspects of experience. For the purposes of illustration and simplification, Table 17.2 provides some examples of commonly used structures for writing for personal development.

Students are challenged on counselling courses when required to use two different writing styles at the same time: academic and expressive. The academic style is totally new to those without any previous higher education experience, and is often perceived and learned as a completely new and different language: 'Academically we are inclined to a rather pedestrian prose tone as if writing is something to be done only from the loftiest of motives, a kind of distillate of rationalism trickled onto the page' (Cameron 2000: 2). Even graduates and postgraduates often find the process of writing in the mixed academic and personal style required on counselling courses alien and contrary to their previous training. Another required style of writing is the expressive or journal style where trainees are asked to write genuinely for themselves, but simultaneously to meet academic criteria. This seems to be a contradiction and causes some confusion. For example, one trainee noted the

Table 17.2 Methods of personal development involving writing

Narrative	This may involve simple, brief autobiographical sketches or more extensive life histories. It can focus on particular events, life stages or recurring themes.
Stream of consciousness	Writing anything that comes to mind, indifferent to spelling, apparent significance, etc.
Dream recall and associations	It can be useful to keep a regular dream diary. Reflect on your dreams from time to time, seeing if any links and meanings appear for you.
Poetry and creative writing	Regardless of what talent you think you have, writing in poetic or story form can indirectly help you express significant feelings.
Specific, structured exercises	
Letter to oneself	This can be addressed to your 'inner child', 'fearful self' or any other 'sub-personality'. Use photographs as aids.
Unsent letter to others	Try addressing a letter to your mother, father, or anyone significant, whether living or dead, whether they would actually understand and value it or not.
Your own obituary	This can help you focus on your self-image and on what you consider your most important values.
Self-characterisation	Taken from personal construct psychology, this involves writing a description of yourself from the point of view of someone who knows you well.
Dialogue	This can be used creatively, for example in the form of your beautiful self writing to your ugly self, your shy self to your extraverted self, etc.
Best experiences and worst memories	Write as freely and fully as you can about these. A time limit is useful.
Planning diary	Declare your aims for the coming week, month, year or five years and record your progress, setbacks or changed plans.
Hopes and fears	Write about what you most fear and what you most hope for.

difficulty of 'making links with the assignment'. If provided with a series of questions, for example the 'template for a daily journal' suggested by MacMillan and Clark (1998: 76), students may tend to see the journal as being symbiotic with the course but often fail to integrate their reflections and learning into their lives. Goldberg's rules of writing practice (1991: xiv), used and developed by many other authors on creative writing, include a time limit (five to seven minutes) and a theme in the form of a title or unfinished sentence – for example, 'My home', 'I dislike', 'My ideal life'. These have proved popular as a group exercise to get learners started and used to the idea of this rather different style of writing.

There is a particular value in bringing the often solitary experience of journal writing to the group to allow individual approaches and difficulties to be shared and discussed. Sometimes the group can encourage individuals to link their difficulties with their ongoing personal development issues. When we asked our trainees what would help them make more of their personal journal the predominant response related to a) making a regular/focused time to write and b) sharing ideas on progress, the process and structure. Some identified a workshop as a means to do this, others requested further input on creative writing. Sources of inspiration and support were identified by our trainees not only in the form of books (poetry, the Bible; 'self-help, personal growth and fantasy' books), music and art (colour, texture) but also in the form of meditation, walking and relationships.

Conclusions

There are good reasons for promoting the increased use of reflective and therapeutic writing in counselling training. Mackaskill (1999) argues that in the light of a lack of evidence for the effectiveness of personal therapy and groups for trainees, journal keeping could offer an effective and far more economic alternative. Progoff (1992: 13), pioneer of therapeutic journal keeping, takes a radical view:

> The *Intensive Journal* method has been described as a method that is beyond psychotherapy because it take a transpsychological approach to what had been thought of as psychological problems. Here the word *transpsychological* means a process that brings about therapeutic effects not by forcing an individual to passively accept so-called treatment, but by providing active techniques that enable an individual to draw upon his inherent resources to become a whole person.

Given that many trainees are new to higher education, there seems to be some need for relearning the value of writing (MacMillan and Clark 1998; Cameron 2000). There is ample supporting evidence for the cathartic benefits of writing as a means of emotional expression (Dunn *et al.* 1996; Pennebaker 1997). The narrative turn in counselling and psychotherapy suggests that many practitioners are benefiting from working with clients to help them re-author their life stories, scripts and schemas (McLeod 1997). Among the burgeoning of new qualitative research methods favoured by counsellors Richardson (2000) commends the writing process itself as a major research tool. Better links have yet to be made between reflection in personal journals and its impact on trainees' lives and practice. Research is needed to determine the usefulness of personal development writing within training and its sufficiency or otherwise as a therapeutic tool. We believe the time is ripe for therapeutically orientated writing not only to help inform the training process, but to become a part of the new wave of innovative personal development strategies which include time-limited and online counselling. Trainees', counsellors' and clients' highly idiosyncratic learning styles and needs are likely to be better accommodated by such a range of strategies.

References

Bass, E. and Davis, L. (1988) *The Courage to Heal*. London: Cedar.

Cameron, J. (2000) *The Right to Write*. London: Pan.

Dryden, W. (1991) *A Dialogue with John Norcross: Toward Integration*. Buckingham: Open University Press.

Dunn, S., Morrison, B. and Roberts, M. (eds) (1996) *Mind Readings: Writers' Journeys Through Mental States*. London: Minerva.

Goldberg, N. (1991) *Wild Mind*. London: Rider.

Hay, L. (1984) *You Can Heal Your Life*. London: Eden Grove.

Irving, J. and Williams, D. (1999) Personal growth and personal development: concepts clarified, *British Journal of Guidance and Counselling*, 27(4): 517–26.

Jeffers, S. (1991) *Feel the Fear and Do It Anyway*. New York: Arrow.

Johns, H. (1996) *Personal Development in Counsellor Training*. London: Cassell.

Mackaskill, A. (1999) Personal therapy as a training requirement: the lack of supporting evidence, in C. Feltham (ed.) *Controversies in Psychotherapy and Counselling*. London: Sage.

McLeod, J. (1997) *Narrative and Psychotherapy*. London: Sage.

MacMillan, M. and Clark, D. (1998) *Learning and Writing in Counselling*. London: Sage.

Mearns, D. (1997) *Person-Centred Counselling Training*. London: Sage.

Page, S. (1999) *The Shadow and the Counsellor*. London: Routledge.

Pennebaker, J.W. (1997) *Opening Up: The Healing Power of Expressing Emotions*, revised edn. New York: Guilford.

Prochaska, J.O. and DiClemente, C.C. (1986) Toward a comprehensive model of change, in W.R. Miller and N. Heather (eds) *Treating Addictive Behaviors: Processes of Change*, pp. 3–27. New York: Plenum.

Progoff, I. (1992) *At a Journal Workshop*, revised edn. New York: Tarcher/Putnam.

Richardson, L. (2000) Writing: a method of inquiry, in N.K. Denzin and Y.S. Lincoln (eds) *Handbook of Qualititative Research*, 2nd edn, pp. 923–48. Thousand Oaks, CA: Sage.

Wilkins, P. (1997) *Personal and Professional Development for Counsellors*. London: Sage.

Wosket, V. (1999) *The Therapeutic Use of Self: Counselling Practice, Research and Supervision*. London: Routledge.

Chapter 18

The uses of writing in the supervision of cognitive analytic therapy

Anthony Ryle

Introduction

The supervision of psychotherapists is a crucial aspect of training and some continuing access to it is considered valuable by most experienced practitioners and professional associations. There are three main aims in supervision:

1. Seeking to develop the therapist's understanding and application of the model of therapy.
2. Helping the therapist to become aware of, and make use of, their counter-transference reactions.
3. Noting recurrent problems, whether these stem from the therapist's difficulties, from particularly disturbed patients or from unsatisfactory aspects of the model.

This chapter will describe how these functions can be carried out either wholly or partly through written communications and how this allows teaching and supervision to be carried out by email. The retention of written communications between therapist and supervisor is also of value where research into the process or outcome of therapy is undertaken, contributing to the assessment of the therapist's adherence to, and skill in delivering, the model.

Face-to-face supervision and the use of audiotapes

The traditional style of supervision in psychodynamic therapy has been dependent upon the therapist bringing to individual or group supervision a detailed verbal report of a session. This should include a clear summary of the content, describing the episodes, stories and dreams brought by the patient, a detailed account of the mood, style and non-verbal communications of the patient and a description of the therapist's spoken and felt responses during the session. Where the supervisor is skilled and the relationship with the supervisee is such that idiosyncrasies, errors and omissions can be openly acknowledged, this mode of supervision can be a powerful learning experience and can ensure that good therapy is done. But this is not always the case and a number of problems can arise, some due to the relative vagueness of theories, some reflecting the supervisee's wish to present a 'correct' account in terms of the model's orthodoxy and some due to the fact that memory is unreliable, especially as note-taking during sessions is normally discouraged. Moreover, attention and memory are always selective and trainees cannot report what they did not notice. For this reason, accurate, detailed supervision is best achieved by audiotaping. Therapists frequently dislike this, at least until they have tried it. Patients, on the other hand, in the author's experience, are usually happy to have their sessions audiotaped, especially if they are offered the right to listen to the tapes or make their own copies.

Listening to tapes is a basis for therapists' self-supervision and either random or selected transcribed excerpts can be studied in more detail and brought to supervision; selected excerpts may focus on particular phases of the session or on particular topics. In group supervision, copies of the excerpts can be provided for all members to be discussed in the context of the verbal report of the session. Listening to a whole session on audiotape is, of course, most informative but is too time-consuming for routine use. During training, however, therapists may transcribe and comment upon whole sessions, and supervisors may write detailed critiques, especially if the therapy appears stalled or the therapist appears to be failing in some respect.

Supervision of cognitive analytic therapy using writing

Many of the features of the cognitive analytic therapy (CAT) model make reliance on writing in supervision practicable. The model itself has clear guidelines (without being manualised) and involves the extensive use of writing by therapists and patients; such writing can be copied and provides direct evidence of aspects of the interchange. With trainees early in their career, part of the task of supervision is educational, serving to ensure that the model is understood and adhered to; failures in this respect may derive from unfamiliarity but in many instances are a manifestation of unrecognised countertransference.

In CAT there are established rules or conventions guiding therapists' writing. For example, the reformulation letter (described in Chapter 6) should be constructed as follows:

- The letter, when first presented to the patient, should be described as provisional, the possibility of revision after discussion being emphasised.
- The main problems which have led to consultation at this time should be briefly summarised. There is no need to detail the story but its implications and meaning should be simply expressed.
- In most cases memories of childhood will point to experiences which shaped personality and patterns of relationships. These can be simply but provisionally described and should be phrased in ways that do not imply that the memories

are necessarily accurate – for example, by writing 'you told me that you always felt criticised and had to strive hard and achieve to win your parents' love' rather than 'your parents were critical and demanding'.

- The procedures developed in response to this early experience should be described; in most cases they can be explained as having been necessary means of coping rather than as defences.
- The ways in which these coping procedures may manifest themselves in their relationship with the therapist should be indicated.

In addition to reformulation letters, no-send letters, midway letters and goodbye letters (more fully described in Chapter 6) all provide supervisors with direct evidence of how far the formal requirements are observed and of how sensitively the material is presented. Patients' writing can also be copied to the supervisor.

Termination is never easy; the fact that the therapist's draft goodbye letter can be discussed in supervision before being read to the patient means that supervisors can ensure that accurate accounts of what has and has not been achieved are given, rather than bland or over-optimistic ones, and that the patient's actual or potential reactions to termination are named in ways encouraging neither denigration nor idealisation.

Distance supervision

The use of audiotapes and transcripts to supplement face-to-face supervision opened the way to the reliance on such records where meetings between trainers and supervisees were impossible. The demand for training in CAT has grown rapidly and has been met by the setting up of a number of courses in different parts of the UK and abroad, despite which there are many trainees who are out of reach of the existing training sites.

Initially, distance supervision was only offered when supervisees moved away after a period of attachment to a service and when a personal relationship already existed between supervisor and supervisee. Nowadays, if this is impossible distance supervision may be offered even where no prior relationship has been established. In such cases it is essential that the trainee has a basic professional qualification, has read appropriate CAT texts and has attended introductory workshops. There should be a trial period before a definite commitment is made, to ensure that the supervisee can offer adequate reports of sessional events and feelings and that the supervisor is found to provide relevant and useful comments. Such trainees should be working within a professional service which accepts overall clinical responsibility.

The 'microsupervision' of transcripts of parts of sessions, involving the detailed linking of reported events and in-session enactments to the appropriate parts of the reformulation diagram, can reinforce the trainee's assimilation of the model and ensure that the diagram becomes an available, shared part of the therapeutic discourse (e.g. see Ryle 1997: 73–5 and 112–14).

Two illustrations of how issues may be addressed will now be given. The therapists had provided summaries of the weekly sessions and copies of draft letters and diagrams. Details which might identify the trainees or patients have been modified.

Therapist A (female) with a female patient with borderline personality disorder

This example shows how both technical and countertransference issues can be addressed. After reviewing the reports of the first five sessions the supervisor wrote a commentary highlighting the following issues:

- The therapist had paid attention to the accurate naming of affects but had not linked the feelings to the reciprocal role patterns with which they were associated.
- A sequence was observed and clearly described more than once whereby the patient's recognition of a new understanding was followed by a period of confusion and self-criticism, after which she became either blank or hyperactive. This sequence, however, had not been spelled out or described in the letter or the provisional diagram.
- The diagram was over-complicated and was not based on clear sequences or on reciprocal patterns.
- Despite the patient's criticism of past counsellors and despite her failure to complete agreed homework tasks and her late cancellation of two sessions the diagram did not record any negative procedures, notably not referring to the pervasive pattern of passive resistance.
- The therapist had responded to the missed sessions by offering a range of alternative times and had not explored how far fear and hostility to her might be being expressed in this way.
- Faced with this evidence of how transference and countertransference issues were reflected in deficient CAT tools and collusive responses, a simple working reformulation was suggested in terms of two complementary dilemmas, one describing the patient and one the therapist. The patient's dilemma was 'it is as if I am either overwhelmed by fearful exposure or remain out of reach and unhelped' and the therapist's was 'it is as if I must be either amiably collusive or cruelly intrusive'.

Therapist B (male) with a young man with borderline personality disorder

In this example the main emphasis in the supervision of the first four sessions was on the creation and use of an adequate diagram. Four issues were addressed:

- The patient had a history of destroying objects and of physically harming a schoolmate but in the reformulation letter and diagram there was no reference to violence.
- During a session the patient had shown very rapid shifts between contrasting states ('whirlpooling'); it was suggested that, in order to understand these and construct a diagram, it was necessary to take control of the pace of the session so as to allow a detailed analysis of short sequences.
- It was suggested that the therapist needed to explain how the procedures described in the developing diagram offered not only a description of how the patient acted and of how others responded but also of how the diagram represented a 'template' through which he was liable to interpret events in a distorted way.
- Keeping a diary linking episodes of confusion to the emerging diagram was negotiated as a homework task.

The Melbourne study

A systematic experience of distance supervision has been provided by involvement in a randomised controlled study in Melbourne (Australia) assessing the impact of CAT in adolescents considered to have, or to be likely to develop, borderline personality disorder. The project is directed by a psychiatrist, Dr Andrew Chanen, and therapy is provided by three clinical psychologists (Louise McCutcheon, Helen Nistico and Dominic Germano) none of whom had any prior training in CAT but all of whom were experienced clinicians. After two initial five-day workshops, one in Melbourne and one in London, training and supervision of the therapists has been provided by CAT supervisors in the UK (Anthony Ryle, Eva Burns, Dawn Bennett and Jackie Withers).

Each therapist treated one case under supervision before the commencement of the research project. Referral and assessment data, weekly session reports and copies of letters and diagrams were emailed to supervisors and were commented on within a few days. In addition, the therapists met weekly and consulted the supervisors by telephone either as a group or individually.

In addition to the transmission of written accounts of sessions and the copying of documents, therapists were asked to conclude sessions with a four- to five-minute review with the patient of the most important aspects of the meeting. An audio recording of this summary recapitulation was transmitted by email. The intention was that this would offer therapists a chance to repeat, or name for the first time, how reported events or transference enactments might be understood by reference to the diagram. Comments on the sessional reports and ratings of how adequately the end of session recapitulation was done were sent by email before the telephone consultations. Being rated was not very popular with the supervisees, but in the supervisors' opinions it did reveal, initially, significant problems in making such links. In addition, the audio excerpts provided supervisors with a sample of the tone and style (and accents!) of both therapists and patients.

To give some impression of the scope of this emailed supervision, the topics covered in a sequence of supervision emails to the three therapists towards the end of the first year are listed below. Details are altered in all cases. Earlier in the project more attention was paid to the 'technical' CAT procedures, notably letter writing and the construction of diagrams. As these skills were consolidated and as the email relationship developed, transference-countertransference themes got more attention.

Supervision themes

The following examples provide a sense of the range of themes taken up in supervision:

- the need to clarify management and therapy roles where the structure of the service involved some overlap of functions;
- the need to revise a draft reformulation letter of a borderline patient who constantly accepted exploitation and use from others, in order to point more clearly to her active contribution to these experiences;
- the need to be cautious in the face of a patient's blissfully optimistic response to the early sessions by spelling out her idealisation and referring to the anticipated disappointment;
- faced with a patient alternating between quiet compliance and increasingly severe self-poisoning, the need to clearly name his despair but to focus on his anxiety-provoking and controlling behaviour and to liaise with other involved agencies;
- suggesting that 'despair' or 'emptiness' were more appropriate descriptions than 'depression' in a borderline adolescent;
- noting with approval how the patient's very positive mood at a pre-termination session (which had been shared by the therapist) had been acknowledged and related to real changes but had also been questioned because of the absence of any report or anticipation of doubt or disappointment;
- noting how the draft diagram of a patient with a history of out-of-control anger failed to include this and linking this omission to a previously identified countertransference tendency in the therapist;
- suggesting that the phrase 'struggled with dysthymia' in a draft reformulation letter should be amended using direct, non-professional language;
- proposing that attempting to construct a diagram was premature; the first need was to complete the assessment and the reformulation letter in order to clarify the relation of two major abandonments at different ages to the patient's current procedural problems.

Conclusion

The CAT model, because of the use of writing by patients and therapists, has advantages over most therapy models when it comes to distance supervision. In particular, therapists' reformulation and goodbye letters and diagrams provide direct evidence of how far the formal requirements are observed and of how accurately and sensitively the results of the patient's and therapist's joint work are recorded.

The value of supervisors writing to trainees parallels the value of therapists writing to patients; in particular, the written word is usually more considered and more precise than the spoken and it is available for repeated reading. This is important, as the comments made by supervisors are, inevitably, largely focused on technical failures or on unrecognised countertransference and as such can be difficult to hear and assimilate.

There is, of course, a place for acknowledging or praising good work and the ability to report on the emotional impact of the relationship. Trainees who have had little prior experience of working with transference and countertransference can find it difficult to recognise the power of the therapy relationship for both the patient and themselves.

It is obviously easier to achieve a good working relationship between supervisors and trainees on the basis of direct contact, but as long as trainees have good basic clinical skills and an open relationship can be established, supervision depending on writing has some advantages and relatively small losses. Through it, geographically distant trainees can be satisfactorily taught and supervised.

References

Ryle, A. (1997) *Cognitive Analytic Therapy and Borderline Personality Disorder: The Model and the Method.* Chichester: Wiley.

Chapter 19

Black and blue: writing for reflective practice

Gillie Bolton, Heather Allan and Helen Drucquer

> Reflective practice is key to the meaningfulness of therapeutic endeavour.
>
> (O'Loughlin 2002)

Introduction

This chapter examines the use of expressive and explorative writing for reflective practice for professional and personal development. It draws upon my own (Gillie Bolton) experience running groups for therapists, counsellors, clinical psychologists and other clinicians. It also draws upon practising psychotherapists Heather Allan and Helen Drucquer's experience of using writing for their own reflections upon practice. The processes of writing, and making reflective use of that writing, are examined, and examples of writing and their effect are given.

Reflective practice writing

A reflective practitioner examines their practice, and their approach to practice, using their full range of critical, affective, spiritual, practical and knowledge-based faculties. Using reflective practice writing effectively is even better than driving with all-round vision. Big shiny rear and wing mirrors, a well-washed windscreen and rear window are all working for you to enable all-round vision. You can angle the rear-view mirror to see the children on the rear seat when you stop at traffic lights, or towards your face to take the eyelash out of your eye. But using writing within reflective practice adds an extra dimension – that of being able to apprehend what another road user might do before they do it, and what your own instinctive reaction is likely to be.

Reflective practice

Reflection upon action was a process identified by Schon (1983): a process of deeply considering events afterwards in order effectively to enhance practice. Critical reflection upon situations of unfamiliarity and complexity is a vital component of professional practice. It can enable the:

- sensitive, fruitful review of 'forgotten' areas of practice;
- critical study of personal decision-making processes;
- constructive awareness of relationships with fellow professionals;
- analysis of hesitations, skill and knowledge gaps;
- relief of stress by the facing of problematic or painful episodes;
- identification of learning needs;
- dissemination of experience and expertise to colleagues;
- increase of confidence in professional practice.

The reflective practice process described here is an open questioning approach, one which will raise questions rather than simple answers. A prerequisite is the willingness to lay one's own practice and understandings open to question: a willingness to 'risk abandoning previous "truths" and sit with *not knowing*' (Gerber 1994: 290, original emphasis). Practice is like therapy: there are no simple answers. In order for it to be effective the reflective practitioner needs to be open to uncertainty:

> The goal of education, if we are to survive, is the *facilitation of change and learning*. The only person who is educated is the person who has learned how to learn: the person who has learned how to adapt and change; the person who has realised that no knowledge is secure, that only the process of seeking knowledge gives a basis for security. Changingness, a reliance on process rather than on static knowledge is the only thing that makes any sense as a goal for education in the modern world.
>
> (Rogers 1969: 152, original emphasis)

Reflective practice has been much written about. Many diagrams and stages have been identified in an effort to help the practitioner to reflect (e.g. van Manen 1995 reporting Dewey's five steps; Morrison's 1996 four-stage process developed from Habermas; Tripp's 1995 lists; Johns' 1995 development of Carper's four ways of knowing; Kolb's 1984 learning cycle; and Mezirow's 1981 levels).

Reflection is a natural process; it needs to be carefully facilitated and supported. Programmed methods can be disrespectful of the practitioner and can result in mere box ticking or rote exercise-doing. In a properly facilitated forum, where effective processes are used, experienced practitioners and students naturally reach deep levels, work their way round and round cycles, and up steps, and could tick off all items in a list if it was not a waste of time to do so. If practitioners are respected, treated with unconditional positive regard (Rogers 1969) by supervisor or tutor, and guided towards listening to, and rewriting their own stories (and of course within them the stories of their clients), they will reflect effectively and fruitfully.

The reflective writing process

Creative writing processes, used within reflective practice, enable practitioners to express whatever needs expressing graphically, clearly, concisely and readily. They also enable in-depth exploration of areas of experience to which it might otherwise be difficult to gain access. Accounts are written, drawing upon the experience of practitioners; these can occasionally skim the surface of experiences, offering little insight, but then the group or supervisor can sensitively support the writer to go back to the writing and extend and develop it.

This silent reflective writing process, in which the writer is communicating initially solely with themselves, is perhaps similar to the *internal supervisor* recommended by Casement (1990).

The initial creative process of writing is an aesthetic-synthetic one rather than being logical and analytic. This is the 'artistry' Schon (1983) said reflection upon practice required. Reflective practice writing is not a process of thinking reflectively about issues within practice and then using writing to record those thoughts, but of consciously *not* thinking, while allowing the writing hand to express and explore that which needs expressing and exploring. It is more akin to image-making in painting or drawing than to intellectual thought.

Writing is useful for stress management, helping to avoid burnout and lowered performance: 'Writing is a disinhibition strategy, as it anchors people to a safe present while they re-experience a past event, providing optimum distance possibilities and hence cathartic reset' (Evison 2001: 256).

This initial writing stage is followed by a more cognitive process of reading and redrafting the writing to make sure it covers as much range as possible. Reflective practice writers need to ensure they've covered what they *did*, what they *thought* and what they *felt*. There follows the stage of reading the writing aloud to peers in a trusted, carefully facilitated forum. The audience are using artistry in their response. Here is Rose Flint, an art therapist and poet, who uses poetry writing in her reflective practice:

> I try to reach a place of creative introspection and response in which to write or draw as freely as possible how I experienced the session on an inner level. I do this for both the patients and for myself, perhaps in the spirit of *physician, heal thyself*. It not only gives me a deeper insight into the patient's experience but it provides me with space where I can let go of any projection that I have picked up that does not belong to me. It helps me to separate from the often disturbing content of a session and it enables my search for meaning to go deeper, as I understand more of that which affected me in the session. The making of a poem or picture clarifies the counter-transference and I can then use that as a mirror to reflect back to the process that the patient or group was engaged in. And most importantly I can allow my emotions, my creativity, my deep self to be present to witness the mystery and not-knowing of the metaphoric level . . . When I engage in the process of creative introspection, I

> often find a deep sense of beauty, of something numinous, held at the centre of the session, something utterly human yet transcendent . . . In this indwelling reflective place, there is a task of retrieval of experiences, metaphors and images, which is akin to the shamanic journey made to affect a soul-healing. The use of and familiarity with the power of imagery and metaphor has always linked poets and artists to healers.
>
> (Flint 2002: vi, original emphasis)

Helen Drucquer reflects upon her reflections:

From the same source

Exposed.
Feel windswept, wordsnatched.
Words rise from the same source
But stutter out
through fingers, pen.

Reading them later
with GPs, Gillie:
gagging on them.
I gasp inside to hear myself:
intimate consulting room words:
reworked for all of us
from the same source
as the pen
and re-spoken : thrice worked!

Twenty-seven years writing.
'Notes'. Psychotherapy notes.
Case notes. My God.
I'll tell you why.
NOTES WORK.
The word, this one now in black or blue
on white
from the same source
re-does the work, till black and blue
creates and recreates
spins new webs of insight.

Bad news!
Courts like them!
Protocols, proceedings,
Implications!
Facts only!
No opinions without reason!

Reason? Nice and tidy. Example:
'She reports that she vomited.'
Not, 'sicking up the vile bilious stuff of force fed
foul centuries old
fear and only way anger
to say NO.'

No. No more notes.
Too careful, fearful even.
My forcefed protocol sits
Lumpen in my throat, on my pen.

But here you see it.
Unreasonable; on the page.
Nervous notes, tumbling honestly
all from the same source.

Helen Drucquer

A reflective practice writing group

Helen Drucquer is a therapist in a general practice health centre. She belongs to one of my primary care reflective practice writing for professional development groups. The above poem reflects upon her experience of writing for the group, and sharing that writing with us.

Nine primary care practitioners (most of the others are GPs) attend the group to which Helen belongs, once a month. They each bring and read to the group a piece of writing – a story, poem or reflective passage – which expresses and explores an area of current concern. A discussion follows each piece of writing: supportively drawing out whatever issues seem to be relevant to the writer. These might involve particular patients, relationships with colleagues, relationships with higher authorities or more personal issues with a bearing on clinical practice. The group members offer their own ideas, making connections to other areas of experience in an intense and lively discussion. As well as knowledge and skills, they are also not afraid to touch upon feelings, spiritual values and personal territories where appropriate.

Group members then return to their work with fresh insight, supportive advice from colleagues, a sense they are not the only ones struggling with certain issues, and, perhaps most importantly, deeper levels of understanding and wider perceptions with which to practise. The ways in which these affect practice are then brought back to the group to be discussed and reflected upon further. This is a process of reflection being a way of working life, rather than an exercise undertaken for a course.

Members of the group have said that the process offers help with the often unfinished and seemingly unsustainable nature of their work. They also appreciate its creativity as a form of exploration and expression. This kind of writing takes them by surprise: it tells them what it wants to be and do, and it tells them what areas of their experience they will explore. One group member said: 'things come out because the story lets them out'. Another, who had just discovered poetry writing, said: 'I like poetry because I can't make it do what I want. It has to do what it wants.' And another: 'this writing enabled me to find what I had never lost but didn't know was there'.

A group of clinical psychologists from a different group commented how 'time efficient' the process is, and that 'unconscious links are made conscious on the page'. They also found reflective writing 'physically exhausting' and very 'affective' as well as 'effective'.

Reflective practice writing: an example by Helen Drucquer

Christine wrote a letter.
Dear God, let me slip away.
I am ready to go.
People up there, dear God,
will they love me for myself?
Grant courage, God, to end it;
I have nothing left.

Will they love me for myself up there?
Not what I could give?
I have only lived to give.
I have nothing left.

I laid his clothes out
I ran his bath,
put toothpaste on the brush;
cleaned, cooked, cared, controlled.
I ask you, now, God,
Let me leave this world.

I have nothing left.
Are you ready for me?
Will they love me for myself?
Help me, God. Help me, Helen,
I have nothing left.

Will they love me, God?
I am all alone.
Please love the kids for me.
I brought them up alone:
one day they'll understand.

I need to flee from home;
it's no longer mine.

I have nothing left.
Have you room for me?

I have nothing.
No one cares for me.
Give me space.
Let me home.
I can't go out.
I tremble, pant.
I can't meet,
I choke
choke
heart bangs.
Let me out,
let me home.
Let me out
let me home.
I have nothing left.

I brought them up alone,
I'm crying, God, at last.
Last week, Mum said, 'You? Ill?
You've others to look after.'

I can't believe she said it.
I have nothing left.
I want to be alone.
I'm looking now for love.

Dear God, dear Helen, doctor,
let me slip away.
Please love me for myself.
Let me out
let me in
let me out
let me home.
I am desperate alone
Your disciple, Chris

Fairly early on in therapy, Christine wrote a letter beginning 'Dear God', and ending, 'Your desperate disciple'. She felt it was the best way to convey her desperation to me and she was right. She doesn't feel the need to mention it in the letter but she had been attacked at work and her whole world came tumbling down. She became severely agoraphobic and suicidal. Her children were around 20 and she had brought them up alone for the past 12 or so years.

For our homework for Gillie's group we had to write on 'love' or 'home'. I sat with Christine's letter in front of me and started to write it again, feeling my way into her skin. Some of the words are hers and some mine and they become more and more interchangeable as the poem goes on. By the end I was in tears, really feeling how she had come to the end of all that giving. Would anyone ever love her for herself, not for what she could do for others? She could only feel safe at home, away from others, but at the same time she felt suffocated by her new imprisonment. There was nowhere to turn, except to a God she didn't even know if she believed in and then only in the hope that He would take her out of life.

When I read my poem to the group, we sat in silence and I had the same feeling I had when Christine had shown her letter to me: emptiness; where on earth do we go from here; let me in, let me out! No one tried to offer any solutions which was a blessed relief. We just sat and then we talked a bit about what it is like to feel at the end of the line. I had seen this flicker over people's faces as I finished reading, just as Christine must have seen it flicker over mine. No one is trying to be a clever clinician. Through the writing we find the place which touches something that happened on that day in that clinical moment and in recreating it we create something new. And there's no doubt that I take that 'something' back into the surgery.

Looking back at the poem after several months, I am still intrigued that the two parallel themes of *home* and *love* are intertwined. I had never thought they were until I started letting the letter write itself through my pen rather than hers. She has not done any since, but I have only just realised that it is Christine who has initiated a poetry wall in the group room at the practice, where patients are free to come and add something which is meaningful to them. It's getting rather full.

This is *such* useful work for me.

How to start writing

The initial write is a brief six-minute dash with no subject, no thinking, no pausing – free-flow writing. The aim is to allow the writing hand to record whatever flows in and out of the mind as it happens. The writer must say to themselves that this writing is not for sharing with anyone: the thought of a reader other than themselves might well inhibit the free flow as it can seem utter rubbish, or deeply personal. The six-minute write has three functions: to begin to mark that blank, white page (always a bit scary to any writer: where do I start?); to note down issues which need to be pushed out of the mind for the time being (e.g. what on earth can I buy Joe for Christmas *this* year?); to capture essential ideas and images otherwise lost. Here is Helen Drucquer (musing in an email):

> I always do my six minutes, but then I screw it up and throw it away without reading it. I realised when you said you should read it through that while I am doing my six minutes, which is complete and utter garbage and can even include a shoppping list, weird exclamations and verbal tics, I also have another current slowly going along in my mind which is deciding what to write about in the next bit of writing and then I sit at the end of the six minutes and think,

> oh THAT is what I am supposed to do. Sometimes I don't want to do it and I try to do something different but it is the thing that has appeared in the six minutes that is very insistent and demands to be written.

Then the writer focuses upon a single event or incident, writing a story with as many details as come to mind; abstract ramblings (such as 'how I learn things', 'the nature of gifts and gift giving', 'the kind of people who are important to me') may seem easier to write, but offer far less insight. This *showing* the reader an incident, rather than *telling* the emotions or feelings is also a keystone of literary writing.

Recreating in writing enables a mental recreation of the event, which in turn can offer new depths of insight into the experience. Helen Drucquer expresses this succinctly: 'This word / this one now in black or blue on white / from the same source / re-does the work, till black and blue / creates and recreates / spins new webs of insight.' The play on 'black or blue on white' (ink on the page) and 'black and blue' (bruising) is particularly effective.

The next stage is for the writer to reread and reflect upon their writing to prepare themselves to share it with colleagues or a supervisor. They might then develop the writing: redrafting it to fit even more closely with their own experience: adding in forgotten sections; rounding out the description with smells, tactile observations, precise sounds. Details can affect the significance of an account (just how did she carry herself as she walked into the room; what were the precise words he shouted; what was that expression in her eyes?), just as detail is vital in building up suspense in a well-written thriller, or unravelling a complex therapeutic situation.

Reading to other(s) and reflecting with them upon the writing can develop writers' understandings in a closed, confidential, carefully facilitated forum. This stage is often critical and analytic as well as creative: helping the writer to think upwards, outwards and more deeply from the event or problem upon which they initially focused. Group members, or a supervisor, might offer clinical, legal, professional (from a different knowledge, skills, and experience base to the writer) or personal advice and support.

Experiences of writing

Reflective practice, using this creative writing process, can potentially draw upon all areas and levels of experience, knowledge and skills. It can offer contact with vital elements of practice most needing to be reflected upon. It is often just these areas to which the thinking mind does not offer ready access – perhaps because they are difficult, painful or personally problematic; but they can be available to the creating pen or pencil (as they might also be to the paintbrush). After the deep quiet which the whisper of pens and pencils across pages and the silent rereading to the self engenders in a group however large, I'll ask: 'What did that writing feel like? How did it feel to reread to yourself what you have just written?' And people reply: 'It's taken me by surprise: I don't know where this has come from, I certainly didn't think I was going to focus upon that.' What has been forgotten, or not thought about, is likely to be central to understanding, such is our self-protective instinct; and writing can be a doorway to it.

Many therapists, counsellors or clinical psychologists in my groups also often write about a very much remembered and thought about pressing problem or dilemma, which they have found unshareable or difficult to share. The writing process can open up not just memories, thoughts and experiences which have been forgotten, but also ways of sharing hitherto unshareable areas.

The reflective practice writer therefore needs to be able to embrace that uncertainty which is central to all effective therapeutic and educational processes. People have no idea before they start what they are going to write – like Bilbo in Tolkien's *The Hobbit*, putting one foot in front of the other when he set out, not knowing where his adventure would lead him. I have often been asked how I can introduce people to such a dangerous process: what if material comes up with which the writer is unable to cope? 'It could be like opening a can of worms' is what they often say. Well, how do we dare step out of our front door in the morning, when life is so dangerous; or face deeply troubled clients with the potential to set off all sorts of countertransferences? We have to have faith in our own strength and capabilities. Also, if we work with clients we have to have the courage to tackle any issues which bother us, or which hold us up in our explorations with them.

But although this kind of writing can bring one face to face with oneself, it is a kind, gentle and knowing process. We are not used to trusting our bodies (our writing hands); we are not used to trusting our creative selves. But they are entirely trustworthy. This is how poets and playwrights have been writing for thousands of years, and novelists and story writers since there have been such forms. It is only a borrowing of their methods; our society would be impoverished indeed if it wasn't for these artists' willingness to enter such 'dangerous waters'. I use the metaphor of water as it is one many writers I have worked with over the years have used: 'it's like coming up for air'; 'it's like coming to the shore after a long refreshing swim'; 'it's like I feel after a long dreamy bath'.

Participants do need to have the courage to be willing to share vital elements of their reflection with peers. Practitioners often report how the processes of writing, and rereading it silently to the self, offer insight and affect, but that interaction with the other participants in a carefully facilitated forum greatly increases the depth of the reflection.

At a recent day course, one therapist wrote about a childhood bereavement which had clearly had a massive impact upon his life. The writing was clear, full of meaning and depth. The small group sat stunned after hearing it: it was so beautiful – a privilege to hear. And it was clearly of such enormous value to the writer to write. Every therapist has bereaved clients; coming to terms with one's own losses is essential to being able to support and help others (see also Bolton 2001: 17–19).

The writer said he could never have intended to write about that subject, and in fact wouldn't have done so, if I hadn't forgotten to mention before they wrote that I would be asking them if they would like to read their writing out to their small group of six. I was on poor form, my daughter in hospital and my mother having just died. He had felt secure in the privacy the paper and pen offered him. But he did choose to read it, despite my clearly saying that we'd all understand if anyone said their writing was too personal to share (it is always important to stress this, even when I have remembered to inform them of the reading and sharing stage). The hearing of another's writing can feel like a privilege and is a deeply informative window onto the experience of others – it can set off fruitful trains of thinking into one's own experience.

Reflective practice writing: other experiences

Bennett-Levy *et al.* (2003: 145) found that trainee cognitive therapists reported a 'deeper sense of knowing' of cognitive therapy (CT) practices as a result of a form of reflective practice using writing. The process involves 'self-practice/self reflection: SP/SR', in which:

> trainees practise CT techniques on themselves (SP), either from workbooks on their own, or they do 'co-therapy' with a training partner. Then they reflect in writing on the sessions (SR), looking at the implications for themselves, for their clients, and for cognitive theory

Bennett-Levy found that the written reflections were crucial, enabling in-depth work.

Bennett-Levy quotes Skovholt, who has undertaken considerable research into therapist development, as saying: 'A therapist and a counsellor can have twenty years of experience or one year of experience twenty times. What makes the difference? A key component is reflection' (Skovholt *et al.* 1997: 365).

Davidson (1999: 120) reports using a reflective writing approach to support and develop his practice within an eating disorders unit:

> Through reflection and writing, we can struggle to get a conceptual grip on the situation. With a leap of faith we can open ourselves to honestly experiencing what is going on in our relationships. Even if the resultant understanding and experience is partial, it should yield a point of leverage where something that we can *do* is revealed. And if it transpires that what we do does not have the desired result, then at least we have new information with which to enhance our experience and aid further reflection.

Gerber has used writing to help him understand and come to terms with his psychotherapeutic work with South-East Asian refugee patients (Gerber 1994, 1996).

Reflective journals are often used. Best (1996: 298) stresses the value of a journal 'as a process of integration'; for *containment*, and *therapeutic space*: it is a safe place to put experiences and emotions, however bad. These can then be reviewed more safely at a later date: the material will have remained the same on the page in the interval, but the writer will have moved on and be able to reassess the situation, their feelings and thoughts about it. She also calls it a *play space*: 'space to explore and confirm'.

Writing: why and how

This privacy is one of the reasons that writing works. The primary interlocutor to a piece of writing is the writer themselves. They can decide if they will share it with another, and who that listener should be; they can even choose to throw it away unread. They can keep it unread and unshared for as long as they like before reading or sharing. The therapist who wrote privately about his childhood bereavement could have taken it home, and read it to a relative, friend or supervisor later. If he did, I'm glad he shared it with us first.

Reflective writers need to trust the writing process. In a group setting a facilitator is fairly readily given that trust if they show themselves to be competent, authoritative and experienced. So the therapists and counsellors who attend my courses learn the easy way really – from me at first hand. It is more difficult for people to begin to do it from reading about it. But follow the suggestions below and have a go: trusting the process and having faith in yourself.

We've looked at two prerequisites for successful reflective practice writing: trust in the process and faith in oneself. The third is love. It is a loving, gentle, giving process. Therapists and clinical psychologists have remarked how *self-indulgent* it feels to allow themselves to *write without inhibitions – for themselves*. They never usually do this in a professional setting. It had never occurred to them that this might be a way into effective reflective practice. It is like a gift. If we don't love and endeavour to understand ourselves, how can we lovingly support our clients? It is also a gift in that each piece of writing belongs to, and expresses and develops its writer. So much of therapy and counselling is giving to others.

Davidson (1999: 122) comments on how, when introducing colleagues to reflective writing, people 'say how it helped their writing to know it was acceptable to write in forms of their own creation, and as a way of expressing their experience. The norm seems more often a feeling of intimidation at the prospect of using a foreign tool with stuffy rules.'

And it's enjoyable. In the groups I run we laugh quite a lot, as well as cry. And people feel enriched by having created, and by being involved in the creativity of others.

How to start

- Only 20–30 minutes is needed to do a useful piece of writing: if much longer is set aside, much of it will be wasted in fiddling about without starting to write.
- You will write the right thing, no matter what you write; you can't write the wrong thing.

- Write without thinking: let the writing hand take charge.
- Forget all the rules of grammar, structure, form and spelling ever learned. If these do need sorting out before the writing is shared, it's easily done later.
- First write whatever comes into your head for six minutes without stopping, and without thinking. There is no theme or subject for this stage: the aim is to capture those images which flash in and out of the mind with little or no attention paid to them. This might come out like lists, scattered bits and bobs, or even be fairly incomprehensible.
- Now take a theme, such as: *a time I learned something vital*; *a gift*; *someone who was very important to me*. Tell a story or write a poem about *a time when* . . . Write for about 20 minutes or more.
- Read it all through silently (including the six-minute scribble). Improve upon the content if that seems right, but give no thought to grammar, construction or spelling yet. Look out for useful connections between the six minutes and the longer writing.
- Share it with another, if and when that seems right.
- Now this is an exciting stage, if you venture this far: write a fictional story or poem which complements the original one. Write in the voice of the person at the centre of the original account: the patient, the colleague or the relative. Or rewrite giving the account a satisfactory ending instead of a horrid one, or switching the gender of the main characters. Or write in another genre: Mills & Boon, thriller, detective, fantasy . . . There are as many different ways to write another story or poem as there are writers: experiment, have fun. This is a very instructive stage.

Reflective practice writing: an example

Heather Allan is a therapist who has been very involved in the use of the arts in therapy. Here she contributes an experience of using writing to enable her to reflect effectively upon her practice. She is not primarily a poet or creative writer, any more than Helen Drucquer is; she uses writing creatively in her practice and in her reflection upon it.

On a Mountain at Night: Heather Allan

I found this poem by chance, in a folder from 1977. I had completely forgotten it, yet when I read it the whole situation immediately came to mind. It interests me partly because I write hardly any poems and yet I wrote a poem about this. Why? At that time I had no involvement in psychoanalysis; nor any therapeutic role with the young woman who recounted the incident.

But I understand the writing of this poem, and remember it as a quite spontaneous attempt to contain my confusion about something my student told me, so I could reflect upon its meaning for her, and the meaning of her communication with me.

I was a young college tutor; she was a student I was fond of, whose boyfriend did this, in Switzerland. It was the quality of the young girl's telling me which so affected me. I felt it was much more than gossip: a mixture of bravado and fear. Who was feeling the doing of this, in her recounting the incident? I felt drawn into this emotional confusion, and I wrote the poem to clarify, separate and offer space for the emotional meaning to be shared between us. The girl was scared, but she sounded boastful.

Fragments of well-known words (such as from Shakespeare), nursery rhymes and the writing form are my attempt to put this grotesque incident into the containment of my own culture and knowledge. That's partly what a therapist does. The girl and I could then think about what the incident might signify (other than you shouldn't do drugs on a mountain at night!). I was interested to read the somatised object relations expressed in the poem, before I had any formal knowledge of the theory.

On a mountain at night
in the snow a young man high
on hallucinogens pushes his hand
into his mouth and forces his arm
down his throat up to here
as if trying to ingest his own body.
Because what is inside cannot come out
he tries to put what is outside in;
because his gut is full of emptiness
a hollow passage seeping fear
he tries to absorb the familiarity
of his own flesh,
the reassurance of his own known skin.
Like an infant grasps the world
in his mouth;

the lover needs to know the Other
in the hot clasp of the cunt.
And alone and cold
on the bare mountain poor Tom
puts in his thumb
and sucks himself to sleep.

Conclusion

Reflection is essential for effective practice. A clinician needs to be able to reconstruct a situation (whether clinical, or an event with colleagues, or one which does not at first sight seem to relate to the professional). A purely critical, rational, analytic approach will only access some of the experiences which need to be examined, and will only examine part of them. This is because the more tricky areas of our experience, those which are perhaps the most troubling, or the most difficult for us to sort out, are hidden from our immediate critical, rational analytic processes.

This parallels the experience of our clients. They need the help of therapists, counsellors or psychologists to reflect upon their experience in order to understand it and relate more effectively and happily to themselves and the world. They might also indeed need the help of the arts, such as in art or writing therapy. Clinicians also need help to reflect upon their experience; this can be offered by supervisors and peers. Expressive and explorative writing is a time-efficient, cheap and effective method which can be accessed at any time.

References

Bennett-Levy, J., Lee, N., Travers, K., Pohlman, S. and Hamesnik, E. (2003) Cognitive therapy from the inside: enhancing therapist skills through practising what we preach, *Behavioural and Cognitive Psychotherapy*, 31: 143–58.

Best, D. (1996) On the experience of keeping a therapeutic journal while training, *Therapeutic Communities*, 17(4): 293–301.

Bolton, G. (2001) *Reflective Practice Writing for Professional Development*. London: Sage.

Casement, P. (1990) *Further Learning from the Patient*. London: Tavistock/Routledge.

Davidson, B. (1999) Writing as a tool of reflective practice, *Group Analysis*, 32(1): 109–24.

Evison, R. (2001) Helping individuals manage emotional responses, in R.L. Payne and C.L. Cooper (eds) *Emotions at Work: Theory, Research, and Applications in Management*, pp. 241–68. Chichester: Wiley.

Flint, R. (2002) Fragile space: therapeutic relationship and the word, *Writing in Education*, 26: ii–viii.

Gerber, L. (1994) Psychotherapy with southeast Asian refugees: implications for treatment of western patients, *American Journal of Psychotherapy*, 48(2): 280–93.

Gerber, L. (1996) We must hear each other's cry: lessons from Pol Pot survivors, in C. Strozier and F. Flynn (eds) *Genocide, War, and Human Survival*, pp. 297–305. New York: Rowman & Littlefield.

Johns, C. (1995) Framing learning through reflection within Carper's fundamental ways of knowing in nursing, *Journal of Advanced Nursing*, 22: 222–34.

Kolb, D.A. (1984) *Experiential Learning*. London: Prentice Hall.

Mezirow, J. (1981) A critical theory of adult learning and education, *Adult Education*, 32(1): 3–24.

Morrison, K. (1996) Developing reflective practice in higher degree students through a learning journal, *Studies in Higher Education*, 21(3): 317–31.

O'Loughlin, S. (2002) Attending to the patient within us. Presentation to Warwick University Department of Clinical Psychology Conference: Reflective Practice.

Rogers, C. (1969) *Freedom to Learn: A View of what Education might Become*. Columbus, OH: Charles E. Merrill.

Schon, D.A. (1983) *The Reflective Practitioner: How Professionals think in Action*. New York: Basic Books.

Skovholt, T.M., Ronnestad, M.H. and Jennings, L. (1997) The search for expertise in counselling, psychotherapy and professional psychology, *Educational Psychology Review*, 9: 361–9.
Tripp, D. (1995) *Critical Incidents in Teaching*. London: Routledge.
van Manen, M. (1995) On the epistemology of reflective practice, *Teachers and Teaching: Theory and Practice*, 1(1): 33–49.

Chapter 20

After the session: 'freewriting' in response

John Hilsdon

Introduction: session notes – neglected terrain?

'After a client has left,' Sue told me, 'I have fifteen minutes before the next one – just enough time for a drink, and a chance to scribble some notes.' Sue is one of nine counsellors I talked to during 2001 and 2002 about the topic of making session notes. The group, although small, have a broad variety of theoretical orientations and working practices. The majority reported experiences similar to Sue's: they rarely have more than 15 minutes between clients, and less in some cases. All write at least something after each session, albeit just rough notes or *aides-mémoire* for when they record the session later. They all emphasised the importance they attach to session notes, though the purposes of their notes can vary according to their method of working.

All respondents were trained to at least diploma level and the descriptions they gave of their approaches to the work included person-centred, integrative, existential, humanistic and psychodynamic methods. A striking similarity among them was the comment that their counselling training had not included much – or, in some cases, *any* – explicit content concerning the theory or practice of making notes in response to client sessions. (The exception was a colleague trained as a psychodynamic psychotherapist.)

A review of the growing body of literature on counselling in the UK also yielded little on this topic – although recent concerns about legal and ethical issues have resulted in the production of some helpful material by the British Association for Counselling and Psychotherapy (BACP) (BACP 2002; Coldridge 2003). At the time of writing, however, I found little other than an article on creative uses of notes (Smith 2001), and a short section in a book about starting a counselling practice (McMahon 1994). Like Smith, I found that the major text books designed for trainee or novice counsellors contained scant advice about writing or using session notes – often relating only to first session history-taking. For example: 'So long as it neither becomes too intrusive nor has a negative impact on the client, note taking may be helpful for remembering details of the client'. (Nelson-Jones 1982: 284).

For readers thinking about this area for the first time, I have listed some questions below to indicate the range of issues implied – including legal and ethical issues.

Awareness of relevant legislation and ethical integrity in practice are clearly crucial – and I wish to emphasise that in considering use of any of the ideas in this chapter, readers should make sure that their own approaches conform to both the Data Protection and Human Rights Acts (Jenkins 1997; Bond 1999), and the BACP's own *Ethical Framework* (2002).

In exploring the subject of note-making, the following questions need our attention:

- Is it (always) necessary to make session notes?
- For whom? Who owns them? Client, counsellor or both (ethical and legal connotations of ownership are equally implied here).
- For what reasons, other than recording personal data such as address, age, name of GP, relevant medical history, etc. do counsellors make notes – and how might they use them?
- How do different note-making strategies link to the orientation and theoretical approach of the counsellor or therapist?
- What about the use of diagrams, doodles, sketches or other symbolic material in notes? (I usually draw a genogram – a diagram of family structures – in the first session, and have a number of shorthand devices, developed over time. One of my respondents uses different coloured pens to represent information of different types.)
- How long should be spent on notes, given limited time?
- How long after the session is the ideal time to write?
- What do we actually write in our notes and how do we select material? What gets left out?

Of these, it is the last three – and especially the last – which are addressed directly by this chapter.

Introducing freewriting

This is a brief account of the technique. My version of freewriting is largely borrowed from the work of Peter Elbow (1998), whose book *Writing Without Teachers* was designed for general educational contexts. Elbow uses the term to mean setting pen to paper, or fingers to keyboard, for a specific, timed period, in response to a stimulus 'trigger' word or phrase. The writer follows a set of guidelines designed to capture thoughts and ideas exactly *as they come to mind*, with no conscious 'censorship' or selection; no revision, correction or editing. For example:

- determine a 'trigger' word or phrase;
- set a time limit (e.g. three or five minutes);
- write whatever comes to mind without stopping, censoring, judging or thinking about it; don't worry about grammar, spelling or style;
- if your mind goes blank, write the trigger phrase – again and again, until ideas arrive;

- don't stop until the time is up;
- don't go back to edit, 'correct' or change anything.

For some few years now, I have used this exercise with university students in various subjects as part of experiential essay-writing workshops (Hilsdon 2002). Participants report that freewriting helps 'getting started', coping with feeling 'blocked' and avoiding procrastination. Many say it also assists in planning and thinking through subject matter and 'brings up' relevant issues that were not previously in conscious awareness. Significant improvements appear in the quality and depth of argument in the finished essays.

'Journalling', story composition and other forms of writing have also been suggested as therapeutic tools for clients: see elsewhere in this book and, for example, Lange's account of narrative therapy (1996) or McKinney's account of 'free writing' (1976). Although not suitable for everyone, certain of my own counselling clients have benefited from freewriting. It affords opportunities for catharsis, where unheard or unacknowledged inner 'voices' are given permission to express themselves. It can also help trace the nature, history and patterning of feelings, beliefs and views, thus enhancing self-awareness and understanding. It is crucial, however, to offer guidelines to clients about staying safe (see below), and to warn that unexpected, painful, frightening or otherwise difficult material may emerge.

For counsellors, the experience of limited time between sessions, reported above, is very common. Freewriting offers a way to respond quickly to a session without the need to consciously analyse or select material. It can form the basis of notes to be written up later, taken to supervision or, where appropriate, shared with clients.

Here is the approach suggested to the counsellors who were consulted for this chapter:

- As soon as possible after the client leaves, jot down the words and phrases uppermost in your mind. Pick three or four of these. In a person-centred way of working, it may be most appropriate to choose exact words or phrases used by the client. If your approach is psychodynamic, however, you might be just as interested in working with words or phrases you used in responding to what the client said, or to what happened in the session. Such methodological issues need a rather fuller treatment than is possible here, but the point is made to illustrate that freewriting can serve counselling work of varying traditions.
- The words or phrases picked become 'triggers' from which to write. Depending on the time available, allow between one and three minutes to write about each, using the guidelines above.

Background and rationale for freewriting

McLeod (1998) reminds us that there is a strong tradition in counselling of using methods and techniques from drama, literature and the visual arts to help clients express their meanings, make sense of experiences and work through them. He lists techniques such as autobiography, journalling, poetry and 'bibliotherapy' (Greening 1977; Progoff 1992; Winter *et al.* 1999; Bolton 2001).

Freud famously made use of 'free association' as a key tool of psychoanalysis, and freewriting could be seen as a written version of this method. The idea was taken up by surrealist poet and thinker André Breton in the 1920s. Breton experimented with 'automatic writing', hypothesising that it might bypass thought. His aim was to clear the mind of conscious thinking, to produce material directly from the unconscious. After some study, Breton admitted that it was not neurologically or existentially possible to 'turn off' faculties such as moral and aesthetic judgements – but the method retains some interest for artists and others looking for hidden resources in the psyche that might help uncover meaning and significance (Breton 1936).

The Freudian rationale is the access to unconscious material that free association affords: as a form of dialogue between analyst and patient, free association results in what may seem to be merely coincidental or adventitious connections – but as a phrase or sentence is articulated, between one word and the next, the emerging links, slips or incongruities, it is argued, can reveal something of the client or patient's unconscious. Examination of the resulting material – images, metaphors, riddles or multiple meanings – is the business of psychoanalysis (Phillips 2000).

I believe that other approaches to working with clients, such as humanistic or existential counselling, can also make use of such a technique – albeit in different ways. Freud's concern may be said to have been his particular interpretation of how rationality can be our aim, despite our irrational and unconscious 'drives'. In my counselling work, it is the clients' interpretations and the development of their own meanings in relation to experience that I wish to facilitate. Freewriting offers me a way to record counselling sessions while leaving open a channel for material outside my conscious awareness – the results of which help me see how my own processes of perception and interpretation may be influencing the work.

Exemplifying freewriting

In reading it back to myself, I felt the previous section was not as intelligible as it might have been. I got up from my computer, took a sheet of paper and 'freewrote' the following:

> I think of Prince the musician. How embarrassing !! But let's go on – he plays all the instruments himself, records each part separately, then puts his songs together . . . that's a bit like how I write . . . an academic paper, say. Work it all out then put it together to make it come out . . . coherent . . . neat. Smooth over wrinkles. But my experience of *being conscious* is not like that – different tunes are going on at the same time . . . Partly that's me choosing, but lots does not feel like I'm choosing – it's just going on in my head – awareness of ideas and feelings. When I'm talking – say teaching – I shut bits out and try to say one thing at time. In writing it's all carefully constructed, edited and

> reworked. But normally thoughts, feelings, memories, images and sensations all happen together – maybe awful cacophony going on – maybe harmony sometimes . . .

This reminds me that I use freewriting after counselling sessions to enable what might otherwise become a too consciously constructed account of the session to be creatively disrupted. This disruption can admit more than just rational, linear and chronological information. Emotions, images, intuitions and feelings can be more easily acknowledged too. The interruption of a conscious 'voice' (the voice holding the 'turn', to use an expression from linguistics) by another, bubbling underneath, or set off by an element of the first voice, allows at least some of my multifaceted, multilayered experience of myself-with-my-client, and her or his reality, to 'break in' to my session notes. This material can then legitimately populate the mental terrain of me-as-counsellor-in-reflection, and therefore become part of the ground I am trying to map with my client.

Freewriting has been particularly useful in bringing to my awareness features of countertransference – unconscious, unacknowledged or hard to identify reactions to a client. In becoming more conscious of such feelings, reactions and assessments, I've been better able to discard or make use of them as appropriate. An experience of discomfort in a client's presence, for example, that I initially attributed merely to a physical characteristic and told myself to 'ignore', was revealed in freewriting to have triggered feelings relating to someone else of significance in my life. This understanding enabled the association to be first acknowledged, then examined for relevance and finally removed.

One morning I awoke and remembered a dream which instantly triggered thoughts about a counselling session from the previous evening where my client had described a dream of her own. I quickly freewrote the piece below, transcribed from my notebook:

> **My dream of the wolf and X's dream**
>
> X dreamed she had an exciting painting of her life, yet she feels fake, upset with herself – because it was a picture she didn't ever really see – she knew it was in a frame – gilt – ornate. She had people to carry it for her – and when she caught a glimpse she saw . . . shifting colour. Finally she *sold* it – was talked into it by men in suits, almost without realising.
>
> I dreamed I shot a beautiful grey wolf. Woke quite shocked feeling I had committed gross . . . destruction . . . thinking instantly of client X and her painting dream – she sold her life-painting, imaginative possibility – it was a shock to me – parallel my shock – I coerce wolf violently out of existence – deep regret.

This piece of freewritten work was taken to my supervisor and was also described in part to the client it concerns. It has also been the basis of therapeutic work for me.

I feel that a number of important issues arise from this example. My client had described her dream to me at the end of an evening counselling session. I had been tired after the session and had not given it much attention in my notes. On waking the next morning, my own powerful dream of shooting the beautiful grey wolf was shockingly present. I remembered my client and her dream without making any conscious connection or interpretation. I chose to do the quick freewriting (above) because, in my experience, such impressions are easily forgotten. The result gave me some clear leads into possible connections between my own and my client's dream, and into how I might work with my client.

For me, the freewriting brought to consciousness feelings of anger and resentment I had yet to deal with. Making myself 'tame' and respectable in response to certain social fears and anxieties had led me to repress some 'wildness' (I shot that wolf – and then felt profound regret at this 'gross' and 'destructive' act). After untangling issues from the dream relevant for my own therapy, my supervisor and I identified a number of possible areas to pursue with my client:

- X had previously talked of choices in her life she felt had been taken away by 'boring' people she 'had to' please (who are the men in suits? Boring, but powerful?).
- Was the painting her life? Though potentially exciting ('shifting colour'?) and valuable ('in a frame – gilt – ornate'?), it is not available for her to see – and others carry it (can't she live her own life?). She doesn't 'know' those people (alienation, isolation, loneliness?).
- She has felt upset at being 'fake' (not authentically herself? how could she change that?). Then before she could even 'look at' her picture (know herself better?) she is persuaded to 'sell' it by the men in suits (why did she sell it? Is it 'selling out' in some way?).

Over a number of further sessions with this client these ideas allowed some very productive work. Other counsellors report that, in freewriting, as in the example above, their own personal issues emerged alongside and entangled with material concerning clients. For some, this may be seen as a worry and a potential distraction from the core business of the work. My response is that any approach to counselling needs a mechanism to clarify and deal with the counsellor's own issues, whether we refer to these in terms of 'countertransference' or 'authenticity'. Freewriting can have a useful role as a tool to reveal such issues.

I have found supervision invaluable in exploring freewriting, although I have also shared writing with clients where it has felt appropriate. Most recently, when using a psychosynthesis approach with a particular client, sharing some freewritten responses to sessions with her triggered useful exploration of her 'sub-personalities' (Assagioli 1993). This enabled the client to compose some highly revealing and helpful descriptions of some aspects of her character, of which she had not previously been fully aware.

Staying safe

There may be a temptation to see freewriting as light-hearted, entertaining and fun. It can, of course, have these characteristics, but it is certainly not to be treated as a party game. This activity has the ability to release powerful feelings, memories or experiences with the potential for causing great distress and pain where adequate support and preparation has not been set up.

An essential step to take before using freewriting is to ask yourself (or your client) if there are issues you are aware of that could cause distress, or that you (or they) would be unwilling to confront. If such things can be identified (clients do not, of course, have to reveal the actual subject matter to you) it is then useful to prepare a phrase to use in writing that will direct attention away from that subject matter. The writer and therapist Caroline Wilson recommends using 'I am aware of X but I'm not going to write about him/her/that now'. Despite its simplicity, this device works extremely well to defer any unwelcome subject matter – and may be repeated as often as necessary during an exercise (Wilson 1997).

In using the approach for the first time, or recommending it to clients to use at home, it is advisable to ensure that a supportive and trusted person is present or available to be contacted for support if necessary. While this might seem unwarranted to some, I can report from experience that such precautions are by no means disproportionate.

Sharing with clients: another version

David Acres, a person-centred counsellor whom I consulted about the idea of freewriting, uses an approach which is both similar to and different from the one described above. In a workshop he calls 'Capturing our Voice', Acres describes how he has used the writing of 'verse' to record experiences, not only of counselling but also of supervision and training. He attributes this method to Anne Hughes, a bereavement counsellor, and explains his approach as follows:

> I use between one and four handwritten words per line and 'tumble' them down a sheet of A4 paper in columns: longer 'verse' (if that's what it is) occupies four columns or more. At a subsequent meeting, I offer to read it aloud to the person(s) involved and offer it to them as a record of my experience of being with them. They are not edited or amended to attempt to 'improve' them into better verse, grammar or whatever. They stand as my response to the meeting.
>
> (Acres 2002)

A contrast between this method and the one described above is that Acres' free verse is written specifically *for* his clients and is offered to them at the subsequent meeting. He explains that his journey to this approach started from an absolute refusal to make notes about his counselling sessions. This was because he did not want to engage in a process outside of the relationship and that was not shared with the person he was working with. After experimenting with verse he found it to be a way of recording his experience with clients which is fully congruent with a person-centred philosophy: 'not subtracting from the relationship with the other person, honouring it, fully acknowledging it – deepening it' (Acres 2002).

Conclusion

The introductory account of freewriting in this chapter is designed to encourage you to experiment – not necessarily in the ways I have described, but I hope that you will find your own (legally and ethically considered) uses for the technique. The only strong claims I want to make for freewriting at this stage are first its authenticity in representing counsellors' experience of their work and second its ability to bypass internal 'censorship' processes and thus facilitate the admission of material that might otherwise be excluded from consideration. For these reasons I value its help in recording, interpreting, processing and responding to sessions with my clients. Whether or not it will work for you is, of course, for your own judgement. The various colleagues I consulted and interviewed about the approach did *not* all find it helpful – but those who did were very enthusiastic! They divided into two roughly equally sized groups in their views, with half saying they would use freewriting to help record and process sessions, and the other half saying the method did not suit them. This may simply reflect that, for some of us, writing is a primary means to elicit deeper levels of thought, understanding and creativity, while for others it plays a lesser role and these things are achieved by other means.

References

Acres, D. (2002) Unpublished interview, Plymouth, March.

Assagioli, R. (1993) *Psychosynthesis, Principles and Techniques*. London: Thorsons.

BACP (British Association for Counselling and Psychotherapy) (2002) *Ethical Framework for Good Practice in Counselling and Psychotherapy*. Rugby: BACP.

Bolton, G. (2001) *Reflective Practice: Writing and Professional Development*. London: Paul Chapman.

Bond, T. (1999) *Confidentiality: Counselling and the Law*. Rugby: BACP.

Breton, A. (1936) *What is Surrealism*? in F. Rosemont (ed.) *What is Surrealism? Selected Surrealist Writings*. New York: Pathfinder Press, 1978.

Coldridge, L. (2003) *Making Notes of Counselling and Psychotherapy Sessions*. Rugby: BACP.

Elbow, P. (1998) *Writing Without Teachers*. New York: Oxford University Press.

Greening T.C. (1977) The uses of autobiography, in W. Anderson (ed.) *Therapy and the Arts: Tools of Consciousness*. New York: Harper & Row.

Hilsdon, J. (2002) Writing unbound – freewriting in academic contexts. Paper delivered at the Discourse, Power and Resistance conference, University of Plymouth, April.

Jenkins, P. (1997) *Counselling, Psychotherapy and the Law*. London: Sage.

Lange A. (1996) Using writing assignments with families managing legacies of extreme traumas, *Journal of Family Therapy*, 18: 375–88.

McKinney, F. (1976) Free writing as therapy, *Psychotherapy* 13: 183–7.

McLeod, J. (1998) *An Introduction to Counselling*. Buckingham: Open University Press.

McMahon, G. (1994) *Starting your own Private Practice*. Cambridge: National Extension College.

Nelson-Jones, R. (1982) *The Theory and Practice of Counselling Psychology*. London: Cassell.

Phillips, A. (2000) *Promises Promises*. London: Faber & Faber.

Progoff, I. (1992) *At a Journal Workshop*. New York: Tarcher Putnam.

Smith, M. (2001) Bringing case notes alive, *CPJ Counselling and Psychotherapy Journal*, 12(5): 15–16.

Wilson, C. (1997) *Writing Therapy, Holistic Nurse*, ND.

Winter, R., Buck A. and Sobiechowska, P. (1999) *Professional Experience and the Investigative Imagination – the Art of Reflective Writing*. London: Routledge.

Chapter 21

Writing in a reflective practice group for staff working with people with dementia

Lisa Heller

Introduction

Two o'clock on a warm May afternoon; the small, silent, newly painted room is a little too hot. No one moves to open the window wider, everyone is sitting bent in concentration. From the corridor outside, we can hear voices, the telephone, a carpet cleaner, and occasionally a door handle being rattled. Inside, the atmosphere is calm and expectant. It seems that for this brief time, the six people in here with me are not distracted by noisy demands, but relish the peace in the room. They are nursing and therapy assistants, who work on Woodside Ward. Some are weary after an early shift; others have done almost a full day's work at home before coming on duty. This is *their* time: one hour, once a month, when they can shut the door of the little room and stay together, because it's time for their reflective practice group. They are engaged in a piece of writing about someone they enjoy caring for, and are describing the ways they think that they may be like that person. Some find this writing easy, bringing a poetry and unselfconscious lyricism to their words. Others regard it in the same light as other writing that they do, as useful and functional, but hardly enjoyable. But together, they are bringing their work to life in a way that simply talking about it had never done previously.

This chapter explores the experience of a reflective practice group for unqualified staff from a hospital ward. The nursing and therapy assistants face the challenge of being alongside vulnerable people, whose disability from dementia is severe. The experience of those they care for may be painful, hurtful and frustrating. A reflective practice group was established to help unqualified staff develop their skills, empathy and practice, and become increasingly 'person-centred' in their work. The group started writing after a period of using other group-work techniques. After some time, the group had become 'stuck'. The use of reflective writing enabled significant amounts of self-reflection to happen and facilitated honesty and openness. Writing also helped group members to improve their ability to understand and support each other in their work.

The story of Woodside Ward

Woodside Ward is home to 18 people who have dementia and very complex needs. It is sited in a modern hospital building which, in spite of being pleasantly decorated and furnished, retains some unmistakable elements of the old traditional institution which it replaced. Locked doors, long corridors and staff uniforms are still in evidence. Several members of staff have been employed by the organisation for many years. They may have found it hard to cope with the many waves of organisational and cultural change. Expectations of them have also changed, and grown.

Paradoxically, as the culture of care advanced in line with modern thinking, many care facilities, including Woodside, were having to tighten their belts in terms of expenditure and reducing staff numbers. Those who kept their jobs had to work harder and faster to keep up with tasks, coping with an increasing sickness rate and consequent rapid turnover of staff. Attention to delivering care in a person-centred way was relegated to an ever lower place on the agenda. (*The National Service Framework for Older People* 2001: 23).

What was happening to the people who form the regular staff on this ward? How could they possibly meet all the needs and expectations of the people they cared for? How could they work here day after day, in an increasingly demanding but uncertain role? It was becoming clear that Woodside Ward was suffering from staff demoralisation and widespread 'burnout' (Kitwood 1997a: 106).

The reflective practice group

As part of a wide-ranging ward development plan a 'reflective practice group' was established and I became its facilitator. This group met once a month for one hour, just after handover time. It was precious time to the ward, but the only time available for the group (Palmer *et al*. 1994: 7). All of the available 16 regular unqualified staff of the ward attended the group whenever they were on duty at the time. At the first meeting we discussed ground rules, and immediately some important issues concerning the working lives of the unqualified staff members emerged. It was obvious that there was much for them to talk about.

Over subsequent meetings, a pattern emerged. Group members began with overt support for each other, following which came expressions of anger, frustration and of a sense of injustice about aspects of the work, which seemed to be out of their control. For several months, members told their stories. Following diplomatic discussion with the manager, some improvements were made to their conditions at work, and these were acknowledged to be achievements of the group.

But was this reflective practice? Were lessons being learned to help inform us of new ways to handle situations? Were the group members beginning to make sense of things, in order to give them insights which would help improve the care on the ward? Were staff avoiding reflection because it was too sensitive?

Over the next few months, the group tried a variety of methods and exercises designed to stimulate reflection, but we were not progressing to a deeper understanding of the work, or of the situations those involved were in. No new insights were being gained. The question of how group members felt when Freda asked repeatedly to let her go out of the door seemed to them superfluous: 'You just have to get on with it', would have summed up most of their answers to this and similar questions.

What happens when Pete dismantles the bed you have just made? 'You put it back. That's the job, isn't it?' I asked a variety of questions designed to stimulate reflection, which all met with similar responses, sometimes a little humour, some cynicism, and often blaming someone for a failure to do the job *they* are supposed to be doing. Other questions met with stoic defence: 'What can you expect? These people can't help themselves, and we have to put up with everything they do.'

I was beginning to feel anxious about the group. I had no new perspectives to offer, and feared that the group would have to be abandoned. We had been meeting for a year when I asked the members what they valued about the group. The response was, 'A chance to talk', 'Our space'. They enjoyed the group, and it was a chance to let off steam. Perhaps I should try harder, or hand it over to someone else?

Beginning to write

The breakthrough came when I asked the group members to write a piece, to share if they wished, describing what they felt they had to offer to their work. The results were truly astonishing. They had fended off such questions over a period of a year, but what they entrusted to paper, and then to each other that day, was a complete revelation. They loved their work; they felt compassion for the people they cared for, sadness for the relatives, guilt at not being able to do more, gladness and satisfaction when someone went quietly to sleep after a calm evening. The feelings bubbled out of the writing. I could not wait to get to the next group.

I suggested they write about their favourite patient, and what they liked about him or her. The result was again astonishing. They wrote about people who were important to them, and about themselves. We all began to see things in a different light. One support worker wrote about Pete. He described how Pete's strength and fitness chimed with his own, how they shared the habit of being active, rather than being content to sit quietly. Pete's refusal to conform to the confines of the patients' routine was similar to his own tendency to initiate activity in order to prevent boredom. He had never found routines easy:

> Another thing, you have to be very careful when you shave Pete, he's very fussy, and you have to choose your moment. But I know what that's like, I broke my arm once coming off my bike, and I *hate* being shaved by someone else.

One wrote about Freda, whose family had been so important to her:

> She's like me with my family. They are the most important thing in my life. I live for them. The children are growing up now, and one of them is married, but I love the days they come home and we can be a family again.

Following this, she and the others in the group observed how Freda watched for her daughters, how she sought affection from staff and fellow patients and how positively she responded when spoken to about her family.

> It must be terrible to be away from them and not to understand why. It must feel like she's done something wrong, maybe she even wonders if people think she's harmed them, and so they keep her away from them. She must worry about them, because she can't remember that they are grown up, and that the little ones [the grandchildren] have their mothers to take care of them. No wonder she's always asking to go. She wants to get to them, to feel useful and needed, which she thinks she is.

The insights which the writing brought allowed group members to share a deeper understanding of their patients. It also allowed them to see aspects of themselves and each other never before explored.

During subsequent sessions, group members wrote about themes such as an ideal day, the worst day, what helps you through the day, what you enjoy doing outside work. They wrote about an occasion when they learned something important, about what they imagined themselves to be doing in five years' time. They wrote notes, poetry, letters and stories. Group members decided whether or not to share their writing, and to read it out to the others, but they were almost always ready to share the content. Writing about what helps you learn, one member volunteered:

> Sometimes you learn from people, and sometimes you learn from the things that happen. The most important lessons I have learnt have been when someone was there at an important time. Sometimes it has been when I needed something to happen to change the situation I was in.

The subsequent discussion focused on how a combination of the right person being present at the right time can have a profound effect on learning, and also on relationships.

The way that the experience of group members mirrored that of their patients was something that began to emerge. Who was around for the patients now they were in hospital, so disabled? Who could influence their lives now? Did relatives sense that this was necessary, and at the risk of being labelled 'awkward' take things into their own hands at times? Did the patients also take risks and cause things to happen in order to try to precipitate action by others? Debbie Everett, a Canadian chaplain, is quoted in John Killick and Kate Allan's book on communication with people with dementia, describing people with dementia as 'magic mirrors', who have a capacity to show us things about ourselves and our humanity and personhood (Killick and Allan 2001: 38).

The members of the group began to demonstrate that they could put themselves in another's shoes, and learn from doing so.

> When Stan calls out, I sometimes really want to help him. Sometimes though, when you are tired and when you have been with him all morning, you want to pretend you haven't heard him (which would be difficult!). Or you want to pretend you have got something far more important to do. But what must it be like for him – bed, wheelchair, chair – if he's lucky, then wheelchair, then bed. And he can't always go in the garden because he's got to have someone with him all the time. And he doesn't even get any company in the dining room because the others don't like sitting with him. If I were in that chair day in day out I'd be shouting out too, most probably.

This member observed that there was little inherently challenging in what Stan did. How to find ways of including Stan, making him feel a part of things and making him feel valued, were the questions which needed to be addressed. Another member suggested:

> It's easy to forget about Stan's life, his personality. His sense of humour and his brother are two key things with Stan. It helps if you talk about his brother and when he's coming next, but it's really best if you can have a laugh with him, because then he really seems different, and he's more alert and more with it, which helps with everyone else as well.

Does this enhance Stan's relationships with staff? Do they feel better about being with him if they can have a laugh with him? What about when they can't have a laugh with him? Another member said,

> He really does me good. He is so appreciative of any little thing you do, and when I have had a laugh with him, I sometimes tell him he's done me good, and he holds my hand really gently, not tightly like he does when he wants something.

It seemed that Stan was telling his carers something, and also that he had something to offer to them. One member described how taking a patient out to the garden to smell the herbs on a warm afternoon brought *him* a sense of calm and well-being as well as his patient. Another described the fun and pleasure of an evening dance when she had partnered an old gentleman who had obviously been, and still was, an excellent dancer.

Group members began to describe in detail what happened when they felt sad about the situation of someone they cared for. One wrote, 'It's not something we talk about or generally admit, but when I look at Peggy's face as she walks down the ward, I really want to cry.' The workers are confronted daily by Peggy's grief and distress. They feel sad for her, for her family and for themselves.

Reflecting and learning

The group became used to exploring the meaning of things, to make sense of what is going on for the people they care for, and for their colleagues in the group:

> You get to know colleagues in a different way when you hear what they have written.
>
> I didn't know John [support worker colleague] was so deep, I have learned a lot about him, and I now understand that he is a very thoughtful person, which I never would have known before. I tend to look at all my colleagues now as individuals.

The complexity and diversity of the lives of all the people living and working in the ward has become the source of understanding about a range of perspectives and events. Beverley Taylor discusses the advantages to be gained by nurses from reflection, in learning to articulate what they know, and how they come to know it. They needed a 'kit bag of strategies' for reflection (Taylor 2000: 55, 57). Reflecting about the group, John said, 'Well, I think before I write, I compose it, which I don't always do when I'm speaking, I just blurt it out. I tend to say things in temper.' Another group member felt differently, having written things which 'shocked' her to see written down. She had found the writing profoundly significant, but was glad that the rule of the group was that no one had to share what they had written. It was acknowledged that the writing comes 'from within, it comes from a deeper level'. Another said, 'I really only say anything when I feel strongly, and writing helps you to understand your feelings.'

Through writing, the group members have expressed what lies closest to them: 'Even though we might have been working on the ward for years, it helps you realise what it is you are actually doing, it helps you reflect on your practice, which we all need to do, and can only be a good thing.'

They began to look at things they had written as if they were holding a mirror to the world. As one group member put it: 'It is like you are telling yourself, and you seem to be able to hear it better if you see what you, yourself have written down.' Another said: 'You say things in writing that you would not normally say. It's interesting, but also helps you understand yourself and other people.'

The use of writing opened up the possibility of playfulness and delight in the rewards of their work. Group members laughed together. It was empowering: group members asked me less often to take issues to the managers on their behalf, but instead resolved to do this themselves. By writing about important aspects of themselves and their work, and allowing others to hear what they had written, group members were learning to understand and have a sense of belief in themselves as care workers. In order to be able to give of themselves, staff need to feel they are valued in their work. The group helped staff feel that others valued them, and that they had reason to value themselves. This is at the core of being person centred (Kitwood 1997b: 10).

In this ward, where the experience of the patients was so full of contradiction and unreality, it seemed well worth trying to cultivate the ability to step 'through the looking glass' (Bolton 2001: 31) – to see things from the other side.

Note

All names and details of the ward and people in it have been changed to protect anonymity.

References

Bolton, G. (2001) *Reflective Practice, Writing and Professional Development.* London: Paul Chapman.

Killick, J. (1997) *You are Words: Dementia Poems.* London: Hawker Publications.

Killick, J. and Allan, K. (2001) *Communication and the Care of People with Dementia.* Buckingham: Open University Press.

Kitwood, T. (1997a) *Dementia reconsidered.* Buckingham: Open University Press.

Kitwood, T. (1997b) Cultures of care: tradition and change, in T. Kitwood and S. Benson (eds) *The New Culture of Dementia Care.* London: Hawker Publications.

Palmer, A., Burns S. and Bulman C. (eds) (1994) *Reflective Practice in Nursing: The Growth of the Professional Practitioner.* Oxford: Blackwell Science.

Taylor, B.J. (2000) *Reflective Practice: A Guide for Nurses and Midwives.* Buckingham: Open University Press.

The National Service Framework for Older People, Standard Two (2001) London: Department of Health.

Chapter 22

Conclusions and looking forward

Gillie Bolton and Jeannie K. Wright

Writing Cures demonstrates both the therapeutic potential of expressive and reflective writing in its own right, and the tremendous range of ways in which it is used in the practice of counselling and psychotherapy. Therapeutic writing needs to be widely recognised and used in British counselling, psychotherapy and clinical psychology practice. Whether or not it ever becomes an established complementary therapy like art or music therapy, is open to debate.

What is therapeutic writing?

The term 'therapeutic writing', as we have used it in *Writing Cures*, covers a wide range of provision and enquiry. Writing within cognitive and analytic therapy is different from, for example, journal writing which can be offered within a range of therapies. And these are different again from email and internet relay chat used as vehicles for therapy. 'Interapy', offered over the internet in the Netherlands works through a structured series of writing tasks supported by therapists (Lange *et al.* 2003). But the core of all these projects is the same – that writing is different from talking and has its own particularly powerful benefits. The broad area of therapeutic writing is sufficiently new that a discussion of its definition would be very welcome. Here is a working definition which is open to discussion:

> Therapeutic writing employs processes of personal, explorative and expressive writing, which might also be creative or literary, in which patients or clients are offered guidance and inspiration by a clinician or creative writer, and help in choosing a topic for their writing. This might take the form of approaches similar to 'guided fantasy', or it might take the form of something more like an 'essay topic', or structured writing tasks. Each person is encouraged to work in a way that accords with their own interests and concerns, and according to their own felt wants and needs. Authority and control of each piece of writing always resides with the writer.
>
> Whereas literary writing is orientated towards a literature product of as high a quality as possible (e.g. poetry, fiction, drama), generally aimed at an unknown audience, the emphasis of therapeutic writing is on the process of

writing to create material of satisfaction and interest to the writer, and possibly to a few close individuals. Occasionally no final product may be created.

Therapeutic writing can be the initial stage of literary writing, ensuing stages of literary crafting, redrafting and editing being focused towards publication for the benefit of an unknown readership. The personal nature of the text is reduced: the reader of published literature is not primarily interested in the writer but in what the writer has to say; the reader of therapeutic writing is principally interested in the writer and in their personal development.

Where, by whom and with whom can therapeutic writing be used?

Therapeutic writing is of great value within medicine, healthcare, many branches of psychotherapy, occupational therapy, care of the elderly, substance abuse rehabilitation, community development, social inclusion, race relations, care of asylum seekers and victims of torture, adult education and education of children who have a range of difficulties. This list could be extended to include any form of support of people of any age over 5 who experience any social or psychological difficulties.

But, considering its power, it is not being used enough; it needs to be offered within mainstream provision. It needs to be offered by therapists, clinicians and practitioners such as doctors, nurses and occupational therapists, and included within their training. It needs to be offered by *writers in residence* (professional writers supervised by clinicians) and by specialist therapists.

Online writing has tremendous potential, as the chapters in *Writing Cures* demonstrate. Work in this field is continuing apace, but it needs further development in every way.

Therapeutic writing research

Therapeutic writing is seriously under-researched, and under-reported, especially in British clinical practice. We know many therapeutic practitioners are using the approach with their clients – both on- and offline – because they tell us so, and we read some reports and anecdotal evidence; but there is a great deal of experience *in camera* within therapeutic relationships about which we know nothing. Accounts of experience, which others can learn from, are invaluable. Whatever your theoretical approach, and whichever sections of this book have proved most attractive and useful to you, it may be that the paddle or plunge you have taken has led you to consider research in this area. Both qualitative and quantitative research studies have a part to play. The following may indicate an outline research agenda:

- listening to those who are using therapeutic writing and working with them to record their sense of how and why it works for them;
- case studies, using rigorous methods (Elliott 2002) and as wide a demographic range as possible;

- neuroscientific explorations of the interaction of those parts of the brain involved in language and metaphor;
- collaborative studies with practitioners from other creative and expressive therapies;
- theoretical explanations of how and why therapeutic writing works from different theoretical orientations.

A project

If this book has encouraged you to integrate some new ideas into your practice, we would be delighted to hear about it. If you have been using reflective or any form of writing in the context of your work and have stepped back to see what others are doing, we would also be very pleased to hear your comments. We would like to know:

- Who is using writing in therapy on- and offline and how?
- Who is researching writing in therapy on- and offline: what and how?
- How are text-based counselling services developing and where?

The use of therapeutic writing needs mapping. These questions are only a beginning. Please contact us about your experience of writing therapy:

Jeannie Wright
Senior Lecturer
Unit for Psychotherapeutic Practice and Research
School of Education, Health and Sciences
University of Derby
Chevin Avenue
Mickleover
Derby DE5 3GX

Tel: 01332 592044
Email: j.k.wright@derby.ac.uk

Gillie Bolton
Senior Research Fellow in Medicine and the Arts
Department of English
Kings College, London University
Strand
London WC2R 2LS

Tel: 020 7848 1405
Email: gillie.bolton@kcl.ac.uk

References

Elliott, R. (2002) Hermeneutic single-case efficacy design, *Psychotherapy Research*, 12: 1–23.

Lange, A., Rietdijk, D., Hudcovicova, M., van de Ven, J-P., Schrieken, B. and Emmelkamp, P.M.G. (2003) Interapy: a controlled randomized trial of the standardized treatme nt of posttraumatic stress through the internet. *Journal of Consulting and Clinical Psychology*, 71(5): 901–9.

Index